ORGANIZATION DEVELOPMENT

The Human and Social Dynamics of Organizational Change

Janet Cooper Jackson

University Press of America,® Inc.
Lanham · Boulder · New York · Toronto · Oxford

Library of Congress Control Number: 2006927252
ISBN-13: 978-0-7618-3549-3 (paperback : alk. paper)
ISBN-10: 0-7618-3549-0 (paperback : alk. paper)

CONTENTS

PREFACE

Facilitating and leading change is one of the most exciting challenges facing organizational leaders today. The ability to read internal and external signs to foresee the need for change, the ability to plan for and successfully facilitate change, and the ability to cope with constant change are critical skills.

As a student of organizations or as a practitioner within organizational settings, Organization Development (OD) provides you with methods and practices that focus on improving the effectiveness of the organization. Organization development provides the skills and knowledge necessary for establishing effective interpersonal relationships, diagnosing complex problems, and devising appropriate solutions. As we increase our sensitivity to cultural and social changes in our society, OD can assist organizations in remaining viable and continuing to survive.

The study of organization development includes understanding the nature of planned change, the role of the OD practitioner, the OD consultancy process, including ethical considerations. As important as knowing *what* methodologies to employ when initiating and implementing a change initiative, is recognizing the organization's *readiness level* for change, including when *not* to change.

THIS BOOK

The audience for this book includes students who work in organizations which serves as a learning laboratory; practitioners such as managers, OD consultants and specialists, people engaged in facilitating organizational change; and those who consider themselves scholar/practitioners within the realm of organizational settings. By this, I mean people who see the value of theory as a foundation for application. Specifically, this book is for those who wish to know more about the human and social dynamics of organizational life. This book serves multiple purposes, allowing the reader to:

- develop an understanding of the field of organization development: it's history, basic assumptions, values, characteristics;
- gain knowledge of a foundational framework for the practice of organization development;
- be exposed to fundamental tools of the field;
- develop practical and working knowledge of organization development practices such as the consultancy process, understanding resistance to change, and ethical considerations;
- develop understanding of planned change processes and strategies and the roles of organizational members in change initiatives; and
- develop a personal philosophy of organization development, understand "self as practitioner", and create a platform for the practice of organization development.

How it is Different From Other Textbooks on Organization Development

This book is unique in several ways. It combines theory with practical knowledge; allows the reader to actively engage with materials through cases and activities; provides a path for development of consultancy platform; provides a historical perspective of the field of organization development, underlying principles and current thinking through words of key contributors to the field; provides a strategy for planning organizational change; and is (hopefully) easily accessible (language) to both scholar and practitioner.

Self As Practitioner

Activities are included that are designed to allow you to develop increased self-awareness of yourself as a facilitator of organizational change. This enables:

- understanding of change from an individual perspective;
- therefore increases awareness and understanding of what clients are going through in the change process; which
- hopefully increases effectiveness in the facilitation of client change; and
- develops a personal platform (philosophy) from which to operate as a facilitator of the OD change/transformation process.

Chapters have a common flow, beginning with an activity or case study to introduce you to concepts discussed within. There is a theoretical discussion, and where appropriate, application of theory to practice. Related readings or other activities are located at the end of the chapter.

Layout

The introductory chapter is intended to present some guiding thoughts and questions about the field of organizational change and development. Your part is to think of questions you would like to have answered as you study and learn more about OD. Further definition, characteristics and guiding principles of the field are presented in Chapter 2. Chapter 3 presents a picture of organization development practitioners, examining such factors as types of clients you will work with, type of problems you will encounter, the consulting process, and ethical standards.

Chapters 4 and 5 have a more individual focus. Chapter 4 focuses on the personal side of change. As change begins with the individual and is personal, and directly related to learning, the motivation to learn as well as styles of learning is discussed. Stages of change and transition are examined. Chapter 5 examines organizational learning and creativity, with discussions of creativity from both personal, team, and organizational perspectives.

Returning to the focus of organizational change, Chapter 6 provides a discussion of the dynamics of organizational change, looking at such factors as organizational design and culture and the impact on organizational change. Chapter 7 presents a variety of strategies, both traditional and contemporary, to organizational change. Chapter 8 provides a seven- stage strategy for initiating a change effort.

Chapter 9 examines a philosophy for leading organizational change. It also looks at resistance to change, including examining why people resist change and conditions for reducing resistance. The final chapter provides you with guidelines for creating a strong sense of self-as-practitioner.

It is not my intention to present everything you will ever need to know about organization development. That would take volumes and there are many books available to you to supplement this text. The purpose is to provide you with basic principles of organization development and provide an overview of key strategies and techniques that will assist you in understanding change, both personal and organizational, and facilitating and leading change, large or small, within organizational settings.

I hope you will actively engage with the text. Write in the margins. Do the exercises. You bring to this book your unique experience that enhances the "story." Dig deeper , use this book as a springboard for further exploration.

AUTHOR BIAS AND INFLUENCES

Any book is written with the biases of the author. Mine will become clear as you read, however I present them upfront, as they naturally influence the materials presented.

- Change is not about programs, techniques, or content. Change is personal—it is about each individual choosing to support the change initiative, or not.
- The more we engage those involved in the change, early and upfront, the more we have a chance for success.
- Organization development is not an exact science—it does not come with a money-back guarantee. However, one can become aware of issues that facilitate and hinder organizational change.
- One must develop a personal philosophy and framework for the practice of leadership and organizational consulting. This includes knowing your own biases.

I've drawn heavily from the work of contributors in the field, such as Wendell French and Cecil Bell, William Bridges, Peter Senge and colleagues, James O'Toole, Peter Block, John Kotter, Edgar Schein, and W. Warner Burke. My guides and mentors, including Argentine Craig, Barbara Mink, Frank Friedlander, Peter Parks, and especially my students who are struggling with the many challenges of organizational life, have also influenced me.

ACKNOWLEDGMENTS

I would like to thank the faculty and students in the Organization Development classes at Chapman University for their valuable feedback and input into versions of this manuscript.

I dedicate this book to those who wish to make a positive difference in organizational life. Organizational studies are fascinating. This book takes you on a journey into one of the disciplines within the realm of organizational studies that deals specifically with the people who work (and play) in those organizations. I hope you enjoy your journey.

Janet Cooper Jackson, Ph.D.
Huntington Beach, California
February, 2006

CHAPTER 1:
INTRODUCTION

Organizations are undergoing severe and rapid changes. That statement might sound simplistic, even mundane for those of us who live with these changes. The changes range from small, such as changing the way we process documents, to large-scale change, such as mergers and acquisitions. Technology changes at such a rapid pace that it's difficult to keep current; as soon as you learn a software package, it becomes obsolete and you are forced to change to another.

Some people in organizations thrive on change; they see it as an opportunity to learn new skills and are challenged with the many changes they face. Others, however, are more resistant to change, take longer to adjust to it, feel lost and left out, frightened of a future that seems to be unstable and unclear, and threatened by the ever quickening pace of change.

Much is written about the *technology* of change, analytical techniques like cost-benefit analysis, and fishbone diagrams. Much is also written about the *need* for change, the need to compete in an increasingly global environment. These writings are about the change itself.

Less, however, is written about the *human and social dynamics* of change, the impact of change on organizational members, and the influence of organizational members on the success or failure of the change initiative. As a consultant for a major technological firm, our focus was strictly on the introduction of technology into our client's offices. There was no attention paid to the individuals that were affected by this change. I found myself bewildered and lost when faced with fear, resistance, and even tears of frustration that some of the people felt when they had to change their routine and learn new technology. At that time I didn't know how to help them, other than to listen, describe the benefits of the new technology, and hold their hands while they went through the learning process.

Thankfully now I understand change from the personal perspective—organizational change is a very personal thing!

REFRAMING OUR PERSPECTIVE OF ORGANIZATIONAL CHANGE

The old paradigm of a top-down control-oriented approach to organizational design is changing, at least within organizations that are paying attention. And with these changes comes a need to reframe how we look at change. In the traditional approach, change might be viewed as "the people at the top decide what's best and introduce new ways of doing things," whereupon those below implement it with few questions. In today's more empowered organizations, change can begin anywhere in the organization. In addition, employees at all levels demand to be part of the decisions regarding their workplace and the way they do their work. Table 1-1 lists some of the changes we see in organizations today.

Table 1-1. Characteristics of Old versus New Paradigms in Organizations

Old Paradigm	New Paradigm
Control, regulation	Openness
Management direction	Employee empowerment
Employees treated like children	Employees treated like adults and equal partners, as a community, or a group of all leaders
Short-term goals	Long-term goals that fit into an overall corporate vision
Rigid hierarchy	Flexibility, market orientation, people orientation
Satisfying shareholders	Acknowledgment of all stakeholders
Competition	Cooperation, co-creation, in which relationships within and outside the organization are not just cooperation, but also creative
Aggressive warlike values	Values of openness, integrity, trust, equality, mutual respect, dignity

Adapted from Ray, M., and Rinzler, A. (eds.). (1993). The New Paradigm in Business, New York: Jeremy P. Tarcher/Perigee Books, p. 9.

Many organizational change initiatives fail because of four important factors:

1. The primary focus is on the technology of change.
2. We overlook the importance of the *people* involved in the change, and do not fully address their concerns.
3. We don't assume a *systems* perspective; rather we treat change as though it only impacts a portion of the organization.
4. Implicit within #3 is the fact that we do not acknowledge the difference between *change*, *transition*, and *transformation*.

An example of a failed change initiative was the frequent lack of success with total quality management systems to meet their full expectation and potential. While the process provided such models as statistical analysis, less attention was paid to the human dynamics. Organizational members, once rewarded for their individual contributions, were placed into teams and expected to change the process of doing their work. Few models and tools were given these teams to become a functioning team; it was simply assumed that they would automatically "gel." It was also assumed that "technical" training on

TQMS processes would be sufficient to "transform" the organization into a total quality enterprise.

Peter Senge (1999) argues that organization change fails because of the limitations in the way we think; providing more expert advise, better consultants, or more committed managers will not achieve sustained change. These authors suggest a change in our way of thinking about the transformation process. Leaders should understand the limiting processes that could slow or arrest change. If the "seed" planted by the leader does not have the potential to "grow," no amount of coercion, pleading, or hoping the change will take "root" will help. Such limitations include:

- The prevailing system of management, such as managers' commitment to change as long as it doesn't affect them; the aversion to discussing the undiscussable; and ingrained habits of attacking the symptoms and ignoring the deeper, systemic causes of problems.
- Collective learning capabilities, such as the ability to develop reflection and inquiry skills that enable people to talk openly about complex and conflictive issues without becoming defensive; and the ability to see interdependencies and deeper causes of problems which stems from a systems thinking perspective.
- Failure to develop a thorough understanding of growth processes (forces that aid change efforts and how to capitalize them); the limiting processes (forces that challenge or limit change efforts and how to develop workable strategies for dealing with these challenges); and the inevitable interplay between these two processes.

ASSUMPTIONS ABOUT ORGANIZATIONAL CHANGE

The basic premise of this book is that *people come first* when planning for any organizational change. Addressing human dynamics is crucial for any change initiative to be effective. The second important premise is the need to take into consideration the *whole organization* and understand that a change in any part of the system affects the entire system. Programs that seek to introduce change into an organization will fail if not grounded in a system-wide view of the organization.

A third assumption is that *organizational learning* is a desired state and critical for the success of real change, where people continually expand their capacity to create the results they truly desire, where new patterns of thinking emerge and are nurtured, where people learn how to learn together (Senge, 1990, p. 3). A fourth assumption is that *attracting and nurturing the talent* of all organizational members is critical to the success of organizations in the future. A fifth, and critical assumption, is that we must adapt a *new view of leadership*, away from command-and-control, super hero leadership, and "pseudo" empowerment, to developing a cadre of leaders (O'Toole, 1996) who are willing and enthusiastic to engage in the process of moving the organization forward.

This perspective looks at leadership not as a title or position, but rather a process.

A sixth assumption is that *change is messy*. There is no guarantee that a change initiative will succeed and be sustained. The final assumption is *change is personal*. You can have the best plan for change, transition, and transformation, but unless a critical mass of individuals accepts that plan and make it their own, your chances for success are slim. *People must share a vision* for the future; they must want to pursue that desired future state. As Kotter (2002, p. 1) says, "people change what they do less because they are given *analysis* that shifts their *thinking* than because they are *shown* a truth that influences their *feelings*."

WHY STUDY ORGANIZATION DEVELOPMENT?

Given this, facilitating and leading change is one of the most exciting challenges facing organizational leaders. The ability to read internal and external signs to foresee the need for change, the ability to plan for and successfully facilitate change, and the ability to cope with constant change are critical skills.

Organization development (OD) is an effort which is planned, long-range and organization-wide, supported from the top, designed to increase organizational effectiveness through planned interventions in the organization's processes, particularly through a more collaborative management of organizational culture, using the consultant-facilitator role, applied behavioral science theory and technology.

As a student of organizations or as a practitioner within organizational settings, OD provides you with methods and practices that focus on improving the effectiveness of the organization. Organization development provides the skills and knowledge necessary for establishing effective interpersonal relationships, diagnosing complex problems, and devising appropriate solutions. As we increase our sensitivity to cultural and social changes in our society, OD can assist organizations in remaining viable and continuing to survive.

Most importantly, the study of organization development includes understanding the nature of planned change, the role of the OD practitioner, the OD consultancy process, including ethical considerations. As important as knowing *what* methodologies to employ when initiating and implementing a change initiative, is recognizing the organization's *readiness level* for change, including when *not* to change.

CHANGE, TRANSITION, TRANSFORMATION: WHAT'S THE DIFFERENCE?

Not all organizational change is the same, and require different strategies for planning, leading, and implementing. For example, moving a desk within an office can cause personal angst if the individual is not consulted and comes in one day to the rearranged space, but does not create the same sense of transition as a plant move to another location. There are three basic types of organizational change, as depicted in Figure 1-1[1].

Developmental change is situational, such as a move to a new location, a new boss, or a new policy. Developmental change is the exchange of one thing for another (transactional); the improvement of an existing skill, method, performance standard, or condition that does not measure up to current or future needs. Developmental change is motivated to improve within the framework of what is known, to strengthen or correct what already exists. It is the simplest of the three types of changes. Strategies include (Anderson and Anderson, 2001a, p. 35):

- Training (both technical and personal), such as communications, interpersonal relations, supervisory and management skills
- Problem solving
- Team building
- Processes for increasing cycle time
- Applications of process improvement
- Improving communications
- Conflict resolution
- Increasing sales or production
- Meeting management
- Survey feedback efforts
- Job enrichment
- Expanding existing market

Transitional change is more complex; rather than improve what exists, it replaces what is with something entirely different. Transitional change begins with recognition that a problem or opportunity exists that cannot be resolved within the existing framework. A qualitative shift needs to occur to better serve current and/or future demands. As seen in Figure 1-1, the process involves letting go of the old state, going through a transition period, and entering a new state. Examples of transitional change include reorganizations, simple mergers and acquisitions, installation and integration of computers or new technology that do not require major changes in mindset or behavior, and creation of new products, services, systems, processes, policies or procedures that replace old ones: Planning a strategy for transitional change includes[2]:

- Clearly establishing and communicating the need for change;
- developing a clear plan for change;
- high involvement of those impacted by the change in designing and implementing the plan;
- allowing local control of implementation of the plan; and
- providing adequate support and integration time to ensure that people are succeeding in the new state.

Figure 1-1. Three Types of Organizational Change

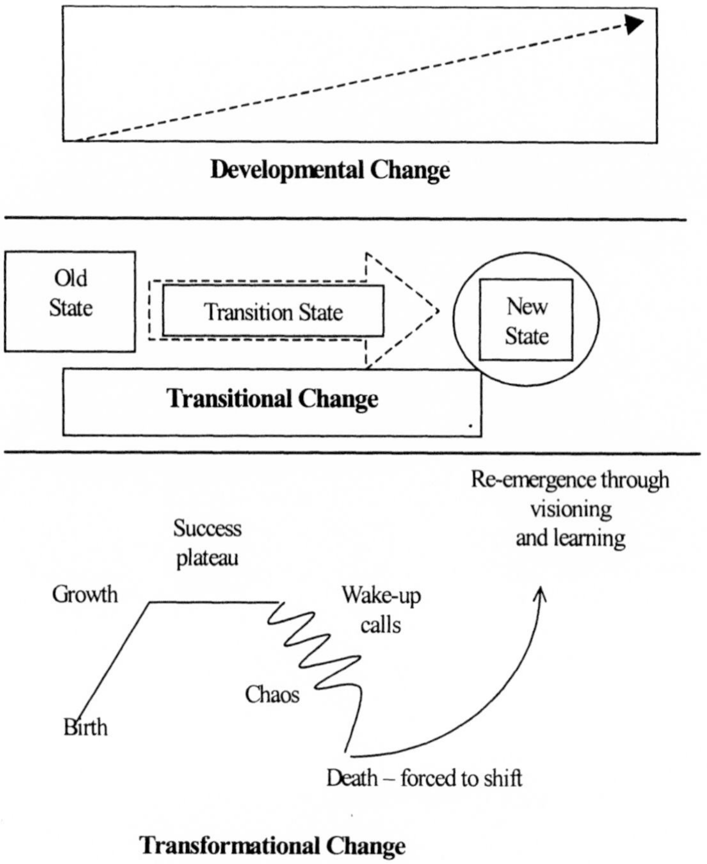

Developmental Change

Transitional Change

Old State

Transition State

New State

Re-emergence through
visioning
and learning

Success
plateau

Growth

Wake-up
calls

Chaos

Birth

Death – forced to shift

Transformational Change

Transformation is a process by which organizations examine what they were, what they are, where they will need to be, and how to get there. Transformation indicates the fundamental nature of the change, in contrast to a mere linear shift from one point to another.

Transformational change is unique in two critical ways. First, the future is unknown at the start of the change process and can only be created by forging ahead with the intent to discover it. Without having a clear goal to manage to, leaders are forced to proceed into the unknown, dependent on broader sources of information and support to formulate a new future. A time-bound predetermined plan is not possible. Secondly, the future state is so radically different than the current state that a shift of mindset is required to invent it, implement and sustain it. This requires all organizational members to transform their mindsets, behavior, and ways of working together. Transformational change results in cultural change; people must change what they do in transformation, but more importantly, they must change the way they think. Transformational change requires different strategies—with a focus on accomplishing this level of personal change across the organization, leaders included (Anderson and Anderson, 2001b).

Anderson and Anderson (2001b) pose two basic questions that determine if transformational change is needed. (1) Does the organization need to begin its change process before its destination is fully known and defined? (2) Is the scope of this change so significant that it requires the organization's culture and people's behavior and mindsets to shift fundamentally in order to implement the changes successfully and succeed in the new state?

In transformational change, the environmental and marketplace changes are so significant that a profound breakthrough in people's worldview is required to even *discover* the new state. The change process takes on a life of its own and the future state emerges out of the chaos of the transformational effort itself. Organizations typically feel a need for transformational change when they have reached a success plateau. Factors, such as those listed below, act as "wake up calls", indications of impending problems (Anderson and Anderson, 2001a):

- Hovering stock price
- Stagnation in product development
- Equipment failure and obsolescence
- Productivity drops
- Loss of control over costs and information
- Dips in employee morale
- Threats from competition
- Inadequate resources and skills
- Loss of market share
- Relentless customer demands

As these difficulties increase, the organization moves into a period of chaos, where various "fix-it" initiatives attempt to maintain some semblance of order and control, such as applying developmental or transitional change methodologies. The true transformational moment occurs when the organizational leaders really listen to the wake-up calls, which catapults them into a breakthrough in their awareness and beliefs. They begin to formulate new intentions about what is possible and necessary for the organization to survive.

SCALES OF CHANGE

Organizational change can be viewed as either first-order (incremental, developmental change) or second-order (planned and intended change). Second-order change views change from three perspectives. The first perspective concerns the source of the driving force behind the change, the second perspective regards the process of change, while the third perspective focuses on the content of change.

Learning to think and compete in new ways is not an incremental alteration (developmental change), but a fundamental, second-order change that requires the critical questioning of current operating assumptions. This is essentially what Argyris referred to as double-loop learning (see Argyris and Schon, 1978).

Single-loop learning occurs when there is a match between the organization's design for action and the actual outcome, or when such mismatches are corrected by changing actions, but without critical examination of the governing variables for action. Double-loop learning, on the other hand, occurs when the correction of mismatches is arrived at by examining and altering the governing variables for action and then the actions themselves. This occurs when organizations learn how to learn (see Chapter 5: Organizational Learning and Creativity).

Transformational change creates second-order changes. Organizational members (including executive leaders) increase their expectations about their contribution in areas that affect them.

EVENTS THAT SHAPED THE FIELD OF ORGANIZATION DEVELOPMENT

There are five distinct stages that describe thinking about behavior and management in organizational settings[3]. The first stage, Mechanical, emphasizes structure and operating principles. People were viewed as organizational components, as extensions of machines, readily and easily replaceable when they became obsolete, discarded when no longer needed. The second stage, Human Relations, working within the structure set forth in the mechanical stage, emphasizes the importance of human relations for strengthening the human environment of work. The third stage, Behavioral Science Theory, seeks to interrelate the previously separate considerations of structure and task, and human motivation. The fourth stage, Organization Development, uses behavioral science-based knowledge to facilitate organization change and improve organizational effectiveness. The fifth stage, which I will call Holistic, is emerging in response to the limitations of technology as a way to drive and sustain organizational change and transformation. The focus is on the human side of change, and incorporates a more holistic approach to change. A chronology of major influences from research, theory, and observations of OD practitioners that helped form the discipline can be found in Appendix A. Let's examine these stages more closely.

Stage 1: Mechanical: Emphasis on Production. The early 1900s focused on the concept of scientific management as a way to organize work and bureaucracy as a way to organize people. Taylor's piecework systems, Weber's passionless bureaucracy, and Fayol's formal principles and plans of action typify this stage. People were regarded as standardized "Xs" to be slotted into formal organizations; nonstandard people were either rejected or hammered into shape. While there were desirable features within this paradigm, there were also inherent flaws. Much of the research, theory and practice since the late 1920s have focused on the shortcomings of these paradigms, and how to overcome their limitations (French and Bell, 1999, p. 63). This stage, however, still has important influences on today's organization.

Stage 2: Human Relations: Emphasis on People. The studies at the Hawthorne Plant of Western Electric in the late 1920s and 1930s were instrumental in changing thought about people in work settings, pointing out the importance of social factors, group norms, and the relationship between supervisor and employee. (See Related Readings at end of Chapter 2.) This stage is almost the direct opposite of stage one; people became the central focus of attention, the structure of organization and work was accepted as a "given." The work of Elton Mayo, Roethlisberger and Dickson, and Kurt Lewin and his colleagues were important contributors to this stage. Human relations became important both in academic studies and in training of managers.

Stage 3: Behavioral Science: Production through People. The 1940s and 1950s brought a behavioral science focus to organizational theories. The emphasis was on theories that deal with cause-and-effect terms, in relationships between formal structure, supervision, and the arrangement of work on one hand; and people, their thinking, feelings, attitudes, and motivations, on the other hand. These theories advocated participative management, greater attention to workers' social needs, training in interpersonal skills for supervisors, and a general "humanizing" of the workplace, and showed these factors had a bearing on performance results. Contributors to this stage included Chris Argyris, Robert Blake and Jane Mouton, Frederick Herzberg, Douglas McGregor, and Eric Trist.

In 1947, the National Training Laboratory in Group Development was established, focusing on interpersonal relations, self-understanding, and group dynamics. The core activity was T-Groups, consisting of 15-20 members (from business, education, government, and religion), meeting each morning for two hours, facilitated by a group leader (mostly academicians). The T-group had no agenda, members had to find a topic to discuss, and at some point towards the end, discussed the process used. According to Blake (1995), this was the first conscious introduction to the use of feedback and critique for social learning in modern times. (Among other contributions to our current learning processes, NTL discovered the need to record things—on blackboards and butcher paper, the precursor to flipcharts, green boards, white boards and other varieties of boards.)

Other contributors to the Behavioral Sciences movement included Abraham Maslow, Chris Argyris, Douglas McGregor, and Rensis Likert. Maslow's theory of motivation became a platform from which worker motivation was examined. His concept of the "need hierarchy" was an easy model for managers to incorporate into their management style. Of particular interest was self-actualization, especially as it related to workers, introducing the concept that individuals are motivated to achieve and reach their full potential. Building on Maslow's work, Argyris further explored the relationship between the needs of individuals and organizational context. Argyris argued against the classical scientific management paradigm that had prevailed in organizations for half a century.

McGregor, also building on Maslow's theory of motivation, proposed two sets of assumptions or orientations towards managers, workers, and the workplace. Theory X assumes people are lazy, lack ambition, need to be coerced into working. Theory Y assumes people want to do well at work, have the potential to develop, and to assume responsibility if given the chance and proper social environment. McGregor introduced the concept of the management role being one of changing organizational structures, management practices, and human resource practices to allow individual potential to be released, in effect operationalizing Maslow's theory.

Likert advanced the concept that social organisms such as the work group could be the source of major blocks of successful organizations, not just individuals, as had been previously noted. He proposed a democratic leadership style to be superior to the classical authoritarian style. He also advanced the notion of the organization consisting of many social organisms linked together by the manager ("linking pin") who plays roles in the work groups of which they are members. Taken together, these humanistic views reflected a prescriptive (as opposed to descriptive) orientation toward organization change and development (Margulies and Raia, 1978).

Stage 4. Organization Development. Organization development (OD), as opposed to individual development, had its beginnings in the 1950s, emerging from the work of the National Training Laboratory (NTL). Richard Beckhard started an OD effort centered on the team as a unit of development and change at Union Carbide. Robert Blake and Herb Shephard, working within Exxon, started an organization-wide OD effort in which all members took part, an effort that encompassed the organization as the unit of change (Blake, 1995). The focus of OD is applied behavioral science, with a systems perspective, using "technology" to facilitate change initiatives.

Stage 5. Holistic Approach to Organizational Change. While OD practitioners continue to rely on traditional techniques of organization development, such as action research, team building, Total Quality Management (TQM), the use of facilitators, process consultation, survey feedback, and participative management, the field has expanded. There is now more focus, both research and practice, on organizational culture, learning organizations, organizational transformation, teams, visioning and future search, appreciative inquiry, and whole systems approach. There is some difficulty in identifying exactly what is and is not organization development, due to the diffusion of OD techniques in such a variety of areas (French and Bell, 1999, p. 50). The human side of change is now recognized as a critical component to the success of organizational change and transformation.

The field has grown and continues to emerge into an ever-expanding number of organizational strategies and practices. The Organization Development Network (OD Network) is a vital learning community that develops, supports, and inspires practitioners and enhances the body of knowledge in human organization and systems development. Its vision is to lead the Organization Development field and its practitioners in creating effective and healthy human systems in an inclusive world community.[4] The National Training Laboratories, American Psychological Association, American Society for Training and Development, and Academy of Management have professional divisions relating to organization development. Several universities offer graduate studies in the field. Organization development is an exciting and changing field of study and practice.

As Senge says, it appears that people seeking change in organizations have different goals in mind, from "accelerating," or "visionary" organizations, to "adaptive," "transformational", or "learning" organizations. Despite the labels, they have a common goal: to respond more quickly to the external environment, and think more imaginatively about the future. To accomplish this, they recognize the need to establish better relationships and partnerships built on trust and openness, and unleash the creative talent and enthusiasm of organizational members. Through this, they strive to shape their destiny and achieve long-term financial success (1999, p. 4-5.)

Organizational studies are fascinating. This book takes you on a journey into one of the disciplines within the realm of organizational studies that deals specifically with the people who work (and play) in those organizations. I hope you enjoy your journey.

SELF AS PRACTITIONER

One of the outcomes of this book is to encourage you to develop and articulate a "personal philosophy" of organization development, a platform upon which to rest your OD practice. This first activity is designed to uncover your personal objectives—what you hope to achieve by reading this book.

Directions:
List below all the questions you can think of regarding organization development. What do you want to know? What will you need to know in order to practice organization development? What assumptions do you have about organization development that you question?

_____

_____

_____

_____

_____

_____

_____

_____

_____

_____

_____

_____

A LIST OF QUESTIONS TO ACT AS THOUGHT-STARTERS

Organization Development

What is it?

What is the purpose?

What are the guiding principles?

Who were the key theorists and writers?

How was the field developed?

What have been the major developments?

What is the major focus?

Where is the field today?

Who are the current theorists and writers?

What kinds of things are they studying and writing about?

What are the major OD projects in organizations?

What are the major issues facing OD today?

Organization Development Practitioners

What does an OD practitioner do?

What training do they need?

Where do they work? Inside organizations? External?

What is the process they use in their work?

How do they gain access to OD projects?

How do they contract for an OD project?

What role do they play in OD projects?

How do I get started in the field?

What do I need to know to get started?

How do I go about advancing in the field?

The Practice of Organization Development

What "tools" do OD practitioners use?

Which of these "tools" are most popular and widely used?

How do you know which "tool" to use and when?

Is there a set of guidelines for what to do and when?

Is there a code of ethics I should follow?

How do you know when to say "no"?

How do you know when to exit?

What happens if the client doesn't accept my recommendations?

What happens if they use my recommendations in a "twisted" way, and cause a greater problem then they started with?

Is it important for me to understand my own orientation toward and methods of change before helping others in the process?

Change, transition, transformation

What is "change"?

What is "transition?"

What is "transformation"?

Are there scales of change?

What is "renewal"?

Why do people resist change?

Why does change seem so difficult for some people but easy for others?

Why do some people naturally embrace change?

What do people go through in the change process?

Does it matter if change is "done to you" versus you initiating the change?

How important is it to have a voice in change projects?

How do people feel when they have a voice in change that affects them?

How do people feel when they don't have a voice in change that affects them?

Why do some organizations involve people in change initiatives early in the process while other organizations tend to "announce" the change after it's a done deal?

Why do most major change efforts fail?

What is involved in a major organizational change/transformation?

Who should be involved?

Who should drive it?

Should it start at the top or can it start anywhere in the organization?

Should there be a sponsor/champion of the change initiative?

What are the major steps in the change process?

How does an organization know when it's ready for change?

How does the OD practitioner solicit support for a change initiative?

How do the OD practitioner and client motivate people to change and get them excited about it?

How do you know when to step back and hold off or stop the change effort?

What happens to an organization if they don't change?

What's the best way to get over "resistance" to change?

Is it best to just tell people to get on board or jump ship?

Is it best to give them a chance to see the benefits and hopefully get on board?

Is it OK to let people grieve the change and what's being "lost?"

Is timing critical in getting the message out about the plan for change?

What's the best way to communicate the plan for change?

What's the best way to sustain change?

ENDNOTES

[1] This section draws from Anderson, D., & Anderson, L. A. (2001). *Beyond change Management: Advanced Strategies for Today's Transformational* Leaders. Jossey-Bass Pfeiffer: A Wiley Company, p. 32.

[2] Anderson, D., & Anderson, L. A. (2001). *Beyond change Management: Advanced Strategies for Today's Transformational* Leaders. Jossey-Bass Pfeiffer: A Wiley Company, p. 36. Also see Bridges, W. (1980). *Transitions: Making Sense of Life's Changes.* Reading, MA: Addison-Wesley Publishing Company; Bridges, W. (1991). *Managing Transitions: Making the Most of Change.* Reading, MA: Addison-Wesley Publishing Company.

[3] See Mouton, J. S., & Blake, R. R. (1972). Behavioral Science Theories Underlying Organization Development. *Journal of Contemporary Business*, 1(3), Summer, pp. 9-22 for discussion of four stages. I have added the fifth to reflect current trends.

[4] www.odnetwork.org. downloaded 7/6/05.

CHAPTER 2:

THE FIELD OF ORGANIZATION DEVELOPMENT

ORGANIZATION DEVELOPMENT VALUES AND ASSUMPTIONS: A QUESTIONNAIRE[1]

This questionnaire is intended to provide an opportunity to examine how much you share the values and assumptions associated with organization development. It consists of a set of prepositions. You are asked to respond to each of the propositions by circling any ONE of the possible answers: Agree, Neutral (or indifferent) or Disagree. This is not a "test" and there is no value placed on your responses.

1.	In the vast majority of organizations, people learn from their experience that their attempts to make constructive contributions are not rewarded, and may even be penalized.	Disagree Neutral Agree
2.	The best way of obtaining solutions to most organizational problems involving attitudes and motivation is for the people involved to alter their relationships.	Disagree Neutral Agree
3.	Emotions are best handled in work organizations by repressing them—feelings are taboo on the job.	Disagree Neutral Agree
4.	What goes on in an individual's work group or team has great significance for the individual's feelings of satisfaction and competence.	Disagree Neutral Agree
5.	Most managerial and administrative groups, teams, and committees lack problem-solving skills.	Disagree Neutral Agree
6.	Improvement in the effectiveness of departments, sections, or units in most organizations requires fuller participation on the part of their members.	Disagree Neutral Agree
7.	In order for a group or team to optimize its effectiveness, the formal leader cannot perform all its leadership functions.	Disagree Neutral Agree
8.	Conflict or competition between either individuals or groups, in which one comes out the winner and the other the loser, is in the long run not an effective approach to solving organizational problems.	Disagree Neutral Agree
9.	What happens in one section, unit, part or sub-system of an organization will affect and be influenced by other parts of the organization.	Disagree Neutral Agree

10. In order for an organization to benefit from an organization development program, its members must value collaborative effort.	Disagree Neutral Agree
11. When provided with a working environment that supports and challenges them, most people will strive to grow and acquire new knowledge, skills, and abilities.	Disagree Neutral Agree
12. The level of trust, support, and co-operation existing between people in most groups and organizations is much higher than is either necessary or desirable.	Disagree Neutral Agree
13. Most managers and administrators need to augment the authority given to them by their positions by developing skills in responding to their subordinates and their needs.	Disagree Neutral Agree
14. It makes most sense to conceive of organizations as consisting of a network of individuals, rather than a network of groups or teams.	Disagree Neutral Agree
15. Most people can help their work group or team solve problems.	Disagree Neutral Agree
16. How a manager behaves in relation to his subordinates is strongly influenced by how his superior behaves in relation to him.	Disagree Neutral Agree
17. Some values must be held in common by protagonists in an organizational conflict if conflict-reducing and problem-solving techniques are to be useful.	Disagree Neutral Agree
18. Organization development practitioners are concerned both with the personal growth of people in organizations and increasing organizational effectiveness.	Disagree Neutral Agree
19. The ordinary organization member inherently prefers to avoid responsibility, has little ambition, and wants security above all.	Disagree Neutral Agree
20. Most organizations will become more effective if they become more responsive to the needs of their members.	Disagree Neutral Agree

21. Understanding people's feelings, and skill in working with feelings, opens up avenues for improved organizational performance.	Disagree Neutral Agree
22. Most people want to be accepted by and interact cooperatively with their work group.	Disagree Neutral Agree
23. A leader may be recognized by the deference paid to him by his subordinates.	Disagree Neutral Agree
24. The average organization member has an inherent dislike of work and will avoid it if he can.	Disagree Neutral Agree
25. Suppressed feeling or emotions adversely affect problem-solving, personal growth, and job satisfaction.	Disagree Neutral Agree
26. One of the most relevant and powerful influences on most people in organizations is the work group or team they are in.	Disagree Neutral Agree
27. Leadership skills may be acquired by most people, regardless of their particular inborn traits or abilities.	Disagree Neutral Agree
28. A major avenue towards increasing organizational effectiveness is through creating conditions under which members can make greater contributions to organization goals.	Disagree Neutral Agree
29. Organizations can be usually characterized as consisting of an overlapping set of groups or teams, with each group's leader serving as the link or anchor man for his team.	Disagree Neutral Agree
30. Most people desire to make, and are capable of making, a higher level of contribution to the attainment of organizational goals than most organizational environments will permit.	Disagree Neutral Agree
31. The extensive use of teams and committees in most organizations usually results in a good bit of wasted time.	Disagree Neutral Agree

Given your responses, review and list assumptions you currently have about organizational life.

_____

_____

_____

_____

_____

_____

_____

_____

_____

_____

_____

_____

_____

_____

Organization development is designed to improve organizational effectiveness. Organization development (OD) focuses on organizational culture, processes, and structures within a total systems perspective.

Organization development emerged in the 1950s and early 1960s as new insights were gained in group dynamics and planned change. It was established to help organizations address and embrace change and see change as an opportunity rather than a threat. The field has evolved to one that offers an integrated framework capable of solving most of the important problems related to the human side of organizations. OD is based on knowledge from the behavioral sciences disciplines of psychology, social psychology, sociology, anthropology, systems theory, organization behavior, organization theory, chaos theory, and management.

Organizations are constantly changing, they are in continuous interaction with external and internal forces, as exhibited in Figure 2-1. Changing customer requirements, new legislation, economic factors, and new technology all act on the organization to cause change from the external environment; obsolescence of products and services, new market opportunities, new strategic directions, and a changing workforce cause change from within the organization. OD provides methods and practices to assist organizations to adapt to these changes.

Figure 2-1. Forces That Create Change Within Organizations

Change has different facets. Change can be deliberate (planned) or accidental (unplanned). The change can be large or small scale. Change can occur rapidly, abruptly, revolutionary style, or slowly and evolutionary. The new state can have a very different nature from the old, as in transformation, quantum, or "second-order" change. Or the new state can look similar to the old with modifications, as in developmental, incremental, "first-order" change. Early OD efforts primarily addressed first-order change; the change was geared to make moderate adjustments to the organization, its people, and its processes. Today's environment demands more second-order change. We see this in organizations that undergo re-invention or re-engineering, redefining their vision and mission.

DEFINING ORGANIZATION DEVELOPMENT

A number of definitions of organization development exist, and while there is no universally accepted definition, there is general agreement on the nature of the field and its major characteristics. An examination of these provides insight into the evolution of the field. Two early authors offer the following definitions:

> Organization development is an effort (1) planned, (2) organization-wide, and (3) managed from the top, to (4) increase organizational effectiveness and health through (5) planned interventions in the organization's "processes", using behavioral-science knowledge (Richard Beckhard, 1969, p. 9).

> Organization development is a response to internal and external changes that affect the organization. It is a complex educational strategy intended to alter the beliefs, attitudes, values, and structure of organizations so that they can better adapt to new technologies, markets, and challenges, and the dizzying rate of change itself (Warren Bennis, 1969, p. 2).

A more recent definition shows the emerging concept of organization development as process improvement:

> Organization development is an organizational process for understanding and improving any and all substantive processes an organization may develop for performing any task and pursuing any objectives . . . A "process for improving processes." (Peter Vaill, 1989, p. 261).

French and Bell (1999, p. 25-26) define organization development as:

> A long-range effort, led and supported by top management, to improve an organization's visioning, empowerment, learning, and problem-solving processes, through an ongoing, collaborative management of organization culture—with special emphasis on the culture of intact work teams and other team configurations—using the consultant-facilitator role and theory and technology of applied behavioral science, including action research.

As you can see from these definitions, organization development is an effort which is planned and lead by managers to achieve long-range and organization-wide goals, supported from the top, designed to increase organizational effectiveness through planned interventions in the organization's processes, particularly through a more collaborative management of organizational culture, using the consultant-facilitator role, applied behavioral science theory, with an emphasis on developing human potential, and scientific approaches that supplement practical experience.

EFFECTIVE ORGANIZATIONS

If the goal of organization development is to improve organizational effectiveness, than it is helpful to have a picture of what an effective organization looks like.[2]

- The total organization is involved in the creation of a shared vision for the organization's future.
- The total organization, the significant subparts, and individuals, manage their work against *goals* and *plans* for achievement of these goals.
- Form follows function (the problem, or task, or project, determines how the human resources are organized).
- Decisions are made by and near the sources of information regardless of where these sources are located on the organization chart.
- The reward system is such that managers and supervisors are rewarded (and punished) comparably for:
  o Continuous improvement performance;
  o Growth and development of organizational members;
  o Creating viable working teams.
- Communication laterally and vertically is *relatively* undistorted. People are generally open and confronting. They share all the relevant facts including feelings.
- There is a minimum of inappropriate win/lose activities between individuals and groups. Constant effort exists at all levels to treat conflict, and conflicting situations, as *opportunities* to explore deep-seated issues.
- There is a high "conflict" (clash of ideas) about tasks and projects (leading to creativity), and relatively little energy spent in clashing over *interpersonal* difficulties because they have been generally worked through.
- The organization and its parts see themselves as interacting with each other *and* with a *larger* environment. The organization is an "open system."
- There is a shared value, and a management strategy to support it, of trying to help each person (or unit) in the organization maintains his (or its) integrity and uniqueness in an interdependent environment.
- The organization and its members operate in an "action-research" way. General practice is to build in *feedback mechanisms* so that individuals and

groups can learn from their experience. The organization practices continual learning.

CHARACTERISTICS OF ORGANIZATION DEVELOPMENT

Organization development has certain characteristics that distinguish it from other models of organizational intervention[3].

- OD focuses on culture, structure, and processes.
- Specifically, OD encourages collaboration between organization leaders and members in managing culture, structure, and processes.
- Teams of all kinds are particularly important for accomplishing tasks and are targets for OD activities.
- OD focuses on the human and social side of the organization and in so doing also intervenes in the technological and structural sides.
- OD calls for participation and involvement in problem solving and decision making at all levels of the organization.
- OD focuses on total system change and views organizations as complex social systems.
- OD practitioners are facilitators, collaborators, and co-learners in the client system.
- An overarching goal is to make the client system able to solve its problems on its own by teaching skills and knowledge of continuous learning through self-analytical methods. OD views organization improvement as an ongoing process in the context of a constantly changing environment.
- OD relies on an action research model with extensive participation by client system members.
- OD takes a developmental view that seeks the betterment of both individuals and the organization. Attempting to create "win-win" solutions is standard practice in OD programs.
- Organization Development practices must be supported from the top in order to be successful.
- Organization Development relies heavily on experiential, action-oriented learning.
- OD focuses more on processes than content. Because it involves a systems approach, it is a relatively long-term process, one that is dynamic and ongoing.

ASSUMPTIONS, VALUES, AND ACTIONS OF ORGANIZATION DEVELOPMENT

The field of organization development is based upon certain values and assumptions about dealing with individuals, group settings, and organizational systems[4]. These assumptions provide the theoretical framework for theories and models found in the field.

INDIVIDUALS

Three major assumptions within organization development about individuals at work are influenced by Maslow's (1954) Hierarchy of Needs theory of motivation, and McGregor's (1960) Theory Y:

- Most individuals desire personal growth and development when placed in a supportive and challenging work environment.
- Most individuals are capable of making a greater contribution to their organizations than organizations are historically willing to permit.
- Most individuals want to have a voice in decisions that affect them and their work. When given a voice, there is a higher likelihood of supporting a change effort.

These assumptions clear the way for organizational management to tap into the creative resources of organizational members, or as French and Bell (1999, p. 67) put it, "Ask, listen, support, challenge, encourage risk taking, permit failure, remove obstacles and barriers, give autonomy, give responsibility, set high standards, and reward success."

GROUP, GROUP MEMBERS, AND GROUP LEADERSHIP

Assumptions of groups and group members at work are influenced by the work of such behavioral scientists as Elton Mayo and the Hawthorne Studies:

- One's work group is extremely important in determining feelings of competence and satisfaction.
- Most people want to be accepted by and get along well with their work group. These work groups can be made more effective if individuals work together more cooperatively.
- Most people are capable of making a greater contribution to the group's effectiveness.
- Teams are often the best way to get work done, and they satisfy social and emotional needs at work. It is in management's best interest to allow teams to flourish.
- Leaders should invest in teams: the time required for team development; training resources to increase team members' skills; energy in creating a positive atmosphere.
- Leaders should adopt a team leadership style and give important work to groups.
- The formal leader of the work group cannot possibly perform all of the leadership functions at all times; therefore, leadership must be shared.
- Group members should receive training in group effectiveness skills such as group problem solving and decision making, conflict management, facilitation, and interpersonal communications.
- Suppressed feelings adversely influence the functioning of groups and organizations. Group climate should be one of increased openness. Group

members should be encouraged to deal effectively with both positive and negative feelings.

- The solutions to most attitudinal and motivation problems in groups require interactive and transactional solutions; group members must accept responsibility for seeking win-win solutions. Rather than seeing the problem as being "within the problem person", a change in perspective to viewing problems and solutions as transactional and as embedded within a system.

DESIGNING AND RUNNING ORGANIZATIONS

Assumptions about designing and running organizations are based on over a half century of research and experience in the field of organization development, and numerous examples of organizations that are both humane and high performing.

- The traditional hierarchy is obsolete and cannot meet the demands of the changing environment. Experimenting with new organizational systems and new forms of authority/management/leadership are imperative.
- Resolving conflict in such a way that one party wins triumphantly and the other loses severely is not a healthy method for solving organizational problems. Cooperative rather than competitive organizational dynamics should be a focus of organizational leaders.
- Development of organizational members is a key assumption within OD. Following the self-fulfilling prophecy, an optimistic, developmental set of assumptions about people is likely to reap rewards beneficial to both the organization and its members.
- Organizations can create an environment that is humane, developmental, empowering, and high performing in terms of productivity, quality of output, and profitability.

ACTIONS CONSISTENT WITH HUMANISTIC VALUES AND COLLABORATION[5]

- The perceptions, feelings, and attitudes of the people affected by a change are viewed as important and are taken into account when that change is planned.
- Those affected by a change are involved in the process of shaping that change.
- Important data about a change are shared with those affected by it.
- Those affected by a change have influence over the nature of that change (*when* and *how* it occurs, and, to some extent, *what* occurs).
- Feedback is elicited from those who might be affected by a change.
- Feedback on the success of a change, the need for corrective action, and the need for maintenance activities are provided to those affected by that change.

ACTIONS CONSISTENT WITH SYSTEMATIC PLANNING[6]

- Study and analysis are used to determine actual problems, feasible solution alternatives, and a ranking of alternatives.
- Objectives are considered in terms of their impact on the total organization.
- Interdependencies are noted and considered.
- Long-range as well as short-range impact is taken into account.
- The effects of a change on tasks, structure, technology, and processes involving people are considered.
- Concern is given to the implementation, review, and reinforcement of a change activity.

The assumptions of organization development provide guiding principles for practitioners. Even though they were developed during the 1950s and 1960s, they remain important today. And while they were thought to be revolutionary at the time, they are widely accepted today. However, values are never static and changes taking place today will force us to examine new definitions, new assumptions about what is "good" organization development practice (French and Bell, 1999, p. 70).

A NOTE ON COLLABORATION[7]

When we say that OD is a collaborative effort, both from the OD practitioner/client system perspective, and from the manager/employee perspective, we recognize there are potential concerns. Operationalized, collaboration means "involvement," "power sharing," "participation," "empowerment" and so on. It is not seen as a true OD effort if all organizational members are not involved, the more democratic and participative the system, the more effective the OD activity.

However, this concept can lead to difficulties. For example, a manager has a range of decision-making options from fully closed to fully open (see the related reading on *Rensis Likert: System 1-4 Management* at end of this chapter). If we take collaboration at its face value, we would encourage the manager to open up, we would offer interventions that build trust in the system, and we would make this a prerequisite to any OD effort. Experience tells us, however, that human nature is slow to change, particularly long-standing behavioral habits that have proved to be effective in the past. An alternative is to allow the manager to see the results of his or her behavior, help him understand the complexity of human aspects of their work world, demonstrate alternatives to his current management approach, and help him understand the most sensible way to deal with change is to be aware of the situation.

Collaboration in decision making also can be misinterpreted to mean the "subordinates" know more than the "managers" and should therefore make decisions for their supervisors. This is demonstrated in the way we practice OD, by encouraging participation, often highlighting the ideas of group members over managers, thus leading to the conclusion that not only does a manager need to involve subordinates in all decisions, but also defer to them in most situations. This practice can be seen as diminishing the leadership role of the manager.

Another misinterpretation in collaboration is that it is the manager's responsibility to develop a more open and trusting relationship in group and intergroup situations. By abdicating this responsibility to the manager, the group members do not feel a sense of ownership over the outcome, and can be passive observers of the manager trying to be more open and honest and soliciting feedback. Again, experience tells us that the more we find the manager distrustful, the more we will not trust his or her efforts, and therefore we will not follow his or her lead. Subsequently, out of frustration, the manager may reduce personal efforts towards openness, demonstrating to the group that he or she was not serious about increasing trust.

The interpretation of collaboration meaning total involvement of all organizational members at all times can lead to frustration and the conclusion that OD is unworkable. The reality is that in most, and certainly large organizations, it is impossible to involve *all* or even most organizational members in decision making. It is also impossible for managers to effect trust and openness without the help of group members. We suggest that collaboration does not necessarily mean constant involvement, and acknowledge that in some cases, collaboration may mean willingness to tolerate the quick and authoritarian actions of those in power that need to move in order to get the job done. We can therefore define collaboration as "a good-faith effort based on trust and a mature understanding of roles and pressures."

BASIC OD PROCESS

The basic process of organization development begins with sensing a need for change, based on a problem or opportunity. A consultant is engaged and the consultant-client relationship is established. The diagnostic phase includes data collection and analysis to clearly understand the problem or opportunity. Many OD consultants use the Action Research methodology (see Chapter 7: Approaches to Organizational Change), which involves collecting data from the organization and feeding it back into the system, followed by developing and implementing action programs to improve organizational effectiveness. Action is planned and taken, followed by an evaluation of the actions taken. Adjustments are made if necessary and if new actions are taken, they too are evaluated. The process is repeated until the problem is resolved, as depicted in Figure 2-2. The goal of the process is to improve organizational effectiveness.

Figure 2-2. Basic Organization Development Process

Organization development involves a systematic planning that allows for and builds on the following factors:
- The client's actual situation versus the desired situation;
- interdependencies in the client system; and
- specific changes required to progress toward the client's desired situation.

ORGANIZATION DEVELOPMENT PRACTITIONERS

Organization development consultants are engaged in the OD process at the first stage of problem awareness. Unlike other organizational improvement programs, the relationship between the OD consultant and client organization is one of collaboration, where the consultant establishes a collaborative relationship of relative equality with organization members. Together, they diagnose the problem, plan and evaluate actions. The OD consultant establishes a learning community where all parties discover what needs to be changed and how to go about getting to the desired state. The role of OD consultants is to structure activities to help organization members learn to solve their own problems and learn to do it better over time. OD consultants typically do not give substantive solutions to problems; rather, in creating a learning environment, they leave organizational members better positioned to go through the OD process on their own.   The aim of the OD consultant is to leave organizational members with key skills and knowledge required for continuous self-improvement.   OD consulting fosters increased competence, growth, learning, and empowerment throughout the client organization.   Further discussion of the organization development consultancy process is discussed in Chapter 3.

ORGANIZATION DEVELOPMENT FOCUS

Organization development is a process that focuses on organizational culture, processes, and structures using a total system perspective.   These key areas are leverage points for determining how well or how poorly the system functions[8].

- **Organization culture** is defined as the values, assumptions, and beliefs held in common by organization members that shape how they perceive, think, and act.   Organization culture strongly influences individual and group behavior—how people act depends on how they perceive and think about things, which is often embedded in the culture.   If real change is to occur within an organization, the culture must be changed.
- **Organizational processes** are how things get done in organizations, the methods employed for achieving results.   Important processes within organizations include communication, problem solving and decision making, resource allocation, conflict resolution, rewards, human resource practices, strategic management, leadership, and self-renewal or continuous learning.   How things are done is as important as what is done.
- **Organization structure** refers to the overall design of the organization, it's "wiring diagram" for how the parts are connected to produce the whole. Structure also refers to how work tasks are designed and how these tasks are integrated.   Organization structure is an active area of experimentation in OD today.

SYSTEMS PERSPECTIVE IN ORGANIZATION DEVELOPMENT

The target of organization development is the whole system, not individual members (even though organizational members are instruments of the change initiatives.) Systems theory recognizes the interconnectedness of various parts of the organization, and acknowledges that change in one area will affect change in another area.   For example, a change in strategy will affect structure, processes, and organizational culture. A sound OD initiative is based on this understanding of the dynamics of systems theory.

A primary goal of OD is to optimize the system by ensuring that system elements are harmonious and congruent.   OD interventions focus on aligning structure, processes and culture, aligning the individual and the organization, aligning organizational elements, and aligning the organization with environmental demands. As organizations are *open systems* (systems interacting with their environment), when the environment changes, the organization must adapt. OD practitioners must be knowledgeable about both systems thinking and open system thinking. There are six organizational components that interact with and affect each other, as shown in Figure 2-3 (Frame, Hess & Nielsen, 1982, p. 10). These elements offer data helpful in the analysis and planning for change:

Figure 2-3. Interdependencies in Organizational Components

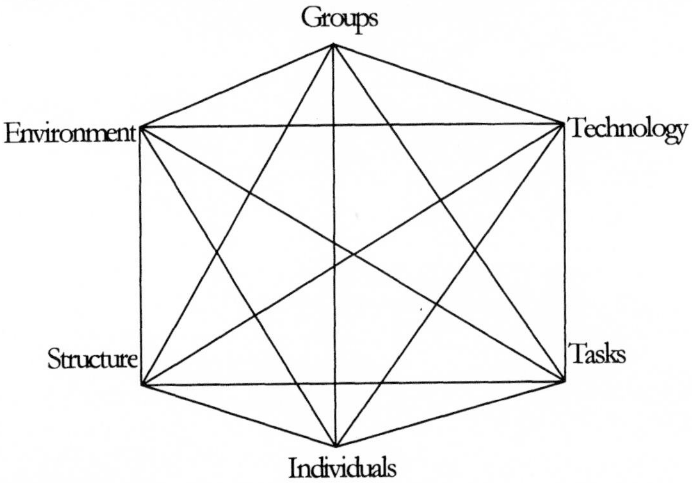

- Groups, analyzed according to norms, relationships, performance levels, work distribution, functions, priorities, and decision making and problem-solving processes.
- Environment, established by market, competitors, related organizations, government regulations, societal values, talent potential, and social responsiveness.
- Technology, consisting of knowledge, equipment, processes, and overall flow of activity.
- Structure, including the reward system, hierarchy, patterns of contact between organizational members, mission and goals of the organization, policy and procedures, financial system, physical setting, decision-making mechanisms, and reporting relationships.
- Individuals, who possess unique demographics, skills, educational backgrounds, needs and motivational patterns, value systems, behavior patterns, and performance levels.

- Tasks, reflecting job-design elements, authority and responsibility, required skills, time requirements, motivational patterns, and work flow.

Change is holistic, change in one area affects and influences the others. While not all changes affect the entire system at the same level of intensity, effective OD work calls for awareness of the interactions. An example of this would be the introduction of new technology that would change the way the individual performs his or her assigned tasks, alter procedures, and influence the attitudes and behavioral skills of the organizational members. Another example would be to introduce skills training based on analysis of individuals without considering the ways in which task and structure might affect the training results. This would result in expenditure of resources with little impact in resolving underlying problems.

ORGANIZATION DEVELOPMENT IS NOT...

Organization development is a collaborative, system-wide approach to improving organizational effectiveness. It is not a program, rather a process. It is not unilaterally imposed upon organizational members, without the collaboration of those affected. The focus is on organization, not individual development, even though within the process of increasing organizational effectiveness, individuals are provided opportunities to grow and learn.

The OD consultant role is one of facilitation of process, not "physician" brought in to prescribe "a cure" for an "unhealthy" organization (Schein, 1997). OD is not a single event, rather an evolutionary process involving a number of interdependent steps or phases, each one building on the previous one, with new learning at each phase. The organization is seen as continually developing, rather than "unhealthy."

Organization development falls within the context of organizational strategy; it serves the organizational purpose, through the exploration of business and people issues.

RELATED READINGS

Hawthorne Studies

During the 1920s and 1930s, a series of studies were conducted at the Hawthorne Works plant of Western Electric Company. The company was interested in the effects of physical working conditions on productivity. Studies included examining how various levels of illumination affected productivity, which failed to yield data showing a relationship. In some groups, productivity increased or decreased at random; in other groups it steadily increased; and in one, productivity increased even as illumination was reduced to the level of moonlight. Another study, led by Elton Mayo, examined the effects of worker fatigue on productivity. Workers were subjected to various rest pauses, lengths of workday, and lengths of workweek, while their productivity was measured. Once again the results showed no direct correlation of fatigue to productivity. Overall, the productivity of the relay assemblers increased over time, regardless of the specific changes made in the work setting.

The conclusions drawn by Mayo and the other researchers were that the new "social setting" was the cause of the productivity increase. They singled out two factors as having special importance. First, there was a positive group development in the test room. The workers shared good social relations and a common desire to do a good job. Second, supervision was more participative with this group. Workers in the test room were made to feel important, given a lot of information, and frequently consulted for their opinion on what was taking place.

Another study at the Hawthorne plant examined the behavior of the work group, with findings that indicated some individuals were willing to sacrifice pay and restrict their output to avoid the displeasure of the group. This led to the assumption that the work group can have both a strong positive as well as negative impact on individual productivity.

The term *Hawthorne effect* has been coined to describe situations in which people are singled out for special attention and increase their productivity only because of the expectancies created by the special situation.

Douglas McGregor: Theory X and Theory Y Assumptions

One of the prominent contributors to the Human Relations movement was Douglas McGregor (1960) who proposed two types of organizational leadership, based on assumptions about human nature at work.

Theory X

- The average human being has an inherent dislike of work and will avoid it if he can.

- Most people must be coerced, controlled, directed, and threatened with punishment to get them to put forth adequate effort towards the achievement of organizational objectives.

- The average human being prefers to be directed, wishes to avoid responsibility, has relatively little ambition, and wants security above all else.

Theory Y

- The expenditure of physical and mental effort in work is as natural as rest or play.

- Man will exercise self-direction and self-control in the service of those objectives to which he is committed.

- Commitment to objectives is a function of the rewards associated with their achievement.

- The average human being learns, under proper conditions, not only to accept but also to seek responsibility.

- The capacity to exercise a relatively high degree of imagination, ingenuity, and creativity in the solution of organizational problems is widely, not narrowly, distributed in the population.

- Under the conditions of modern industrial life, the intellectual potential of the average human being is only partially utilized.

Theory Y offers a more humanistic approach to viewing the organization and its workers. It is assumed that since people are already motivated and desire responsibility, the role of the leader is to arrange organizational conditions so that it is possible for them to fulfill their needs while directing their efforts toward achieving organizational objectives. This theory appears to be correct when the work is valued and the worker has internalized the value of the work effort.

Rensis Likert: System 1-4 Management

Another strong contributor to the Humanist theories was Rensis Likert who suggested that leadership is a process in which leaders must acknowledge the expectations, values, and interpersonal skills of those being led. Likert suggested that management/leadership styles of organizations could be depicted on a continuum from System 1 through System 4 (1967).

System 1 (Exploitive authoritative). Management is seen as having little or no confidence or trust in employees and seldom involves them in any aspect of decision-making. Most decisions are made by key executives at the head of the organization and issued downwards through the chain of command. In System 1 organizations, employees feel they work with fear, threats, punishment, and rare rewards. The need satisfaction (Maslow) is at the physiological and safety levels. There is limited supervisor/employee interaction. An informal organization generally develops in opposition to the goals of the formal organization.

System 2 (Benevolent authoritative). Management is seen as having a condescending attitude towards employees, rather like master/servant. Most decisions are made at the top of the organization; a few are made within a prescribed framework at lower levels. Rewards and punishments are used to motivate employees. When interaction takes place between supervision and employees, it is with a condescending attitude on the part of supervision and fear and uncertainty on the part of employees. Some control is delegated to the middle and lower levels of the organization. An informal organization generally develops, but not always in resistance to the formal organizational goals.

System 3 (Consultative). Management is seen as having substantial, but not complete confidence and trust in employees. Broad policy-making and general decision-making remains at the top, however employees are permitted to make more specific decisions at lower levels. Communication flows both up and down the hierarchy. Rewards, occasional punishment, and some involvement are used to motivate employees. There is a moderate amount of interaction, often with a fair amount of confidence and trust. Significant aspects of the control process are delegated downward. An informal organization may develop, but it may either support or partially resist organizational goals.

System 4 (Participative Group). Management is seen as having complete trust and confidence in employees. Decision making and goal setting are widely dispersed throughout the organization. Communications flows in all directions, up, down, and sideways. Motivation is achieved through participation and involvement, goal-setting, and solicitation of ways to improve methods and processes. There is extensive interaction between supervisors and employees and this interaction is friendly, open, and full of trust. There is widespread responsibility for the control process. The informal and formal organizations are often one and the same.

As you can see, System 1 Management is task-oriented and highly structured with Theory X assumptions, while System 4 Management is relationship-oriented organization based on teamwork, mutual trust, and confidence, and a Theory Y assumption. Systems 2 and 3 are intermediate stages between the two extremes.

ENDNOTES

[1] Adapted from Roy McLennan. (1989). *Managing Organizational Change*, 1st ed. Englewood Cliffs, NJ: Prentice Hall, pp. 104-107. Adapted by permission of Pearson Education, Inc., Upper Saddle River, NJ. Based on Wendell L. French and Cecil H. Bell. 1978, 1984, 1999. *Organization Development*. Prentice Hall.

[2] This list is adapted and updated from Beckhard, R. (1969). *Organization Development: Strategies and Models*. Reading, MASS: Addison-Wesley Publishing, p. 10.

[3] This section draws from French & Bell, (1999), p. 29. Reprinted by permission of Pearson Education, Inc., Upper Saddle River, NJ.

[4] ibid, p. 67-69.

[5] See Robert M. Frame, Randy K. Hess, & Warren R. Nielsen. (1982). *The OD Source Book: A Practitioner's Guide*. San Francisco, CA: Jossey-Bass Pfeiffer, p. 8.

[6] ibid, p. 8.

[7] This section draws from Robert M. Frame, Randy K. Hess, & Warren R. Nielsen. (1982). *The OD Source Book: A Practitioner's Guide*. San Francisco, CA: Jossey-Bass Pfeiffer, p. 1.

[8] French, W. L., & Bell, C. H. (1999). *Organization Development*. Englewood Cliffs, NJ: Prentice Hall, p. 3. Early terms for these three components were: sociosystem, process system, and technosystem. Also see H. Leavitt. 1965. Applied organizational change in industry. In J. March (Ed.), *Handbook of organizations*. Chicago: Rand McNally.

CHAPTER 3:

ORGANIZATION DEVELOPMENT PRACTITIONERS

CASE STUDY: A PROBLEM OF DIMINISHED MORALE[1] (PART 1)

During my (Edgar Schein) second year as an assistant professor at MIT I was asked by my mentor, Douglas McGregor, whether a colleague and I would be willing to take on a consulting assignment at a nearby company. Doug did not have the time himself and was anxious to introduce all of us on the faculty to the experience of consulting.

The assignment was to do an interview survey of the technical personnel in the company's research laboratory. According to the VP of IR and Personnel there was a morale problem in the lab and the laboratory director was interested in finding out what the employees thought so that the problems could be fixed. It was this VP who knew McGregor personally and had asked him either to do it himself or find someone who could. The VP had not only authorized the study but our consulting expenses came out of his budget. He assured Doug that the director of the research labs was on board and was delighted to have the survey done. All of this information came from Doug. We never met the VP but we did talk to the director of the lab and learned that he was in favor of doing the interviews and would set up the process with his technical people.

After some months of careful interviewing, my colleague and I collated the data and wrote a fairly complete report on all of the issues that had been identified by the technical staff. As might have been expected, among the complaints registered were many about the managerial style of the director. We noted these complaints in one section of our report. A feedback session was scheduled with the director during which my colleague and I were prepared to go through all of the data that were contained in the report. We had requested two hours, since there was a lot of information to cover and we wanted to be very thorough in demonstrating how valid the information was by showing various statistics.

My colleague and I walked into the director's office, presented him with a copy of the report (he was the first person in the company to see it), and started our presentation while he leafed through the report. He immediately spotted the section in which his management style was mentioned, read it over quickly and then interrupted us in a rather angry manner with a curt "Thank you", and dismissed us. We had spent no more than 15 minutes with the director and were not invited back either by him or the VP. We never found out what happened to the report that we left with the director.

Level 1 Questions:

1.   What do you think went wrong?
2.   What did Schein and his colleagues do right?
3.   What did Schein and his colleagues do wrong?
4.   What do you think they could have done differently?

The best test, and difficult to administer, is: do those served grow as persons; do they, *while being served*, become healthier, wiser, freer, more autonomous, more likely themselves to become servants? *And*, what is the effect on the least privileged in society. Robert Greenleaf (1970, p. 7)

This quote portrays a guiding principle for the practice of organization development. Organization development practitioners/consultants are typically engaged in the organization at the first stage of problem awareness. Unlike other organizational improvement programs, the relationship between the OD consultant and client organization is one of collaboration, where the consultant establishes a collaborative relationship of relative equality with organization members. Together, they diagnose the problem, plan and evaluate actions. The OD consultant establishes a learning community where all parties discover what needs to be changed and how to go about getting to the desired state. The role of OD consultants is to structure activities to help organization members learn to identify, analyze and solve their own problems and learn to do it better over time. OD consultants generally do not give substantive solutions to problems; rather, in creating a learning environment, they leave organizational members better positioned to go through the OD process on their own. The aim of the OD consultant is to leave organizational members with key skills and knowledge required for continuous self-improvement. OD consulting fosters increased competence, growth, learning, and empowerment throughout the client organization (French and Bell, 1999, p. 3).

In this chapter we explore the role of consultant and the relationship to organizational clients, types of clients and levels of problems faced. We provide guiding principles and a general description of the consulting process. Ethical considerations are presented.

THE ROLE OF OD PRACTITIONER: CONTENT EXPERT VERSUS PROCESS FACILITATOR[2]

Organization development practitioners are continually faced with the dilemma of identifying and solving problems or facilitating the process of helping the organization learn so they can identify and solve problems for themselves. The "consultant as technical expert" and "consultant as process facilitator" present a basic foundation of assumptions and behaviors that affect the consultant-client relationship. In the expert model, the consultant is hired because of specific skills in eliciting information or specific knowledge to solve a given problem. The client decides what to do with that information, if anything. Schein (1978) refers to the doctor-patient relationship where the consultant is hired because the client (patient) admits to not knowing what is wrong, giving the consultant (doctor) broad powers to come into the organization, do a diagnosis, and then implicitly commits to accepting some kind of prescription or remedy. Either way, the consultant is seen as the expert who will come in and fix the organizations' problems.

The process consultation model, on the other hand, puts the "remedy" into the hands of the client. In one version, the catalyst model, the consultant does not know the solution but has skills in helping the client figure out his or her own solution. In the facilitator model, the consultant may have ideas and possible solutions to the problem, but decides a better solution and better implementation of that solution will result in helping the client solve their own problems. An example of this model is the manager who helps a subordinate group reach their own solution by creating a better decision-making process, rather than making the decision personally. Descriptions of the two follow.

TECHNICAL EXPERT MODEL

- The client has made a correct diagnosis of the problem. The client's statement of the problem is either accepted at face value or verified by the consultant on the basis of his or her technical expertise relative to the problem, however it is not in the consultancy contract to verify this.
- The client has correctly communicated the problem. It is not up to the consultant to verify that the problem statement is in fact accurate or not, before going about solving the problem.
- The client organization will reveal correct information to the consultant, information that will allow the consultant to arrive at a diagnosis and cure.
- Little time is spent on developing the consultant-client relationship. The connection is typically short-term and problem-oriented.
- The consultant brings technical expertise to bear on the client's problem(s).
- The solution, or prescription, to the problem is generally developed by the consultant and implemented by the client. The client has thought through and accepted the potential consequences of the help that will be received. The client may not be prepared to accept and do something with information that may not fit with prior expectations.
- The consultant is primarily concerned with increasing the client's knowledge and skill relative to the stated problem(s).
- In general, the consultant does it *for* and *to* the client.

PROCESS FACILITATOR MODEL

- The client's statement of the problem is treated as information. Both the client and the consultant verify the problem jointly. The nature of the problem is such that the client not only needs help in making an initial diagnosis but also would benefit from participation in the process of making that diagnosis.
- A further assumption is that the information relevant to the diagnosis is fairly deeply embedded in the client system and would not be easily elicited by an outsider functioning in a consulting role, but might be more

accessible if the client and consultant are working together to elicit and interpret information.

- Equally important is the assumption that the client would improve his or her capacity for future problem solving through being engaged in the process.
- The consultant-client relationship is viewed as an essential ingredient in the process and considerable attention is given to its development.
- The consultant is an expert on how to diagnose and facilitate organizational processes.
- The major focus of the consultant is to help the client to discover and implement appropriate solutions for him or herself. The client is ultimately the only one who knows what form of solution or intervention will work in the situation.
- The consultant, rather than offering "advice", would be more effective to offer alternatives and encourage the client to generate additional alternatives.
- The consultant is primarily concerned with improving the client's diagnostic and problem-solving skills. If the client selects and implements his or her own solution, the client's problem-solving skills for future problems will increase.
- The goal of process consultation is to improve overall problem-solving skills on the part of the client.
- In general, the consultant helps the client to do it for and to him or herself.

A VARIETY OF CLIENT TYPES

Schein (1997) points out that at times it is confusing to know who is the client, for whom one is working, especially is a large organization where you are engaged in various sub-systems. He says there are six basic types of client populations.

Contact clients - the individual(s) who first contacts the consultant with a request, question or issue.

Intermediate clients - the individuals or groups who or which get involved in various interviews, meetings, and other activities as the project evolves.

Primary clients - the individual(s) who ultimately "owns" the problem or issue being worked on; they are typically also the ones who pay the consulting bills or whose budget covers the consultation project.

Unwitting clients - members of the organization or client system above, below and laterally related to the primary clients who will be affected by interventions but who are not aware that they will be impacted.

Indirect clients - members of the organization who are aware that they will be affected by the interventions but who are unknown to the consultant and who may feel either positive or negative about these effects.

Ultimate clients - the community, the total organization, an occupational group, or any other group that the consultant cares about and whose welfare must be considered in any intervention that the consultant makes.

The contact client usually introduces the consultant to other people in the organization, who in turn, may work with the consultant to plan activities for still others in the organization. As the project proceeds, it is important for the consultant to distinguish between the client types, especially between primary clients who pay for the work and the unwitting and ultimate clients who will be affected by it. As Schein points out, the definition of what is helpful may change depending on the client, requiring the consultant to create broader mental models that permit thinking about social systems, networks, lines of influence, power relations, and other socio-psychological concepts.

A VARIETY OF CONCERNS

In addition to the types of clients, there are also levels of problems and concerns that the consultant must be aware of as outlined below (Schein, 1997.) This indicates the inherent complexity of the consultancy role. A consultant may be working mostly in one-on-one or small group situations, however must be cognizant of whether the person or group is a contact, intermediate or primary client, and whether the problem focus is individual, group, or organizational.

Individual. Comprising of "intra-psychic" issues. Interventions such as career counseling, helping the individual become more effective as a participant of the organization, various forms of coaching, mentoring, training. Can be provided to the contact client, to individuals in the intermediate or primary client system, to members of the unwitting or ultimate client populations.

Inter-personal. Problems or issues that pertain to the relationship between the individual and other members of the organization or client system. The work is either with more than one person at a time, or if working individually, focused on relationship issues, such as the client's roles in various groups, his or her effectiveness as a team member. Interventions described at the individual level may overlap with interventions at this level; the focus is on the impact of the individual's behavior on others.

Face-to-face group. Problems or issues connected with group or team functioning as a group. "Face-to-face" means that the group is conscious of itself as a group, even if not in regular contact or in the same physical location. The consultant's roles include being a non-directive facilitator of meetings, managing the agenda, or helping to structure the work of the group. The consultant may meet individually with members of any of the client types, for purposes of identifying issues or agenda concerns, with the focus on how the group works as a group.

Inter-group. Problems or issues that derive from the way in which groups, teams, departments, and other kinds of organizational units relate to each other and co-ordinate their work on behalf of the organization or larger client system. The consultant is now intervening at the system level and must think in terms of large multi-unit interventions.

Organizational. Problems or issues that concern the mission, strategy, and total welfare of the whole client system, whether that be a family unit, a department, an organization, or a whole community. The consultant may be working with individual leaders, groups or "inter-groups" with the focus on total systems' level problems.

Inter-organizational. Problems or issues that involve members of complete organizational units working in some kind of alliance or joint venture with other units. Many of the same kinds of interventions used at the organizational or inter-group level apply here.

Larger system. Problems or issues that involve the wider community or society where the consultant may be working with social networks, with organizational sets, or with community groups that involve a wide variety of issues pertaining to the health of the larger system.

Schein does clarify that the psycho-dynamics of the relationship between consultant and client remain essentially the same even though the problem focus may shift between levels.

GUIDING PRINCIPLES FOR OD PRACTITIONERS

Again drawing from Schein (1997), there are general principles that govern the relationship of consultant and client, regardless of type of client or level of intervention. These principles and what they mean in practice is discussed.

Principle 1. Always be helpful. Consultation is providing help; therefore every contact should be conceived by the client as helpful.

- This requires consultants to be clear about their motives, i.e., maintaining the relationship to obtain additional income leads to interventions that may not be helpful. Similarly, the need to gather data often serves the consultant's needs more than it does the client's. The consultant should create conditions where the client learns how to gather their own data with the consultant's help, rather than depending on the consultant for this process.

Principle 2. Always deal with reality. You cannot be helpful if you do not know the realities of the client system; therefore, every contact should bring to the surface diagnostic information about the state of client system.

- There is the temptation to define current reality in terms of our own past experience. We "recognize" client problems as being similar to ones we have dealt with before. It is important to engage in a period of exploratory inquiry that identifies as much as is possible the current reality the client is experiencing.

Principle 3. Access your ignorance. You cannot determine what the current reality is if you do not get in touch with what you do not know about the situation and have the wisdom and the courage to ask about it.

- Consultants must learn to identify and accept what it is that they truly do not know about the client situation. Rather than testing hypothesis, asking rhetorical or leading questions, the consultant must engage in genuine exploratory inquiry. Such inquiry, if based on true ignorance, will be helpful; both consultant and client learn new important things about the situation as they explore it together. There is nothing potentially more powerful than the "dumb question", and there is nothing more important than for the client to become a competent and enthusiastic inquirer.

Principle 4. Everything you do is an intervention. Even though the goal of exploratory inquiry through accessing ignorance is diagnostic information, the reality is that every question or inquiry is at the same time an intervention and must be treated as such.

- Everything the consultant does with the client has some impact on the client and the client system. The behavior of both client and consultant affects the system. The reality is, however, only the client knows what the impact is. The consultant must be sensitive to observing client reactions to even initial interventions.

Principle 5. The client owns the problem and the solution. The reality is that only the client has to live with the consequences of the problem and the solution, so the consultant must not take the monkey off the client's back.

- Only the client knows whether a course of action will be helpful to the organization. The role of the consultant is to help the client appreciate what the consequences are. Even though the client owns the problem and the solution, the consultant and client jointly own the inquiry process that will reveal what the correct actions might be. The consultant can never really know the culture of the organization, and must be careful in making assumptions about what will or will not work within the client's culture. Similarly, only the client knows the impact a particular action will have on the organizational system. Therefore, clients must always be involved and be aware that they own all the next steps taken.

Principle 6. Go with the flow, but seize targets of opportunity. All systems develop cultures and attempt to maintain their stability through maintenance of those cultures. Therefore, one must "go with the flow". At the same time, all systems have areas of instability where motivation to change exists. One must build on existing motivations and cultural strengths, and seize targets of opportunity.

- Interventions that work best are ones that have identified and used the current realities present in the client system. The consultant should look for cultural strength to draw on and locate areas of motivation to work with and draw on. Appreciative inquiry[3] and other interventions that focus the client on positive aspirations, ideal states, future states, future targets are helpful and important.

Principle 7.   Be prepared for surprises, and learn from them. Everything that happens is a source of new data, and everything you think you know about the client system is only a hypothesis to be tested through further interventions.

- Things happen that turn out to be mistakes, no matter how carefully the consultant plans the intervention. Clients get upset, reject efforts on the part of the consultant, and in other ways mess things up. Whatever happens, however, is a source of data, ready to be digested and integrated.

Principle 8. Share the "problem". Neither the client nor the consultant can fully understand the reality of the situation; defining that reality is an ongoing joint effort in terms of what to do next.

- Never accept the initial "problem" to be what will ultimately become the target of the joint effort to make changes. The client may be withholding information while he tests the consultant to determine whether the relationship is characterized by sufficient trust to reveal the real problem. The client may think he is being open, but is insufficiently perceptive to see the reality. The consultant and client must work together to search out what is really going on. Additionally, there may be times when the consultant really doesn't know what to do next. Rather than fall into the "expert" trap, and unilaterally decide the next step, it is prudent to share the problem with the client to figure out what to do next. This creates a learning environment in which the client learns how to think more diagnostically about his organization.

THE CONSULTING PROCESS

The change agent can be either an individual external to the organization that is brought in to facilitate the change effort, or an internal organizational member chartered with facilitating the change. The relationship between the client and the consultant/change agent hinges on maximizing the strengths of both sides, while minimizing frustrations, missed deadlines, and products that fall short of expectations.

Block (2000, 2001) provides change agents with a five-phase approach to consulting:

- **Phase 1. Entry and Contracting**. This is the initial contact with the client, including setting up first meeting, exploring what the problem is, establishing whether the consultant is the right person to work on this issue, what client's expectations are, what consultant's expectations are, and how to get started.
- **Phase 2. Discovery and Dialogue**. In this phase, the consultant discovers his or her own sense of what the problem is, as well as helping the client develop this skill. This includes establishing who is to be involved in defining the problem, what methods will be used, what kind of data should be collected, and how long it will take.
- **Phase 3. Feedback and Decision to Act**. Once data is collected, it must be analyzed and reported. This includes decisions on how to involve the client in the process of analyzing the information, and in what fashion it will be reported. The consultant needs to be prepared to deal with resistance to the data, if it deals with important issues. This phase also

includes planning for action, setting ultimate project goals and selecting the best action steps or changes.

- **Phase 4. Engagement and Implementation**. This phase calls for carrying out the plan. The implementation may be done by the client organization, or in the case of large-scale change efforts, the consultant may be involved.
- **Phase 5. Extension, Recycle, or Termination**. This phase begins with evaluation of the implemented change initiative. The decision is made whether to extend the process to a larger segment of the organization. The process may be recycled to previous stages for further data collection and analysis. Or if the problem has been "solved", termination may occur.

ETHICAL STANDARDS IN ORGANIZATION DEVELOPMENT

The values underlying ethical OD practice are honesty, openness, voluntarism, integrity, confidentiality, development of people, and development of client expertise, high standards, and self-awareness. Unethical behavior includes:[4]

- **Misrepresentation of the consultant's skills**, the distortion of one's background, training, competencies, or experience in vita sheets, advertising, or conversation. A subtle form of misrepresentation is allowing the client assume certain skills are present when they are not.
- **Professional/technical ineptness**, using an intervention that has a low probability of being helpful (and may be indeed be harmful), and/or using an intervention that exceeds one's expertise. An example is asking people in a team-building session to provide mutual feedback on leadership style when neither preliminary interviews nor the client group has indicated a readiness or willingness to do so. Another example is to proceed with an intervention with which one has no experience, rather than seeking coaching from a more experienced colleague.
- **Misuse of data** on the part of the client or the consultant. Confidentiality is critical to OD efforts. Examples include: disclosing names of respondents to surveys without permission, disclosing to the boss names of those who provided information about the boss's dysfunctional behavior, disclosing study results of one department to another department without authorization.
- **Distortions of data** are also unethical. Overstating or overemphasizing the dysfunctional aspects of a group to the larger group is not only unethical, but may backfire—the larger group might turn on the consultant and defend the dysfunctional group.
- **Collusion** with members of the group to show deficiencies in other members. For example, setting up a feedback situation in which the deficiencies of a manager will become apparent, particularly to this manager's boss. This collusion is aimed at the deficient manager's undoing, rather than creating a situation where everyone has a chance of improving performance.

- **Coercion**: it is unethical to force organizational members into settings where they are, in effect, required to disclose information about themselves or their units that they prefer to keep private. For example, a manager and most of his or her team members want to go off-site for a problem-solving workshop, but one or two members of the group are strongly resisting. The manager might try friendly persuasion (not painful arm-twisting) addressing the concerns. If this does not work, an alternative might be to indicate that nonparticipation is acceptable and that no one will be subject to recriminations, but non-participants should realize that the group will go ahead and try to reach consensus on action plans for unit improvement without their input.

- **Promising unrealistic outcomes** is both unethical and counterproductive and can lead to reduced credibility of the consultant and the OD field, as well as reduced credibility of the key client within his or her organization.

- **Deception and conflict of values.** Deception in any form destroys trust. An example is when an organization embarks on a major reengineering effort giving assurances of job security, and then lays off a huge part of the workforce. The layoffs come after the company has promoted teamwork and empowerment and engaged employees in streamlining operations. The ethical course of action for the OD consultant is to press top management to look at probably consequences of reengineering, to look at possible options, and be completely open with employees about the implications of whatever change strategy is selected. Under the basic assumptions and values of OD, it is the responsibility of both the consultant and company management to mitigate the impact of any change effort on the lives of individual employees.

WORKING WITH A CONSULTANT[5]

The client must maintain ownership of the project. Whether the change agent is external or internal, the project belongs to the client, even after contracting with a consultant who may do the majority of the work. The client has ultimate responsibility for the project.

Give careful consideration to all written and verbal agreements on project deliverables. All parties must be clear from the beginning about the expected outcomes and exactly what is to be delivered at each step of the project. The clearer these agreements upfront, the less opportunity for misunderstanding further down the line.

Once the change agent or consultant is engaged, compile every bit of documentation and resources that you can, as quickly as possible. This information is often the basis for the consultant's work and absolutely essential before beginning to work on the project.

Accessibility to resources, data, and people is crucial to the success of the project. This point seems almost too basic to bear repeating, but it is often overlooked. Project team members should exchange such basic information as telephone numbers and email addresses. Team members need to know how to get in touch with each other easily and with little effort.

Another high priority is to enlist the active participation of key subject matter experts (SMEs). Involve this group in the project kickoff meeting, and keep them apprised of the project's status. Keep communications channels flowing between all involved in the project. These close ties between the change agent and SMEs make it easier to obtain valuable information.

The project kick-off meeting plays a crucial role in the life of a change project. Often overlooked or set aside for other tasks that may seem more important, this meeting brings the project to life. It is the project's birth. By the way, it is helpful to think of your project as a living being - with a birth, a life span, and a death. At the kick-off meeting, involve all stakeholders, determine project objectives, enlist support, and set time frames for actions.

Allow the right amount of time for the change project to take place. This depends entirely on the project, whether it's a large-scale overhaul of a system or a relatively swift change in a process. Don't rush the process.

It is critical for there to be a close relationship between the change agent and the client project manager. Keep each other informed on all related issues, such as slippages, budget constraints, and other changes. Hold regular status meetings with key project members. Insist that the change agent provide regular status reports.

Midway through the project, it is usually helpful to test your outcome objectives. Conducting a "reality test" reduces undesired results.

Throughout the project, discuss any problems openly and promptly. Do not allow potential problems to become major catastrophes because of lack of communications. Make sure resources remain accessible throughout the life of the project.

If key project team members change, make sure new members are brought up to speed on the project immediately. A "project turnover meeting" is helpful, involving both old and new members and key stakeholders. Make sure the new members have a clear understanding of the project status and direction, and their critical role in the success of the project.

Capture the energy at the end by celebrating the project's completion. Remember that the change agent may feel a certain loss over the completion. Indeed, everyone may feel a sense of letdown when the project ends. Formally end the project with a celebration, including an assessment of those things that went well and those that didn't. That will help both the client organization and the change agent learn from the project.

With these actions, the relationship of the change agent and client organization can be a smooth and productive one.

CASE STUDY: A PROBLEM OF DIMINISHED MORALE[6] (PART 2)

Back to the case from the beginning of this chapter. In retrospect, we had not identified or properly targeted our primary client. Was it the VP, the lab director, or even Doug McGregor? Each of them had a stake in the outcome and each had a problem to solve. But by not inquiring further before leaping into action, we never found out what problem we were really addressing by our survey. We did not really know why Doug wanted us to do this assignment. We did not find out what the VP who was willing to pay for it really had in mind. For example, might he have been gunning for the director and saw this as an opportunity to put him down? Had he been trying to influence the director's management style and saw the survey as a nice outsider intervention to provide a handle on the situation?

We never knew whether the director really favored the project or whether he was "coerced" into it by the VP. And, most important of all, we never found out what the lab director really wanted from the survey. He clearly did not want to hear about his management style. By not figuring out who the primary client was and involving that primary client in designing the project, we fell into a whole series of traps with unknown outcomes.

We never found out what happened to the report, to the director, or to the relationship between the VP and McGregor. In retrospect, had we paid attention to the fact that the project was paid for by the VP, we should have insisted on a session with him to try to learn more about his motives and why he was willing to foot the bill. We should have asked why it was not being charged to the research lab. Our ignorance, and our failure to access vital information, led us to a series of interventions the impact of which we could never determine.

Once the primary client is clearly identified, the consultant must engage in a diagnostic active inquiry process with that individual or group. As the case study illustrates, one cannot take the word of the contact or the intermediate clients on what the primary client might want or need. Getting information directly from the primary client not only guarantees accuracy but also, more importantly, begins to build the relationship that will allow the consultant and the primary client to work together to diagnose the situation and develop further interventions.

Remembering the principle that it is the client who owns the problem, it is essential to avoid the trap of the consultant starting to make suggestions and interventions based on second-hand information. Furthermore, if the consultant moves ahead on her own, the primary client may feel relieved of the burden, may become dependent, and create the inappropriate situation in which the consultant ends up owning the problem

Level 2 Questions:
1. What are the key lessons learned?
2. How would you go about identifying who the primary client is?
3. How would you go about identifying what the "real" problem is?

See the next page for another classic story . . .

CASE STUDY: DRUCKER UNHEEDED[7]

Peter Drucker spent a year at General Motors near the end of World War II preparing recommendations for GM's return to civilian auto production. Drucker was a great admirer of Alfred Sloan and of the influential managerial system that Sloan had created at GM in the early 1920s.

Drucker was then, as he is today, thoroughly imbued with Old World charm. Throughout his career, he has studiously avoided giving offense and is unfailingly positive in his attitude, even when giving criticism. His report to GM's top management was vintage Drucker: respectful, laudatory whenever possible, and accentuating the positive. But when GM's executives looked at the report, all they could see was red. They viewed the study as a condemnation of what they stood for and a repudiation of what they had accomplished. They angrily showed Drucker the door, and to this day, have kept him from darkening it again. (As late as 1985, a young GM manager, ignorant of this history, innocently nominated Drucker to receive GM's highest honor, the Alfred Sloan Award. On hearing this blasphemy, then-CEO Roger Smith flew into a rage—although witnesses recall that neither he nor anyone else in the room could recall why it was de rigueur for GM loyalists to detest Peter Drucker!)

Here is why: in 1946 Drucker had dared to imply that GM must change. Without doubt, Drucker had praised the thoroughly logical theoretical concept of the corporation developed in a study by Alfred Sloan, and had acknowledged that the study had contributed to GM's quarter century of unparalleled success. But Drucker had also dared to ask if Sloan's system would be appropriate for a world soon to be characterized by global competition, changing social values, automation, a knowledge-based economy, and consumer demands for quality. Drucker worried that the bureaucratic hierarchy of commands and controls that Sloan had painstakingly created would be insufficiently responsive to such massive changes, concluding, "G.M. is an organization of managers and management . . .It is not a managerial and *not* an innovative company." Drucker was careful to say this was an observation, not a criticism—many big companies are simply not as innovative as entrepreneurial firms. But that distinction was of small comfort to GM.

Sloan's system anticipated every problem, establishing rules, procedures, checks and balances, and especially committees empowered to handle anything unforeseeable that might fall between the cracks. Drucker was impressed, but he felt obligated to point out that this system left out customers, employees, and society. Hence his major proposal that GM should abandon adversarial labor relations and seek instead to create a sense of community in its numerous manufacturing facilities. He called on GM to draw a lesson from the company's recent wartime experience during which productivity had been higher than before the war, even though the workforce was less experienced and there were many more workers per supervisors, who were also not "majority workers". Drucker asked GMs management to consider why this industrial cooperation had led to higher productivity—and then to ask how they might create a similar culture when their regular workforce was demobilized and returned to Detroit. GM's management rejected Drucker's idea of labor-management cooperation as "hostile to business."

Sloan responded many years later (after the last of his original team at GM was securely in the grave) in a book entitled *My Years with General Motors*, which stands as the clearest expression of managerial philosophy that dominated American corporations for more than four decades, a clear expression of a *value system*. Using calculating language of economizing, utility, facts, objectivity, systems, rationality, maximizing, he clearly demonstrates his relentless commitment to the engineering worldview where the highest goal for the corporation was efficiency. The book became the corporation's bible, as well as guiding curriculum of most of the nation's business schools.

However, success did not remain forever. As Drucker had predicted a quarter of a century earlier, the environment changed radically. The efficient system did not anticipate environmental changes such as the increase cost of gasoline, consumer demands for quality, increasing cost of production, need to become a leader in new technology, a more mobile society, and changing workforce attitudes. A major problem with the system was the inability to accept the need for changing the assumptions, as evidenced by how Peter Drucker's report was ignored. GM, however, became the organizational model for industry and business schools.

Some say it was because Drucker wrote the report and disappeared; in effect, no attempt was made by GM executives to implement the report's recommendations because they saw it as Drucker's report, not theirs. If this interpretation is accurate, Drucker unintentionally created resistance by issuing an outside challenge to the cohesion of the group. He was seen as forcing his ideas on a group that was doing quite well without his interferences.

Drucker's recall of the situation is that he gave them the report, and they treated it like a hot potato, no one knowing quite what to do with it or willing to take any responsibility for it. Not only did they not offer comments on its content, but also they adopted a "don't call us, we'll call you" stance towards its author. As an outsider, a guest in the corporation, he had no leverage to get them to respond or to act. Apparently hoping that the matter would just go away, they didn't even bother to stop him from publishing the report.

Considering these two versions are not completely at odds, let us rewrite the history ourselves . . .

What might have happened had Drucker attempted to create some disciples by allowing the GM executives most open to change to embrace the report as their own? For example, he might have involved them in the writing and presentation of the report. He could have couched the report in terms of their needs, their aspirations, and their values.

Was it simply poor timing? While Drucker felt his timing was poor, and the report was "premature", the problem with the timing explanation is that it can become an excuse. Would-be leaders can too easily rationalize that the time isn't ripe for change. One question we might ask ourselves is: Do leaders have a responsibility to act even when the world isn't ready for change? A practical question is: If they do act, are they merely engaging in a quixotic quest?

Drucker maintained that Sloan was not just a leader, he was an excellent manager. To Drucker, "good leaders without managerial ability rapidly become misleaders," or autocrats. Sloan did not operate a one-person show; he recognized the need to have a team of effective managers at the top of the organization.

Drucker also points out that there were other sources of opposition to his ideas: the union, and the leadership of the National Labor Relations Board, who had a common interest in maintaining labor-management hostility and thus threatened by a community of interest between the worker and the company.

Questions:
1. What are the lessons learned from this classic story?
2. How does it relate to your current experience of organizational life?
3. As an OD practitioner, what must you consider when invited into an organization?

ENDNOTES

[1] Source: Edgar H. Schein. (1997). The concept of "client" from a process consultation perspective: A guide for change agents. *Journal of Organizational Change Management*, 10(3), 202-. http://www.emeraldinsight.com/jocm.htm

[2] This discussion draws from Newton Margulies and Anthony P. Raia. (1978). *Conceptual Foundations of Organizational Development*. New York: McGraw-Hill, p. 113; Edgar H. Schein. (1978). The Role of the Consultant: Content Expert or Process Facilitator? *Personnel and Guidance Journal*, 58, pp. 339-343; and Edgar H. Schein. (1997). The concept of "client" from a process consultation perspective: A guide for change agents. *Journal of Organizational Change Management*, 10(3), pp. 202-.

[3] See Cooperrider, D. L., & Srivastva, S. 1987. Appreciative Inquiry in Organizational Life. In W. Pasmore and R. Woodman. (eds.) *Research in Organization Change and Development*, vol. 1, pp. 129-169. Greenwich, Conn.: JAI Press.

[4] Adapted from French, W. L., & Bell, C. H. (1999). *Organization Development*. Englewood Cliffs, NJ: Prentice Hall, pp. 266-268.

[5] Miller, J. (1994). Getting the Most From Supplier Relationships, Training *& Development*, 48(12), p. 14-15. These ideas are geared towards specific projects, such as development of training program and materials.

[6] Source: Edgar H. Schein. (1997). The concept of "client" from a process consultation perspective: A guide for change agents. *Journal of Organizational Change Management*, 10(3), 202-.

[7] Source: Adapted from James O'Toole. (1996). *Leading Change: The Argument for Values-Based Leadership*, New York: Ballentine Books, pp. 171-188. Also see P. Drucker, (1972). *Concept of the Corporation*, Mentor Executive Library; and A. P. Sloan Jr., (1963). *My Years with General Motors*, Doubleday.

CHAPTER 4:

PERSONAL LEARNING AND CHANGE

LIFELINE EXERCISE

INTRODUCTION

This exercise has many outcomes and can be used in many situations. It is intended to help you understand personal change by examining your life in terms of critical change points.

METHOD

To prepare for creating your lifeline, think of the critical points in your life. Some typical change points are graduation, marriage, birth of a child, moving away from home. However, we all have unique experiences; so do not feel limited by these. Focus on the changes that have had significant impact on the course of your life.

There are no directions or guidelines for creating your lifeline. This is YOUR journey. Your task is to express it as you wish. Use the next page or a separate sheet of paper to graphically depict your lifeline.

After you have created your lifeline, think of your general *experience* of each of the change points:
- How did YOU experience the change?
- What conclusions can you draw about change from your life experiences?
- What conclusions can you draw about yourself in relation to change?

LIFELINE: CRITICAL CHANGE POINTS IN LIFE

We are faced with change almost daily. Changes such as marriage, childbirth, and new jobs, take us out of our comfort zone and place us into a place of discomfort until we adjust. During our lifespan we can expect to pass through various stages of development, each stage requiring us to re-think, re-evaluate, re-assess what we know, what is comfortable, what we're familiar with and adjust to new experiences associated with the stage we're entering.

I became interested in change and transition as I began to experience major personal changes and found myself faced with confusion and anxiety, even when the change was planned and "a good thing". An example of this was when I completed my thesis for my doctoral program. This was supposed to be a period of elation; after all, I had achieved a major milestone. Instead, I became lethargic, directionless, I could barely read a magazine article, certainly not an entire book, and I generally felt that the wind had been taken out of my sails. Only when I turned to the literature and was re-introduced to William Bridges' book, *Transitions: Making Sense of Life's Changes*, did I begin to understand that I was, indeed, in transition and at a point of new beginnings. The realization that I had been through a stage of ending and letting go, as well as the stage of in-betweenness, being lost, what I referred to as my stage of "nothingness", helped put into perspective the unexpected feelings I had experienced.

Before we can lead and facilitate organizational change, we must begin with a personal understanding of change, the personal changes and transitions we have undergone, and attempt to understand how we have experienced these changes. From this personal perspective we are better poised to understand how organizational members are affected by change within their companies. Attempting to change an organization or a management style without first changing one's own habit patterns is analogous to attempting to improve one's tennis game before developing the muscles that make better strokes possible (Covey, 1992).

Additionally, facilitators of change in organizations quickly realize that change begins with the individual who <u>chooses</u> to modify his or her behavior, who <u>chooses</u> to embrace the intended change initiative and adapt it personally. Change usually means learning how to do something new; therefore an understanding of what motivates people to learn and change is important to the success of any organizational change effort. The best programs and strategies will fail if organizational members (people) choose not to go along!

Rapid changes in today's business environment require continuous learning for individuals and organizations. The way we learn or know is central to human development. The way we apply what we know about learning and knowing is central to organization development.

Successful organizations in the nineties will be the ones that have the ability to learn faster than their competitors and discover how to tap people's commitment and capacity to learn at all levels of the organization (Senge, 1990). Understanding how individuals learn can assist in the creation of lifelong learning, both individually and organizationally.

A variety of theories about learning are helpful for understanding the learning process. As an OD practitioner, we need to be able to facilitate learning, especially double-loop learning, which occurs when we *learn how to learn*, with continuous experimentation and feedback. This calls for the OD practitioner to recognize and acknowledge why and how adults learn. In addition to understanding learning, it is helpful to understand the psychological aspects of change and transition.

MOTIVATION TO LEARN AND CHANGE

Most organizational members fall under the category of "adult learners." They have (oftentimes extensive) work and life experience that they bring with them to the learning environment. Working with adult learners shows several factors: (1) adults learn better when they can apply the concepts and material to their experience, their world; (2) adults know what they need to know, or at least think they do; and (3) adults engage in learning to the extent that it helps them in their career, personal and professional development, and life. Drawing from Adult Learning Theory and the work of Malcolm Knowles (1990), there are six crucial principles that inform us of adult motivation to learn and change.

- **Principle #1. Adult Learners Need to Know.**

"*What's in it for me?*" Adult learners need to know *why* they need to learn something before undertaking to learn it. Adults will probe into the benefits gained from learning it and the negative consequences of not learning it.

- **Principle #2. Self-Concept as Self-Directed.**

"*I want to be in control.*" Most adult learners see themselves as being responsible for their own lives and learning decisions. We have a deep psychological need to be seen as being capable of self-direction. Adults resent it when they feel others are imposing their will on them.

- **Principle #3. Experience Plays a Heavy Role**.

"*What about my experience?*" Adult learners enter the learning environment with different experiences than youths, bringing life and work experience with them. However, experience also carries mental attitudes, biases and assumptions that tend to close our minds to new, fresh ideas and alternative ways of thinking. An additional challenge is to help people *open their minds* and discover new ways of thinking and doing things.

- **Principle #4. Readiness to Learn is Key.**

"*I need to know . . .*" Adult learners become ready to learn those things they need to know, and be able to do, in order to cope effectively with their real-life situations. That typically occurs as adults are faced with a move from one stage to the next. Examples include marriage, divorce, a new job, a promotion, being fired, retiring. The more life change events an adult encounters, the more likely he or she will turn to learning experiences directly related, at least in their perception, to the life-change events. Once convinced that change is a certainty, adults will engage in any learning that promises to help them cope with the transition. Learning is a means to an end, not the end itself (Zemke and Zemke, 1984).

- **Principle #5. Orientation to Learning.**

"*I have a problem.*" Adult learners' orientation to learning is typically task- or problem-centered, rather than subject-centered. Adults need to perceive they are learning something that will help them perform tasks or deal with problems they are confronted with in their work situations.

- **Principle #6. Motivation**

"*I want to a better life for myself and my family.*" Adult learners are most motivated by internal pressures, such as the desire for increased job satisfaction, self-esteem, and quality of life. However, in uncertain economic times, people are especially motivated to obtain and maintain jobs, achieve promotions, and secure higher salaries.

An important motivation of adult learners is *prevention of obsolescence*. As the world changes, adult-learners develop a need for on-going training and lifelong learning. Kaizen, a Japanese term meaning continuous improvement, suggests that only those with inquiring minds will be able to prevent obsolescence, those with the ability to find answers on their own, rather than waiting to have facts fed to them. This self-motivation towards learning and inquiry can lead to learning taking place anywhere: in a staff meeting, professional association events, civic clubs, reading the newspaper, radio and television, public discourse, as well as standard educational and training forums.

NEED FOR CHANGE ESTABLISHES NEED FOR LEARNING

Adult learning theory shows that adults are open to learning when they have a problem, a need to know something, or they want to enhance their career. Therefore, as facilitators of change (and learning), we must establish a need for learning. This happens as a result of establishing the need for change.

People will enter into the learning environment if they see a need for change. Conversely, if they do not see a need for change (i.e., they are "frozen" in their current state), they will not be as open to learning ("unfreezing" and change.) Once the need for change is clear, especially change that affects them personally, they willingly engage in learning, especially when the WIIFM question is answered (what's in it for me?)

Organizational members change and learn new skills and behaviors when they share the vision of the intended change, when they embrace the desired future state of the organization. This usually happens when they have had a part in creating that vision, a common theme throughout this book.

Establishing a *need for change* creates a *need for learning*. Once the need for learning is established, we can address the question, "How do adults learn?"

STYLES OF LEARNING

In addition to the motivation to learn, adults have a preferred learning style that affects how they learn. I have observed learners who quickly assimilate the materials into his or her experience. I have also observed learners who reflect and observe quietly, and those who must speak out on every topic. There is the learner who is able to conceptualize ideas well. And the learner who wants to do, act, and "be" with the topic. Some individuals love learning in groups, while others prefer an individual learning environment. By examining David Kolb's learning theory, we develop a picture of an individual's style of learning[1].

Experiential-learning theory is designed to assess the way individuals learn. Experiential learning is conceived as a four-stage cycle: 1) Concrete experience (CE) - immediate concrete experience is the basis for 2) Reflective Observation (RO) - observation and reflection; 3) Abstract conceptualization (AC) - these observations are assimilated into a "theory", from which new implications for action can be deduced; and 4) Active Experimentation (AE) - these implications or hypotheses then serve as guides in acting to create new experiences. According to the theory, this progression mimics the way effective learning takes place and is an on-going continuous process (Osland, Kolb, & Rubin, 2001).

Figure 4-1. Kolb's Two-Dimensional Learning Model and Four Learning Modes

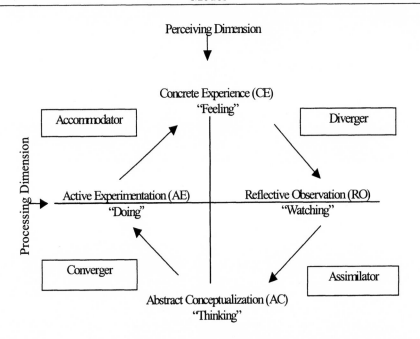

This model reflects two independent dimensions based on (a) *perceiving*, which involves concrete experience (feeling) and abstract conceptualization (thinking), and (b) *processing*, which involves active experimentation (doing) and reflective observation (watching). These two dimensions form four quadrants reflecting four learning modes, as shown in Figure 4-1: accommodator, diverger, assimilator, and converger[2].

- *Accommodators* are people who learn primarily from "hands-on" experience and "gut" feelings rather than from logical analysis.
- *Divergers* are best at viewing concrete situations from many different points of view.
- *Assimilators* are best at understanding a wide range of information and putting it into a concise and logical form.
- *Convergers* are best at finding practical uses for ideas and theories.

Kolb (1976) developed the 12-item self-reported Learning Styles Inventory (LSI) to assess learning modes. People usually see themselves as having a predisposition for one of the four styles; however, the effective learner uses each of the four styles in different learning situations rather than only relying on his or her preferred style[3].

- **Convergence / Deciding.** Key points: Greatest strength lies in problem-solving, decision-making, and practical application of ideas. The *Converger*'s dominant learning abilities are Abstract Conceptualization (AC) and Active Experimentation (AE). This person's greatest strength is the practical application of ideas. A person with this style seems to do best in situations such as conventional intelligence tests, in which there is a single correct answer or solution to a question or problem. This person's knowledge is organized in such a way that through hypothetical-deductive reasoning the person can focus the knowledge on specific problems. Convergers are relatively unemotional, preferring to deal with things rather than people. They tend to have narrow technical interests, and often specialize in the physical sciences. This learning style is characteristic of many engineers.
- **Divergence / Valuing.** Key points: Imaginative ability and awareness of meaning and values; view concrete situations from many perspectives. The *Diverger* has the opposite learning strengths of the Converger. The Diverger is best at Concrete Experience (CE) and Reflective Observation (RO). This person's greatest strength is imaginative ability; they excel in viewing concrete situations from many perspectives. The label "Diverger" was given because a person with this style performs best in situations that call for generation of ideas, such as a brainstorming session. Divergers are interested in people and tend to be emotional as well as imaginative. They have broad cultural interests and often specialize in the arts. This style is characteristic of individuals with humanities and liberal-arts backgrounds. Counselors, organization-development specialists, and personnel managers tend to be characterized by this learning style.

- **Assimilation / Thinking.** Key points: Inductive reasoning, ability to create theoretical models. The *Assimilator*'s dominant learning abilities are Abstract Conceptualization (AC) and Reflective Observation (RO). This person's greatest strength is the ability to create theoretical models; they excel in inductive reasoning and in assimilating disparate observations into an integrated explanation. Like the Converger, the Assimilator is less interested in people than in abstract concepts, but unlike the Converger, the Assimilator is not much concerned with the practical use of theories. For the Assimilator, it is more important that the theory is logically sound and precise; when a theory or plan does not fit the facts, this person is likely to disregard or re-examine the facts. As a result, this learning style is more characteristic of the basic sciences and mathematics than of the applied sciences. In organizations, the Assimilator is found most often in the research and planning departments.

- **Accommodation / Acting.** Key points: Doing things, opportunity seeking, risk-taking and action. The *Accommodator* has the opposite learning strengths of the Assimilator. He or she is best at Concrete Experience (CE) and Active Experimentation (AE). The Accommodator's greatest strength is doing things -- carrying out plans and experiments -- and involving him- or herself in new experiences. This person tends to be more of a risk taker than people characterized by any of the other three learning styles. The label "Accommodator" was given because the person tends to excel in situations in which one must adapt oneself to immediate circumstances. When a theory or plan does not fit the facts, this person will most likely discard the plan or theory. The Accommodator tends to solve problems in an intuitive trial-and-error manner, relying heavily on others for information, rather than on his or her own analytic ability. The Accommodator is at ease with people but is sometimes seen as impatient and "pushy". This person's education is often technical or practical, such as training in business administration. In organizations, people with this learning style are found in "action-oriented" jobs, such as marketing and sales.

It should be noted that Learning Styles Inventory is an indication of how one views oneself. The LSI is not considered a test, and the value is in self-awareness. With this instrument, an individual becomes aware of his primary mode of learning and can develop strategies for employing other modes when appropriate. In addition to learning style, Howard Gardner has shown that there are multiple intelligences that we use to solve problems. These are presented at the end of this chapter.

From this model, we can see the diversity of styles organizational members employ when faced with learning something new and changing. This is a helpful model for organization development practitioners in designing learning experiences that accommodate the needs of participants. It is also a helpful model through which to view reaction to change, how individuals enter into the change process.

Why do some people seem to resist change? What appears to be resistance may be a product of personal style.

PERSONAL STYLE AND CHANGE

Some people embrace change rapidly and with excitement, while others are slower to make changes, and appear to be more resistant. The DiSC Dimensions of Behavior[®4] model is helpful in understanding this difference. The model suggests that individuals have a natural behavioral style with which they are most comfortable when interacting with the world. These dimensions of behavior are based on our individual perceptions and motivations, and how we react to our environment.

Based on the work of William Marston, the model consists of two factors: perception of the environment and sense of self within that environment. Marston suggested that individuals perceive their environment either as favorable (comfortable) or unfavorable (challenging). He also suggested that individuals perceive themselves in terms of power to influence, control, or affect the environment. Those who view themselves as having influence are more likely to take the initiative to achieve their goals through force of will or persuading others; those who view themselves as less influential are likely to achieve their goals by being more accommodating or by adhering to established guidelines to insure quality[5].

The integration of these two factors results in what is referred to as *personal style*, defined as a pattern or group of recurring habits. Sometimes referred to as "behavioral types," personal style influences how individuals respond to the world in order to meet their needs and achieve their goals. Thus, personal style is a contributing factor in understanding why individuals do what they do in the workplace.

DiSC[®] is a widely-used research-based model that describes how people behave as they view themselves in their various environments through patterns of observable, external behaviors[6] resulting in four core behavioral styles: Direct, Interactive, Supportive, and Conscientious[7].

DIRECT STYLE

Individuals with the Direct style are driven by an inner need to be in control of the situation, accomplish results, take charge of people and the situation, and overcome challenges. Their emphasis is on shaping the environment by overcoming opposition to accomplish results. They desire reaching personal goals and demonstrate a bottom-line results-oriented style of behavior. Determined and straightforward individuals, "D's" are motivated by competitive opportunities. Their behavior is exhibited by direct, assertive communications. Short-term and task- oriented, they make quick decisions, and seek frequent change.

Direct style individuals are less inclined to examine alternatives to a situation, build consensus, or take time to win people over to their point of view.

Strengths of "D" Style in Change

- Enjoys being involved in change.
- Freely initiates change.
- High need for specific and concrete results.
- Ability to multitask, work well on several projects at once.
- Thinks in terms of big picture.
- Personal need to lead decisively and direct action for fast results.
- Enjoys challenges and risk taking.
- Likes a quick paced environment.

Potential Limitations of "D" Style in Change

- Plunges into change without much risk-assessing forethought or planning.
- Directive approach, i.e., telling others what the change needs to be.
- Impatience, i.e., "I want this to happen and I want it now!"
- Intolerance to others' transition process.
- Ineffective delegation skills; not knowing when to turn over a project to someone else.
- Does not enjoy attention to detail.
- May have trouble distinguishing the realistic from the awe inspiring.

Strategies for "D" Style to Adapt for Change

- Nurture talent of others; allow them to do things without your excessive control and untimely interference.
- Participate in groups without expecting to always be in control.
- Enlist others' input and support through participative, collaborative actions.
- Praise people for a job well done.
- Let others know that you expect mistakes to happen; and they will be used as learning opportunities.
- Give authority as well as responsibility when delegating.

INTERACTIVE STYLE

Individuals with Interactive as the preferred style are driven by an inner need to be in contact with others, to be where the action is. Their emphasis is on shaping the environment by influencing or persuading others. Their style is demonstrated by outwardly energetic or fast-paced, optimistic, talkative, animated patterns of behavior. "I's" attempt to influence others in a friendly way, focused on positive outcomes. As they are eager to please others, and be liked by others, they seek social recognition. They enjoy trying new things, and dislike repetitive long-term projects.

Interactive style individuals are less inclined to plan or problem-solve. They are less concerned with sharing the limelight with others.

Strengths of "I" Style in Change

- Enjoys being involved in change.
- Readily embraces change.
- Sociable and approachable (therefore good at taking the organizational pulse).
- Bounces ideas off others; freely brainstorms with others.
- Thinks in terms of big picture.
- Creative in approach to new things.
- If the ideas feel right, will pitch those ideas to others to elicit their feedback and enthusiasm.
- Likes a quick paced environment.

Potential Limitations of "I" Style in Change

- Prefers not to dwell on details.
- Gets bored easily; short attention spans.
- May move from project to project without completion i.e., like to start projects and let others finish them.
- May listen to others without checking for themselves i.e., make decisions based on limited information.

Strategies for "I" Style to Adapt for Change

- Attend to key details, when appropriate.
- Improve your follow-through efforts.
- Learn and practice effective time management skills.
- Focus on what is important now.
- Be open to multiple sources of data.

SUPPORTIVE STYLE

Individuals with the Supportive style are driven by an inner need for stable and harmonizing relationships. Their emphasis is on cooperating with others to carry out tasks. They prefer to maintain stability in a relatively constant and secure environment. This style is observed by loyalty, predictability, low-keyed, and dependable patterns of behavior. Preferring listening and doing to talking, they are excellent relaters. "S's" have a high concern for the well being of others; they focus on building trust and long-term relationships.

Supportive style individuals are less inclined to take center-stage and prefer a more balanced share of the efforts and rewards.

Strengths of "S" Style in Change

- Works well with others; excellent team players.

- Thinks deeply about things, logical.
- Thoroughly plans and organizes their work.
- Respects traditions.
- Loyal; prefer long-term relationships with their organizations and coworkers.
- Patience and persistence, especially towards making relationships work.
- Works cooperatively with others to achieve common results.

Potential Limitations of "S" Style in Change

- Uncomfortable with conflict and risk.
- Low tolerance for stress.
- Thinking and planning can limit their actions in the change process.
- Seeks to avoid uncertainty.
- Prefers stability and order.

Strategies for "S" Style to Adapt for Change

- Ask for clarifying information about a change initiative.
- Get involved in new projects more quickly.
- Learn to adapt more quickly to either changes or refinements of existing practices.
- Try new ways of doing your work.
- Become more open to risk.
- Seek support from others; be willing to accept help.

CONSCIENTIOUS STYLE

The Conscientious style individual is driven by an inner need for accuracy and doing things correctly. Their emphasis is on working conscientiously within existing circumstances to ensure quality and accuracy. "C's" are concerned with content, and hold high personal standards. They prefer working under specific, preferably controlled and orderly conditions that result in perfection. Long-term oriented, they gather lots of data prior to making decisions.

Conscientious style individuals are inclined to anticipate the effects of change and try to act to satisfy themselves.

Strengths of "C" Style in Change

- Likes solving problems.
- Concentrates on key details.
- Asks specific questions (often seen as playing "devil's advocate").
- Needs to understand how things work, which allows them to seek the most logical ways to achieve the expected results.
- Logical, analytical in their approach to problems and solutions.
- Checks, rechecks, and checks again.

- Seeks perfection in everything.
- Seeks quality in products and service.
- Thorough planning and preparation in order to minimize the probability of errors; value quality over quantity.
- Intuitive thinkers.

Potential Limitations of "C" Style in Change

- The "collecting data" phase can create frustration from others who wish to know what is going on now.
- The "checking" phase can limit their actions in the change process.
- Low risk-taking tendencies.
- May become bogged down in planning.
- Analysis paralysis may slow down change process by collecting and analyzing data to excess.

Strategies for "C" Style to Adapt for Change

- Share your knowledge and expertise with others.
- Check less often, or only check the critical things (as opposed to everything), allowing the flow of the process to continue.
- Modify your criticism (whether spoken or unspoken) of others' work.
- Accept that you can have high standards without expecting perfection.
- Reduce the tendency to over-prepare.
- Seek realistic deadlines and parameters.

The DiSC model does not presume one style to be better than another style, i.e., it is not a "test." Nor is the point to try and change behavior. The value is in building self-awareness, in order to maximize the strengths of the styles and understand potential limitations.

This is particularly valuable in understanding how individuals react to change. The model suggests that two of the four styles readily seek and embrace change (Direct and Interactive), while the Supportive and Conscientious styles are more slow to change and frequently labeled as resistant to change. Given this, we can foresee some potential problems and offer strategies for dealing with these concerns. For example, D's and I's need to understand that while they feel a sense of urgency to change, planning is important. Considering the whole picture before starting down the path of change will be fruitful. S's would do well to develop an openness to change and be able to articulate their needs, such as needing information about how they will fit into the changed system. C's could do well with development of tolerance to ambiguity, as change is by definition, breaking the mold, experiencing and trying new things. The path to change is often ambiguous[8].

Again, I warn that no one style is the "best style." Each style has its areas of strengths and areas of limitations. The purpose is to understand one's personal style as well as understanding the style of others, in terms of openness to change, tolerance of ambiguity, and developing strategies to maximize strengths and reduce limitations in the change process.

As a facilitator of change, this model is helpful to understand the diversity of behavioral styles employed by organizational members, as it relates to learning new things and making changes. It is also helpful to understand the stages people go through in the change process.

STAGES OF CHANGE AND TRANSITION

Individuals (and organizations) go through a series of *psychological* stages in the change process. Two models help us understand this phenomenon.

THE BEHAVIORAL CHANGE PROCESS MODEL

To understand how change occurs in individuals, groups and organizations, it is useful to examine the model first proposed by Kurt Lewin (1958), and further developed by Edgar Schein (1980, 1987). The change process model addresses three stages through which behavioral change occurs: unfreezing the old behavior or situation, moving to a new level of behavior (change), and refreezing the behavior at the new level, as shown in Figure 4-2. These stages are not discrete, they overlap; and they are based on several assumptions (Schein, 1980):

- Any change process involves not only learning something new, but also unlearning something that is already present and possibly well integrated into the personality and social relationships of the individual and/or organization.

- No change will occur unless there is motivation to change. If such motivation to change is not already present, the induction of that motivation is often the most difficult part of the change process.

- Organizational changes such as new structures, processes, reward systems occur only through individual changes in key members of the organization; hence organizational change is always mediated through individual changes.

- Most adult change involves attitudes, values, and self-images, and the unlearning of present responses in these areas is initially inherently painful and threatening.

- Change is a multistage cycle, and all stages must be negotiated before a stable change can take place.

Prior to change, we are unaware of the need to change. Most of us have habits that make us somewhat less effective than we might otherwise be. Many of these habits are of no concern to us because we don't know we have them, or we aren't aware that they are interfering with our effectiveness. We are *unconscious* of behavior that results in ineffectiveness.

Think of the behavior of one of your associates. You are probably aware of habits that lessen his or her effectiveness in certain situations. As long as that person is unconscious of what you know, she is unlikely to make any effort to change her behavior. There is no motivation to change.

Figure 4-2. Change Process Model

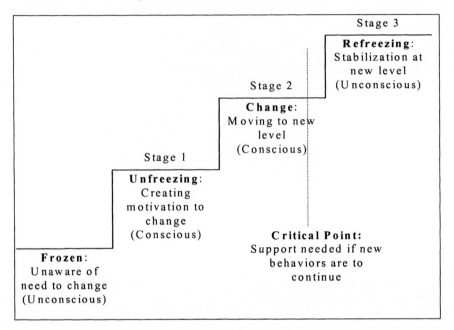

In Stage 1, we are introduced to information that makes us become aware of the need for change.   We become *conscious* of behavior that results in ineffectiveness. This may happen if someone views a video of themselves in a situation, or hears a tape recording of a meeting. Or someone else may point out the particular ineffective behavior to him or her.   From the organizational standpoint, unfreezing may take the form of creating a sense of urgency about the need for change, recognizing that current management practices are ineffective, a merger with another organization, etc.

This new consciousness of ineffective behavior must set up sufficient guilt or anxiety to motivate a change.   This awareness might create the desire to change, especially if there is some support in making this change. If the desire is strong enough, we move to Stage 2. However, we can get "stuck" in Stage 1, either by rationalizing the current behavior as being "not so bad", or by believing that simply wanting to change will in fact create the change.

The process here is to reduce those forces that maintain behavior at the present level (i.e., introduce information that shows discrepancies between behavior desired by organizational members and those behaviors currently exhibited.) The creation of psychological safety is important for reassurance that the change is possible.

The change process begins with identification of desired behaviors and skills, through role models, mentors, friends, or gaining new perspective from another person's point of view. Additionally, gathering data specifically relevant to the "problem" and selection of information from multiple sources provides a mental model for change.

In stage 2, we shift behavior to a new level (i.e., develop new behaviors, values and attitudes.) We are *conscious* in our practice of the new desired behavior or skill. This means taking part of the attention that one normally places on the content of actions, and focusing on *processes*.

During this stage, there is a *critical point* where great support is required to continue on the path of change. In order for real and lasting change to occur, the new behaviors need to fit with our self-concept, and the organizational culture. We need to be able to test whether the new behaviors and attitudes are congruent with our values, with other parts of our personality, and can be integrated comfortably. Additionally, we need to test whether others accept and confirm our new behaviors and attitudes, and if these new behaviors and attitudes move us towards a desired and more effective state. And finally, the organizational culture must correlate with our new attitudes and behaviors in order for the behavior to be stabilized. There needs to be supporting mechanisms that reinforce the new changed state, such as organizational culture, norms, policies, and structures.

It is crucial to get positive feedback on the new behavior. Without this support, there could be a tendency to fall back to the old, familiar ways, particularly if one is under a stressful situation.

In the refreezing stage, we are *unconscious* in our new behavior; we have integrated the change into our behavior mode and no longer need to think about it. The new behavior now comes as naturally as the old once did.

An example of the change process can be found within an organization that has successfully introduced a Total Quality Management System (TQMS). A need is identified for employees to have a greater voice in problem-solving and quality. The organization introduces the concept of TQMS, a shift in attitude towards employee empowerment (unfreezing). New behaviors are developed through training and development (change). Supportive processes are developed and implemented (such as reward systems and teamwork days) in which the new behaviors are recognized and rewarded (refreezing). TQMS becomes a way of doing business, firmly planted within the organizational culture and strategy.

It is often found that programs designed to induce attitudinal and behavioral changes work initially, but fail in the long run. The problem usually is that the new skills learned in training are incongruent with the person's value system and self-concept, or the system to which he or she returns from the training program have not changed. An example is the manager who develops a new and more positive attitude towards subordinates but finds that her own boss is more comfortable with the old subordinate attitudes.

The Behavioral Change Process Model provides us with a basic frame to understand the psychological aspects of the change process. A *critical point* in the process is between the change and refreezing stages. This requires heavy organizational support to ensure the maintenance of the change and assure for future growth. Such support could include continued levels of enthusiasm for the change, and continued monitoring for progress.

STAGES OF TRANSITION

Similar to Change Process Model, William Bridges proposed three separate and distinct stages of transition that individuals (and organizations) go through in various stages of (personal and organizational) life, as shown in Figure 4-3.[9]

Figure 4-3. Stages of Transition

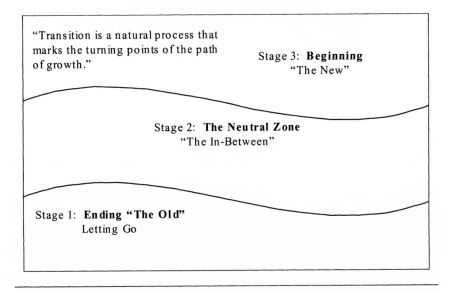

The first stage, ***ending***, is one in which we let go of the old situation. You might find it strange that we begin the process of transition with the ending stage, rather than the beginning. According to Bridges (2004, p. 11), "Every transition must begin with an ending. We have to let go of the old thing before we can pick up the new". For example, when we marry, we must let go of our self-image as a single individual before we can advance to the stage of thinking of ourselves in relation to our mate.

Within the Ending Stage are five components that we may experience, depending on the transition.

- **Disengagement**: a natural tendency to break with the familiar; a signal that a time of transition has begun. Examples of this are divorce, death, job change, move to a new location.

- **Dismantling**: While disengagement is the break, the "movin' on" signal, dismantling is the accompanying emotional process. Bridges calls it the "mourning process" (2004, p. 114).
- **Disidentification**: a feeling of no longer being quite sure of whom we are. We begin to question our identity, our self-image. We are not sure of whom we want to be.
- **Disenchantment**: the discovery that in some sense our world is no longer real. We may become disenchanted with our image of working in a certain environment or industry, or with the people we hang out with.
- **Disorientation**: a time of confusion and emptiness; a time when things that were once important no longer seem to matter. We may find ourselves separating from familiar activities without understanding why.

We experience these feelings when we're in the first stage of transition, the ending stage. We may no longer want to associate with old friends; we may feel that our "dream job" has turned into a nightmare. We often lose touch with whom we really are during this stage, which naturally can cause confusion. Friends may react to us strangely, with such comments as, "You don't seem to be your old self."

The importance of devoting time and energy to endings cannot be over-stressed. Changes that you undergo often force you to abandon habitual ways of working or make changes to those with whom you work. Ignoring the psychological impact of this inhibits the natural progression to the next stage.

Bridges (2004, p. 17) says, "First there is an ending, *then* a beginning, and an important empty or fallow time in between". Stage 2, the *neutral zone*, is a stage of in-betweenness or nothingness, a time "between dreams . . .an empty space . . .within which a new sense of self could gestate" (p. 133). For many this can be an uncomfortable time as we are unaccustomed to "nothingness". Bridges, however, contends it to be an important time for "doing important inner business" (1980, p. 114), and "to deny it is to lose the opportunity it provides for an expanded sense of reality and a deepened sense of purpose" (1980, p. 117).

This stage can be frightening, can cause uncertainty and a great deal of discomfort. These activities help find meaning in the Neutral Zone phase of transition (2004, p. 142-150):

- Accept your need for this time in the neutral zone.
- Find a regular time and place to be alone.
- Begin a log of neutral zone experiences. Journal your thoughts, dreams, etc.
- Write your autobiography, look back to gain insight into the future.
- Take this opportunity to discover what you really want.
- Think of what would be unlived in your life if it ended today.
- Take a few days to go on your own version of a passage journey; allow time to reflect on what was and what can be.

Because the neutral zone is a somewhat uncomfortable stage, people have a tendency to ignore it or rush through it. In doing so, they find themselves "stuck" in the ending and unable to fully engage in a new beginning.

The final stage, *new beginnings*, occurs at a point when there is "a faint intimation of something different, a new theme . . .perhaps in the form of an idea or image" (Bridges, 1980, pp. 136-137). Bridges contends that when we are ready to make a beginning, we will shortly find an opportunity. He offers this advice for the beginning stage (2004, pp. 169-175):

- Stop getting ready and act!
- Begin to identify yourself with the final result of the new beginning.
- Take things step by step - recognize the process.
- Concentrate on the process of reaching your goal, rather than always concentrating on the goal.

Back to my story at the beginning of this chapter, the new beginning came as I joined the faculty of a university, something that had not been planned. By allowing the transition process to occur naturally, the image of myself as a "professor" was allowed to take shape.

TRANSITION CHECKLIST

Bridges (1980) provides this checklist as a tool for understanding and advancing through transition (pp. 78-82). I find it helpful in my own transitions, as well as working with clients undergoing turbulent times.

- Take your time, don't rush the process; it takes time for inner reorientation that brings us back into relation with people and activity.
- Arrange temporary structures - work out ways of going on while working on inner change, i.e., take a temporary job.
- Don't act for the sake of acting - go with the process of bringing something to an end first.
- Recognize why you are uncomfortable - understand the transition process, expect times of anxiety, expect others to be threatened, expect old fears to resurface.
- Take care of yourself in small ways.
- Talk to someone - professional counselor or good friend.
- Discover what is waiting in the wings of your life - allow new ideas to germinate.
- Use this transition as the impetus to a new kind of learning, from your experiences as well as education.
- Recognize that transition has a characteristic shape: disintegration - withdrawal - new orientation.

Bridges' model is useful to understand both personal and organizational transition.[10] Too frequently we think that change and transition start with the beginning, and thereby ignore the letting go process, the process of putting closure to the old. It informs us of the importance of celebrating the old, which often reduces some of the human resistance to change. Also, that important in-between stage allows us to prepare, mentally and physically, for the new.

As Bridges notes, most people do not resist change, they resist *transition*—the process of letting go of the ways things used to be and then taking hold of the way they subsequently become. In between the letting go and the taking hold again, the chaotic but potentially creative neutral zone is the time when things are not the old way, but are not really the new way yet either. Transition is the way we come to terms with change. If transition does not occur, or if it is begun but aborted, people end up (mentally and emotionally) back where they started, and the change doesn't work (Bridges, 2001, p. 2-3).

Transitional change is a psychological process people go through to come to terms with the new situation. Unless people complete their transition, the change will be just a "rearrangement of the furniture."

CHANGE IS PERSONAL

Organizational change begins with the individual choosing to go along with the intended change initiative. How individuals experience change is important to our effectiveness in facilitating organizational change. The stages of transitions and the Behavioral Change Process provide us with psychological background. Personal style of change, based on a behavioral model, helps us to understand "resistance to change," more of which is discussed in Chapter 9.

This chapter began with an examination of your lifeline in terms of change points in your life. It ends with an activity designed to have you look forward, by creating a personal vision statement.

THEORY OF MULTIPLE INTELLIGENCES

Howard Gardner developed a theory that individuals have eight kinds of intelligences, or ways in which we know. Gardner's theory challenges the idea that intelligence is fixed and can be identified through a test. Instead, he claimed there are "intelligences" we use to solve problems and create products, they can be thought of as sets of "know how"—procedures for doing things. Currently, there are eight intelligences that have been identified:[11]

Verbal-Linguistic Intelligence: highly developed auditory skills, love of language and words, love of reading and writing, good memory for names, places, dates or trivia, ability to articulate clearly. Verbal-linguistic intelligence is one of the most highly regarded intelligences and well known since it is an integral part of our traditional educational system.

- For the verbal-linguistic learner, provide mini-lectures, lots of reading materials, topic-related word games, essay assignments and tests.

Logical-Mathematical Intelligence: ability to think conceptually; ability to manipulate the environment and experiment with things in a controlled and orderly way; abstract, logical thinking; questioning everything; love of strategy games. Logical-mathematical intelligence is the combination of logical, mathematical, and scientific ability. This intelligence does not have its origin in the audio or verbal spheres, but rather it is the ordering, reordering, and assessment of various objects and their impact on other objects. The logical-mathematical intelligence is a highly regarded intelligence and is an integral part of our educational system with its focus on tests like the SAT.

- For the logical-mathematical learner, provide the opportunity for abstract thinking, topic-related case studies, problem-related assignments and tests.

Visual-Spatial Intelligence: thinking in pictures and images, love of mazes and jigsaw puzzles, drawing and designing, fascination with machines, ability to recreate aspects of one's experience of spatial relations. This intelligence is the ability to form a mental model of a spatial world, object, or pattern and then maneuvering the image to operate in that environment. Individuals with visual-spatial intelligence are usually described as visual or visionary with active imaginations, and are capable of being able to visualize how something is going to look before it is completed.

- For the visual-spatial learner, provide films, diagrams, charts, multiple visual mediums, problem-related assignments and tests.

Musical Intelligence: used when a person appreciates, composes, or performs using sound. One of the earliest intelligences to emerge, components of musical intelligence begin at a young age with attention to the physical components of music (e.g., pitch, tone, resonance, and timbre) as well as the emotional components created within the music. Specifically, musical intelligence is the process of hearing specific rhythms, instruments, tones, and lyrics and synthesizing how they fit into a selection of music.

- For the musical learner, use music in the classroom at various times, such as background music for individual thinking activity or during breaks; encourage musical learners to use sound in their presentations.

Bodily-Kinesthetic Intelligence: entails using physical actions, including athletics, drama, or building. This intelligence is the ability to solve problems using one's whole body or parts of the body. The core competencies of this intelligence include working skillfully with objects and mastery over one's body movements and using the body for expressive purposes.

- For the bodily-kinesthetic learner, provide time for moving around the classroom; encourage group work; use role-play and dramatic improvisations.

Interpersonal Intelligence: is used when a person attempts to understand and respond to others. This intelligence is described as looking outside of oneself and understanding other people, including the ability to self reflect, analyze emotions, and predict reactions to various situations.

- For the interpersonal learner, allow group activity and problem solving; encourage group facilitations; allow opportunities for community activities such as committees and mentoring programs.

Intrapersonal Intelligence: involves knowing oneself and making decisions based on that knowledge. It is the ability to notice and make distinctions among other individual's moods, temperaments, motivations, and intentions. Intrapersonal skills allow for self-reflection and learning through one's thoughts and feelings (and how they relate to the larger scheme) as well as understanding how people feel about themselves. Individuals with strong intrapersonal intelligence are contemplative, may prefer isolation, possess a certain quality of inner wisdom, intuitive ability; deep sense of self, self motivated to do well on independent study projects.

- For the intrapersonal learner, provide opportunity to pursue independent study, self-paced instruction, and individualized projects; encourage journal keeping; allow self-reflection in assignments.

Naturalist Intelligence: the most recent intelligence to be added to the original seven categories, the naturalist intelligence involves distinguishing among, classifying, and using features of the environment. Specifically, it is the natural instinct to react to the environment and make judgments about survival. People with a highly developed naturalist intelligence are adept at classifying plants and animals.

- For the naturalist learner, provide opportunities for interacting with the environment, such as field trips. Ask participants to bring something in from the environment that represents the learning topic.

We all possess all eight intelligences; we use all eight every day and rarely in isolation (Armstrong, 2000). Unfortunately many traditional learning environments value only language, logic, and analytical skills when deciding what is "intelligence;" devaluing things important to the workplace, such as curiosity, creativity, and originality. To the extent that we acknowledge and support these ways of knowing, we enhance the quality of the learning experience for adult learners.

Additionally, designing instruction for learner populations who choose to learn at some distance from a traditional classroom presents an opportunity to effectively apply the Theory of Multiple Intelligences through the general design of course content, the use of specific instructional activities, general communication, and improved participant interaction. The appropriate use of these eight intelligences will also increase the likelihood that the learner will retain new knowledge and remain an active learner during the entire instructional process. Finally, incorporating Multiple Intelligence theory into the design of instruction can provide multiple avenues for learning based on an individual's preferred style regardless of the discipline or the geographic dispersion of the intended learners (Osciak and Milheim, 2001).

WAYS WE LEARN

There are a variety of ways in which we learn, including:

- Emulation: one emulates either someone one knows or a historical or public figure.
- Role taking: one has a conception of what one should do and does it.
- Practical accomplishment: one sees a problem as an opportunity and learns through the experience of dealing with it.
- Validation: one tests concepts by applying them and learns after the fact.
- Anticipation: one develops a concept and then applies it, learning before acting.
- Personal growth: one is less concerned with specific skills than with self-understanding and the "transformation of values and attitudes".
- Scientific learning: one observes, conceptualizes on the basis of one's observations, then experiments to gather new data, with a primary focus on truth.

Directions:

1. Think of times when you have used each of these learning modes. Journal or discuss with a partner the following questions:

    a. The last important learning experience I had was when . . .

    b. What I learned from that experience was . . .

    c. I enjoy learning new things when I feel . . .

    d. The modes I like to use to learn something new are . . .

    e. In order to feel safe enough to try something new and possibly threatening I need . . .

    f. I have the most difficulty learning something new when . . .

    g. I take the most pride and joy from learning when I have . . .

    h. In a learning situation, I need the support of others by . . .

NOTE: I frequently engage teams in this exercise to start the discussion of team learning.

DRAWING FORTH PERSONAL VISION[12]

Naturally, vision is critical to organization development and change. From a personal perspective, we tend to adapt more readily to change if we share the organizational vision, if the organizational vision is in alignment with our personal vision. We tend to resist change when the picture of the future state does not fit with our self-image, where we want to work, how we want to "be" as organizational members.

Creating an organizational vision is the work of many. Creating a personal vision is individual. Both begin with simple questions such as, "What do we want in the future?" or "What do we wish to see in the future?" Some would think that encouraging people to identify and express their personal vision would lead to anarchy and disarray. However most organizational members are eager to link their personal visions to the team and organization (Senge, Kleiner, Roberts, Ross & Smith, 1994, p. 323).

Roberts, Smith, and Ross offer an effective approach to defining your personal vision, what you wish to create for yourself and the world around you. As personal vision influences most of our decisions, it is considered important to understanding individual change (1994, p. 201-206).

Step 1. Creating a Vision.

The process begins informally, as a private exercise. Making yourself comfortable, and giving yourself a block of time (at least an hour with no interruptions), begin by bringing yourself into a reflective frame of mind. Take a few deep breaths, let go of any tension as you exhale, so that you are relaxed, comfortable, and centered.

Imagine achieving a result in your life that you deeply desire. For example, imagine that you live where you most wish to live, or that you have the perfect job. Ignore that little voice that speaks of "possible" or "impossible." Imagine yourself accepting, into your life, the full manifestation of this result.

Describe in writing (or sketch) the experience you have imagined, using the present tense, as if it is happening now.

What does it look like?
What does it feel like?
What words (or pictures) would you use to describe it?

Step 2. Reflections.

Now pause to consider your answers to this first step. Did you articulate a vision that is close to what you actually want? There may be reasons why you find this challenging:

- "I can't have what I want." Perhaps your experience is such that what you want doesn't really matter.

For this exercise, try to suspend your doubts, worries, fears, and concerns about the limits of your future. Try to imagine real life could live up to your deepest wishes: What would happen then?

- "I want what someone else wants." Some people choose their visions based on what they think other people want.

For this exercise, concentrate on what *you* want.

- "I already know what I want." You may feel you already have your personal vision.

For this exercise, you may create a new sense of what you want, especially if you haven't asked yourself this question in some time. A personal vision is not a finished product, it is something you create, and continue to re-create, throughout your life.

- "I am afraid of what I want." You may feel afraid that if you let yourself start wanting things, things will get out of control, or you will be forced to change your life.

Since this is your vision, it can't "run away" with you; it can only increase your awareness. However, we suggest that you set your own limits on the exercise.

- "I don't know what I want." You may be unsure of what, specifically, you want.

We all have a vision within us, even if it is not well developed or articulated. For this exercise, feel free to express what you *hope* for the future.

- "I know what I want, but I can't have it at work." Some people fear that their personal vision won't be compatible with their organization's attitudes. Their fear of jeopardizing their job and position keep them from articulating their personal vision.

For this exercise, suspend your fears. However, this perception is worth investigating. You may find that your organization is more accepting of your goals and interests. If you find your perceptions are correct, your vision might include finding another place to work that will allow you to grow and flourish.

Step 3. Describing Your Personal Vision.

Now that you have reflected on the above, answer these questions. Use present tense, as if it were happening now. If the categories do not quite fit your needs, feel free to adjust them. Continue until you have completed a picture of what you want.

- Imagine achieving the results in your life that you deeply desire. What would they look like? What would they feel like? What words would you use to describe them?

Self-image: If you could be exactly the kind of person you wanted, what would your qualities be?

Tangibles: What material things would you like to own?

Home: What is your ideal living environment?

Health: What is your desire for health, fitness, athletics, and anything to do with your body?

Relationships: What types of relationships would you like to have with family, friends, coworkers, and others?

Work: What is your ideal professional or vocational situation? What impact would you like your efforts to have?

Personal pursuits: What would you like to create in the arena of individual learning, travel, reading, or other activities?

Community: What is your vision for the community or society you live in?

Life purpose: Imagine that your life has a unique purpose, fulfilled through what you do, your interrelationships, and the way you live. Describe that purpose.

Step 4. Expanding and Clarifying Your Vision.

Return to your list and expand and clarify each dimension of your vision. Ask yourself the following questions about each element:

- If I could have it now, would I take it?

Some elements of your vision don't make it past this question. Others may pass the test conditionally: "Yes, I want it, but only if . . ." Others pass, and are clarified in the process.

- Assume I have it now. What does that bring me?

This question allows you to develop a richer and deeper image of your vision. Continue to ask "And what does that bring me?" until you have reached the depth of your real desire. You may find that many components of your vision lead you to the same two or three primary goals.

ENDNOTES

[1] See Osland, J.; Kolb, D. A.; & Rubin, I. M. (2001). *Organizational Behavior: An Experiential Approach*, 7th ed. Prentice Hall; Kolb, D. A. (1976). *Learning Styles Inventory*. Boston, MASS: McBer and Company; and Kolb, D.A. (1985). *Learning Style Inventory*. Boston: McBer and Co.; Osland, J.; and Kolb, D. A.; & Rubin, I. M. (2001). *Organizational Behavior: An Experiential Approach*, 7th ed. Prentice Hall.

[2] Kolb, D. A. (1976). *Learning Styles Inventory*. Boston, MASS: McBer and Company; and Kolb, D.A. (1985). *Learning Style Inventory*. Boston: McBer and Co.; Osland, J.; Kolb, D. A.; & Rubin, I. M. (2001). *Organizational Behavior: An Experiential Approach*, 7th ed. Prentice Hall.

[3] Adapted from Kolb, D. A. (1976). *Learning Styles Inventory*. Boston, MASS: McBer and Company; and Kolb, D., Rubin, I., & McIntyre, J. M. (1984). *Organizational Psychology: An Experiential Approach to Organizational Behavior*. Englewood Cliffs, NJ: Prentice-Hall.

[4] For information on DiSC® Dimensions of Behavior Learning Approach, see Inscape Publishing at www.inscapepublishing.com.

[5] See Marston, W. M. (1928). *Emotions of Normal People*. New York: Harcourt, Brace Co.; Personal Profile System Facilitator's Manual, 1996; and Bridges, W. (2000). *Transition: The Personal Path Through Change*. Carlson Learning Company, pp. 36-39.

[6] Behavior may change when the environment changes, and therefore people's perceptions and reactions to it change. However there are consistencies in behavior across a variety of situations and the DiSC model reflects these consistencies as well as adaptations of behavior.

[7] I have altered the names assigned to the styles to reflect more "user-friendly" terminology. The original names are: Dominance, Influence, Steadiness, and Conscientiousness. Although some aspects of the four styles are present in each of us, we tend to select one or two primary styles with which we interact with the world. Combinations of the four styles can also be categorized into 15 patterns, similar to the Myers-Briggs Type Indicator. Descriptions are drawn from Personal Profile System Facilitator's Manual, 1996; and Bridges, W. (2000). *Transition: The Personal Path Through Change*. Carlson Learning Company, pp. 36-39.

[8] Draws from Allesandra, T., & O'Connor, M. J. (1994). *People Smarts. Bending the Golden Rule to Give Others What They Want*. San Diego, CA: Pfeiffer & Company.

[9] See Bridges, W. (2004, 1980). *Transitions: Making Sense of Life's Changes*. Reading, MA: Addison-Wesley Publishing Company; Bridges, W. (1991). *Managing Transitions: Making the Most of Change*. Reading, MA: Addison-Wesley Publishing Company; Bridges, W. (2001). *The Way of Transition: Embracing Life's Most Difficult Moments*. Cambridge, MASS: Perseus Publishing; and www.wmbridges.com.

[10] For a more organizational focus, see Bridges, B. (1991). *Managing Transitions: Making the Most of Change*. Reading, MA: Addison-Wesley Publishing Company; Bridges, W. (2001). *The Way of Transition: Embracing Life's Most Difficult Moments*. Cambridge, MASS: Perseus Publishing. See also www.wmbridges.com.

[11] See Armstrong, T. (2000). *Multiple Intelligences in the Classroom*. Alexandria, VA: Association for Supervision and Curriculum Development; Gardner, H. (1983). *Frames of Mind: The Theory of Multiple Intelligences*. New York: Basic Books; and Gardner, H. (1999). *Intelligence Reframed*. New York: Basic Books.

[12] Adapted from The Fifth Discipline Fieldbook by Peter M Senge, Charlotte Roberts, et. Al, copyright © 1994 by Peter M. Senge, Charlotte Roberts, Richard B. Ross, Bryan J. Smith, and Art Kleiner.   Used with permission of Doubleday, a division of Random House Inc.

CHAPTER 5:

ORGANIZATIONAL LEARNING AND CREATIVITY

WHAT IS THE CREATIVITY CLIMATE IN YOUR ORGANIZATION?

Think about an organization with which you are familiar and answer the following questions.

1. Who are the creative people and how do we know they are creative?

2. What opportunities exist for creative people in this organization?

3. What barriers have we placed in front of creative people?

4. In what ways do we reward creativity?

5. Do we embarrass, ridicule, ignore, or reject those people who experiment and try new approaches?

6. How do we specifically encourage and promote experimentation and independent thinking?

7. Do managers usually make all the important decisions? What types of decisions are non-managers encouraged to make?

8. Are meetings typically agenda bound, tightly structured, time constricted, and dominated by critical, control-oriented managers who have little tolerance for diversion from the agenda?

9. How can we encourage *all* organizational members to be more creative?

10. What creativity and innovation training do we offer?

From your responses, how would you rate your organization in terms of tapping into the creative talents of its members?

> In an uncertain world, where all we know for sure is that nothing is sure, we are going to need organizations that are continually renewing themselves, reinventing themselves, reinvigorating themselves. These are the learning organizations, the ones with the learning habit. (Charles Handy, 1993)

Along with individual learning, it has become clear that organizational learning is essential for an organization's survival. The ability to adapt quickly stems from an ability to learn, i.e., the ability to assimilate new ideas and to transform those ideas into action faster than a competitor. Organizational learning is generally defined as "the process by which an organization obtains knowledge about the associations between past actions, the effectiveness of those actions, and future actions" (Bedeian, 1987). Senge (1990, p. 3) describes learning organizations as places . . .

> where people continually expand their capacity to create the results they truly desire, where new and expansive patterns of thinking are nurtured, where collective aspiration is set free, and where people are continually learning how to learn together.

Organizational learning is the basis of successful organizational change. Learning takes place at individual, team, and organizational levels. Individual learning occurs each time an individual reads a book, collects new data, try's something new, gets feedback. Team learning occurs when team members learn from experience or activity, involving new ways of doing things or new ways as interacting as a team. Organizational learning occurs when the organization develops systemic processes to acquire, use, and communicate knowledge. People, teams, and organizations do not, however, automatically learn; many have learning disabilities that disable the learning process.

ORGANIZATIONAL LEARNING DISABILITIES

Peter Senge[1] (1990, pp. 18-25) describes learning disabilities that result in a non-systems perspective and thereby inhibit creativity and learning. Many of these stem from the traditional structure and management philosophy found in large, complex bureaucratic organizations.

- **I Am My Position**: People tend to see their responsibilities as limited to the boundaries of their position. "It's not my job".
- **The Enemy is Out There**: A by-product of the above, people do not see how their own actions extend beyond the boundary of their position.
- **The Illusion of Taking Charge**: We often take proactive action against "the external enemy", which is, in reality, reactiveness. Changes are made to effect external, not internal states.

- **The Fixation on Events**: We make changes based on events, such as last month's drop in sales, or new budget cuts. Changes are made in reaction to the events, not the system.
- **The Parable of the Boiled Frog**: Unable to see slow, gradual processes, we react to events, making changes only on events, not on the very things that are the most threatening.
- **The Delusion of Learning From Experience**: The most powerful learning comes from direct experience. However, if we have what Senge refers to as a "learning horizon", we can only assess our effectiveness within a limited time and space. One usually hears as a resistance to change, "We've always done it that way and it works". Senge suggests that we learn best from experience but we never directly experience the *consequences* of many of our most important decisions. Critical change affects the entire system, but the people making the change are only able to experience the consequences within their particular division or department.
- **The Myth of the Management Team**: While this group is tasked with bringing forth good decisions and effective change, within the traditional organization, the management team is highly ineffective due to "turf" protection, self-promotion, and maintaining the *appearance* of effectiveness. When managers assume a "turf protection" stance, they are much less interested in the global effects of the change. When a management team is interested in maintaining the appearance of effectiveness, people are required to squelch disagreement, avoid public statements of reservation and accept compromise.

A learning environment requires systems thinking. The opposite of linear thinking, in which one sees un-related parts of the whole, or static snapshots of an event, systems thinking views the organization as an integrated whole, seeing interrelationships, and patterns. For this we again turn to Peter Senge.

FIVE DISCIPLINES OF ORGANIZATIONAL LEARNING

Senge contends that we can build learning organizations where people continually expand their capacity to create the results they truly desire, where new and expansive patterns of thinking are nurtured, where collective aspiration is set free, and where people are continually learning how to learn together. We do this through the practice of five disciplines, which he defines not as "an enforced order or means of punishment, but as a body of theory and technique that must be studied and mastered to be put into practice. A discipline is a developmental path requiring certain skills or competencies . . . To practice a discipline is to be a lifelong learner. You never arrive."[2] Senge describes the disciplines of the learning organization as follows:

Personal Mastery. The discipline of continually clarifying and deepening personal vision, of focusing energies, of developing patience, and of seeing reality objectively. This calls for learning to expand our personal capacity to create the results we most desire, and creating an organizational environment that encourages all its members to develop themselves towards the goals and purposes they choose.

Mental Models. Mental models are deeply ingrained assumptions, generalizations, or even pictures or images that influence how we understand the world and how we take action. This discipline calls on reflecting upon, continually clarifying, and improving our internal pictures of the world, and seeing how they shape our actions and decisions, both positively and negatively.

Building Shared Vision. This discipline calls for building a sense of commitment in a group, by developing shared images of the future we seek to create, and the principles and guiding practices by which we hope to get there. When there is a genuine vision, people excel and learn, not because they are told to, but because they want to.

Team Learning. Transforming conversational and collective thinking skills, so that groups of people can reliably develop intelligence and ability greater than the sum of individual members' talents. When teams are truly learning, not only are they producing extraordinary results but also the individual members are growing more rapidly than could have occurred otherwise.

Systems Thinking. A way of thinking about, and a language for describing and understanding, the forces and interrelationships that shape the behavior of systems. Systems thinking is a conceptual framework, a body of knowledge and tools to make the full patterns clearer, and to help us see how to change them effectively.

Through the practice of these disciplines, organizations move towards creating an environment in which learning (personal, group, and organizational) is explicit and intentional. The model assists in the facilitation of developing a systems perspective so important to the success of organizational change and transformation.

Another critical aspect is enabling creativity and innovation. How do we get organizational members to think creatively about certain organizational problems or future vision? A key question for those seeking to improve organizational effectiveness is, "Why are some organizations able to foster creativity and innovation among organizational members, while others are not?" Most experts agree that each of us has the ability to be creative and innovative, to some extent, within our particular domain. Given the tools and an environment that is conducive to innovation, most employees can come up with new and useful ways of handling situations and solving problems. It has been found that the work environment can influence both the level and frequency of creative behavior. As innovation is vital for long-term organizational success, understanding the "social psychology of creativity" is important.

CREATIVITY AND INNOVATION IN CONTEXT

Amabile first introduced the idea of a social psychology of creativity in 1983, aimed at identifying particular social and environmental conditions that positively or negatively influence the creativity of most individuals.[3] Many researchers have contributed to the literature on environmental factors found to influence the creative process. Figure 5-1 depicts a contextual view of organizational creativity and innovation, useful to assist our understanding of organizational innovation[4].

Figure 5-1. A Contextual View of Organizational Creativity and Innovation

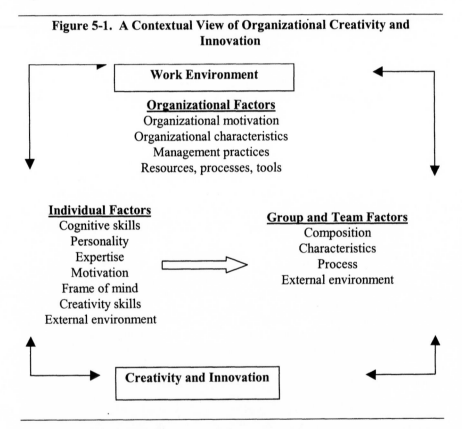

This model proposes that individual creativity and innovation is a function of cognitive skill and ability (e.g., divergent thinking, ideational fluency); personality factors (e.g., thinking and behavioral patterns); relevant knowledge (e.g., intelligence within a particular domain); motivation (e.g., intrinsic); internal frame of mind (e.g., mood, current feelings); creativity skills (e.g. creative problem solving); and external environmental factors (e.g., social influences and rewards, and contextual influences such as physical environment, task, and time constraints).

Group creativity and innovation is a function of individual factors; the interaction of group members (e.g., group composition); group characteristics (e.g., norms, size, degree of cohesiveness); group processes (e.g., approaches to problem solving); and environmental influences (e.g., the larger organization).

Organizational creativity and innovation is a function of individual and group output; organizational motivation (e.g., a culture of risk-taking); organizational characteristics (e.g., rewards, strategy, and structure); management practices (e.g., empowerment); and resources, processes and tools (e.g. training).

The individual creates both independently and dependently within group settings. The group takes on its own characteristics and develops methods of problem-solving and innovation. The organization provides the climate and tools for innovation to occur.

CHARACTERISTICS OF INNOVATIVE ORGANIZATIONS

Albrecht (1987) suggested that creativity is a behavior pattern -- a form of activity. Amabile (1983, 1996), among others, asserts that certain environmental factors exist that can be manipulated to increase the likelihood of creative performance. Organizations can "learn to learn" and become open to innovation and creativity[5]. Characteristics of static (segmentalist) organizations include[6]:

- **Structure.** Rigid: much energy given to maintaining permanent departments; committees; reverence for tradition; constitution and by-laws. Hierarchical: adherence to chain of command; roles narrowly defined. Structured boundaries; limited flow of information.
- **Atmosphere.** Task-centered; impersonal; cold; formal; reserved; suspicious.
- **Management philosophy and attitudes.** Control through coercive power. Cautious - low risk-taking; avoid errors. Emphasis on personnel selection. Closed system regarding sharing of resources. Low tolerance for ambiguity. System trusted more than organizational members.
- **Decision making and policy making.** High participation at top, low at bottom. Clear distinction between policy-making and policy-execution. Decision making by legal mechanisms. Decisions treated as final.
- **Communication.** Restricted flow. One-way -- downward. Feelings repressed or hidden.
- **Change.** Anti change; maintain status quo.
- **Problems.** Problems seen narrowly with no connection to other problems.
- **Innovation.** Difficult to transmit innovative ideas; "If it ain't broke . . ."
- **Rewards.** Rewards after the achievement; no power given to potential innovators.

Characteristics of innovative (integrative) organizations include[7]:

- **Structure.** Flexible: much use of temporary task forces; easy shifting of departmental lines; readiness to change rules and depart from tradition. Multiple linkages based on functional collaboration; roles broadly defined. Invisible organizational boundaries to enable shared information.
- **Atmosphere.** People-centered; caring; warm; informal; intimate; trusting.
- **Management philosophy and attitudes.** Release of energy of personnel; supportive. Experimental - high risk-taking; learn from errors. Emphasis on personnel development. Interdependency, open system regarding sharing of resources. High tolerance for ambiguity. Belief that organizational members can be creative and innovative.
- **Decision making and policy making.** Relevant participation at all levels. Collaborative policy-making and policy-execution. Decision making by problem solving. Decisions treated as hypotheses to be tested.
- **Communication.** Open flow - easy access. Multidirectional - up, down, sideways. Feelings expressed.
- **Change.** Change seen as opportunity to grow and test limits.
- **Problems.** Problems viewed as wholes, related to larger wholes.
- **Innovation.** Continuous improvement upon existing things and conditions.
- **Rewards.** Rewards before and during the innovation process; incentives for defining new problems or pet projects to work on.

Innovative and integrative approaches build support and cooperation and are more beneficial to organizational learning and creativity. Kanter (1983) suggests the following strategies of integrative approaches:

- Frequent mobility, including lateral moves, circulation of people through various departments of the organization. This results in movement of information to different areas of the organization; retaining contact with people in neighboring areas in order to gain needed information or support; making new contacts (creating links) and getting fresh ideas; and exchanging favors with old and new contacts.
- Employment security, resulting in the elimination of fear; increased output; and creation of an atmosphere for innovation.
- Team approach, which enables immediate exchange of support and information at middle and upper levels; successful problem solving and innovation; diversity of sources and variety of ideas; carrying out major tasks which are spread evenly throughout the team; and a clearer understanding of what is happening at different levels.
- "Cross pollination" permitting cross-cutting access, i.e. manager to upper level management or cross functional teams. This creates inter-unit contact between managers; enables working relationships (both formal and informal) with persons from other functions or disciplines; mobilizes support or resources in order to facilitate a desired result; and provides alternative sources of power.

One of the major characteristics of innovative organizations is the way in which it is organized. Closed bureaucratic systems were geared to the industrial age when the workforce was comprised primarily of uneducated immigrant workers. Today's workforce is very different, in terms of economic status, education level, and diversity. The values and assumptions of bureaucratic organizations that served us well in the past are now problematic, particularly when it comes to organizational learning and creativity.

An open systems model allows organizations to become flexible and respond to internal and external pressures, while maintaining stability. An open systems view does not reject being organized. Rather it presents a way of understanding and developing organizations so that management processes and individual human potential work together instead of against each other (Mink, Shultz, and Mink, 1991). McWhinney (1992) suggests the following as avenues to open systems organizations:

- Various configurations, not always hierarchical;
- Participation in decision making;
- Work design in response to individuals' psychic and physiological needs for social interplay;
- Power sharing, such as employee stock option plans or similar modes of participation in ownership;
- Sensitivity to the environment;
- Openness to external influences, such as the customer and the community; and
- Openness to and encouragement of change.

In the past, the challenge was to "get organized." Today, organizations need to find ways in which to remain open to continuous self-organization[8].

CREATIVITY AND INNOVATION DEFINED

Creativity is the production of novel and useful ideas (Amabile, 1983, 1996). Organizational creativity is the creation of a valuable, useful new program, product, service, idea, procedure, or process by individuals working together (Woodman, Sawyer, and Griffin, 1993).

Creativity is the first step in the innovation process. Many creative ideas do not make it to 'reality', not due to the idea itself, but due to a lack of process to carry the idea forward.

Innovation is the process of transforming creative ideas into a "marketable" program, product, service, or process[9]. While the terms "creativity" and "innovation" are often used interchangeably, it is generally agreed that creativity is one aspect of the innovation (application) process.

People have the ability to be creative, particularly within a domain of specialty. Organizational members could be considered the expert on his or her segment of the business (Clark, 1980). If we assume this to be true, that all organizational members are creative and vary only in the degree of their creativeness, then all organizations must be considered creative; some will simply be more creative than others (Van Gundy, 1987).

There is a creative process, which can be described. There is also an innovation process that can be described. Creativity and innovation can at least partially be learned; there are tools, methods, and processes that help increase the creative and innovation processes.

The creative and innovation process can also be inhibited. For example, in traditional education we are trained to think in terms of reaching the "correct" answers, not always the "best solutions." Individuals may also be inhibited by the desire to please others, not make waves, and thereby maintain the status quo. For example, in a meeting, if an idea is introduced and someone challenges it, the person with the idea becomes embarrassed or frustrated and refrains from further creative offerings.

Some say creativity in business is a way of life, an ongoing process, not a series of isolated aberrations, that it is a productive attitude developed by individuals throughout their business lifetime, not a random good idea that happens to work.   Some propose that creativity is more individual than organizational, and that while it is easier to be creative in a company whose policies invite it, corporate policy is not a requirement for individual creative expression (Ray and Myers, 1986). However, considerable research shows that the social (work) environment has heavy influence on creativity and innovation in organizations.

FACTORS THAT IMPACT INDIVIDUAL CREATIVITY

Research suggests a cluster of factors that are related to creativity and creative problem-solving to varying degrees. For example, one study reported that some of the geniuses of mathematics were of intuitive inclination and others were analytic (Hadamard, 1945).   Maslow (1968) discerned two types of creativity—one based on talent, the other on intuitive originality. Other research has shown four common creative traits: 1) Courage—willingness to dare new tasks and risk failure; 2) Expressive—willingness to express thoughts and feelings; 3) Humor—willingness to view ambiguity and incongruity with humor; and 4) Intuition—acceptance of intuition as a legitimate aspect of personality, as well as a drive to find order in chaos, an interest in finding unusual problems as well as solutions, the ability to balance idea creation with testing and judgment, and motivation by the problem or task itself rather than external rewards.

Characteristics that are related to individual creativity include absence of repression and suppression; feminine and aesthetic interests; self-esteem and self-confidence; tolerance for ambiguity; willingness to take risks; ability to use convergent and divergent thinking; originality; ideational fluency; elaboration; independence of judgment; dual-brain hemispheric dominance; and perseverance; opinion flexibility; semantic flexibility; positive orientation; sense of humor; investigative orientation; and resistance to enculturation[10].

Motivation is a key factor in individual and small group creativity. There is evidence that people will be most creative when they are primarily intrinsically motivated by work that is interesting, engaging, exciting, satisfying, or personally challenging. People are more creative when they are interested in the work, regardless of external rewards.

People are less motivated with extrinsic motivators such as competition with peers, dictates from superiors, or promise of rewards. Studies report that the "means-end" work environment, doing the task in order to get a reward, undermines creativity. There are, however, times when extrinsic motivators enhance the creative process, such as perception of promised reward (i.e., constructive feedback on the work from an esteemed colleague) for working on a project where the interest level (intrinsic) is high (Amabile, 1997).

COMPONENTIAL THEORY OF INDIVIDUAL CREATIVITY

To some extent, intrinsic motivation resides in an individual's personality. Amabile and her associates found, however, that a person's social environment can have a significant effect on level of intrinsic motivation at any point in time; and that the level of intrinsic motivation can, in turn, have a significant effect on that person's creativity. This theory has three major components that address individual and small team creativity (Amabile, 1997).

- **Expertise**: the foundation of all creative work; can be viewed as the set of cognitive pathways that may be followed for solving a given problem or doing a given task. The expertise component includes memory for factual knowledge, technical proficiency, and special talents in the target work domain.
- **Creative Thinking**: the "something extra" of creative performance. Includes a cognitive style favorable to examining new perspectives on problems, an application of techniques for the exploration of new cognitive pathways, and a working style conducive to persistent, energetic pursuit of one's work.
- **Task Motivation**: determines what the person will actually do, the extent a person will fully engage his expertise and creative thinking skills in the service of creative performance. This component is most heavily influenced by the social (work) environment. Two types of motivations positively affect creativity: Internal level of intrinsic motivation, such as passion for the work; and the type of extrinsic motivation such as feedback that confirms competence or provides important information on how to improve performance (informational extrinsic motivators), or recognition that directly increases the person's involvement in the work itself (enabling extrinsic motivators). Controlling extrinsic motivators, such as constraint on how the work is done, negatively affects task motivation.

FACTORS THAT IMPACT TEAM OR GROUP CREATIVITY

The assembly of people in a group often impacts creative behavior, which is partially determined by the composition and characteristics of the group. Characteristics in effect during the creative problem-solving process in group settings include (see Van Gundy, 1984):

- **Group-member gender**—in general mixed-gender groups produce higher-quality and more creative problem solutions than same-sex groups;
- **Group homogeneity-heterogeneity**—diversity with respect to personality seems to promote group creativity;
- **Group cohesion**—members of highly cohesive groups are generally more motivated to participate in the activities and identify with group success than members of less cohesive groups;
- **Group compatibility**—groups that are more compatible are generally more effective in achieving group goals; and
- **Group size**—while the literature is inconclusive on the 'perfect group size', it is generally proposed that a smaller group (6 to 8) is more effective for creative tasks.

Another factor that influences team innovation is maturity or the **stage of group development** (Tuckman,1965, 1977). A group begins with the initial *forming* stage, in which the group is orienting to its goals and procedures; the relationship behavior is testing and dependence. This is followed by the stage of *storming* where the group task is to develop roles and responsibilities; there is resistance or emotional response to task demands, with intragroup and interpersonal hostility in relationships. The *norming* stage is one where the group learns how to express opinions; acceptable behaviors are developed as teams begin to become cohesive. The stage of *performing* is when the group senses an emergence of solutions and problem-solving becomes creative; group effort is mobilized to achieve group goals. The final stage, *adjourning*, is when the group terminates task behaviors and disengages from relationships.

The probability of creative outcomes may be highest when **leadership** is democratic and collaborative, **structure** is organic rather than mechanistic, and groups are composed of individuals drawn from **diverse** fields or functional backgrounds (Woodman, Sawyer, and Griffin, 1993).

CREATIVITY AND INNOVATION PROCESS

Individuals go through a process of creativity and innovation, however the process may vary for different individuals and within different situations. This also applies to creativity and innovation in groups, in which one process may work well for one set of circumstances but not for another. There are four basic steps to the *individual* creative process.

- The first step is **preparation**, when one actively seeks problems to be solved and information about these problems. One gathers information from all available sources, to the point of saturation.

- The second step is **incubation**, when one puts the problem to rest and turns to other activities. Any technique of relaxation of the conscious cognition (left brain) which would allow subliminal processes (right brain) to operate, such as dreams, daydreams, fantasy, meditation, and play, is helpful for this stage (Wallas, 1926).
- The third step is **illumination**, which typically brings the "aha!" when one receives an answer unexpectedly and without effort.
- The fourth step is **verification**, when one tests and verifies the ideas for viability through various implementation stages. Within this step are two additional steps: **refinement**, a process of modification and refinement to get ideas into a salable form; and **selling**, the process of getting someone else to buy the finished product (Albrecht,1987).

There is also the element of **encounter**, in which the creator becomes absorbed in the object at hand. The intensity of the encounter, also referred to as absorption, leads to a heightened consciousness that is exhibited in neurological changes such as a quickened heartbeat, higher blood pressure, increased intensity and constriction of vision, and lessening of appetite as we become oblivious to the surroundings. Rollo May contended that while we cannot "will" creativity, we can *will* to give ourselves over to the encounter with intensity and dedication and commitment (May, 1976).

Groups are also seen to follow a process while in a problem solving state, which includes four basic steps[11]:

- **Problem awareness and identification**: a group becomes aware of the problem and begins the analysis of identifying the underlying causes of the problem.
- **Idea proposal**: the group generates ideas on potential solutions and goes through a process of analyzing those ideas.
- **Idea adoption**: The group selects a solution to the problem and begins the process of planning for its implementation.
- **Idea implementation**. The final step is the implementation of that idea, or transforming the ideas into "reality."

A critical factor in the success of team creativity and innovation is the awareness of the *process* used (Albrecht, 1987), with the understanding that innovation is a continuous dynamic set of activities, deals with the concept of newness relative to a particular organization, and is stimulated by a perceived gap in performance (a problem) (Van Gundy, 1987).

DIMENSIONS OF TEAM INNOVATION MODEL[12]

Teams often become frustrated and non-productive because they get "stuck" and unable to come up with new ideas, or they are unable to advance or move ideas forward. There often is friction between team members who feel that an idea won't work or isn't thought out thoroughly before being implemented. The Dimensions of Team Innovation Model proposes that we each have a natural style with which we are most comfortable in the innovation process. These styles are based upon the way we think and the way we choose change-oriented behavior.

The Dimensions of Team Innovation Model suggests that 1) there are roles within the innovation process that individuals are most comfortable in assuming; 2) teams must recognize the idea cycle and develop strategies to manage ideas; and 3) a team is more effective in the innovation process if it maximizes the individual strengths of team members.

The model is based on work developed by Fahden and Namakkal (1993) to explain the distinct behavioral and cognitive patterns of individuals in group or team settings. Like others, they observed that each team member demonstrates a preference for performing certain roles over others, and related these roles to the innovation process[13]. These authors combined the two basic factors of behavior and thinking because in innovation, thought carries as much weight (someone thinks of an idea) as behavior (someone implements or kills the idea with their behavior)."

- The **thinking factor** is comprised of a continuum from conceptual to linear. Conceptual thinking, often referred to as divergent or creative thinking, reflects the tendency to think dimensionally or "sideways." Persons who utilize conceptual thinking are comfortable with dealing with ambiguity, and the ability to link disparate elements to form new patterns. A conceptual thinker uses a more intuitive, digressive approach to problems and challenges. Linear thinking, or convergent, critical thinking, reflects the tendency to think systematically and deliberately, taking a stepwise approach to problems and challenges. A linear thinker tends to like clear, well-defined problems and issues, and prefers to address one thing at a time.
- The **behavior factor** is comprised of a continuum from initiating to adopting. Initiating behavior preference reflects a tendency to instigate change, either by creating or advancing new behavioral tendencies. Persons with initiating behavior originate, recognize, or adopt new trends very early, and favor fresh perspectives. Adopting behavior preference reflects a tendency toward cautiousness, clearly assessing the pros and cons of proposed change. Persons with adopting behavior preference display a careful and deliberate manner in responding to change.

The Dimensions of Team Innovation Model, measured by the Team Dimensions Profile®, proposes that individuals display a preference along both the behavior continuum and the thinking continuum and that the intersection suggests one's natural "style" in the innovation process. The model identifies five primary dimensional patterns of innovation: Creator, Advancer, Refiner, Implementer[14], and Facilitator, which represents a blend of the other four. The model also describes combination patterns that identify a blend of two dimensions, e.g., Creator-Advancer pattern[15].

Figure 5-2. Dimensions of Team Innovation Model

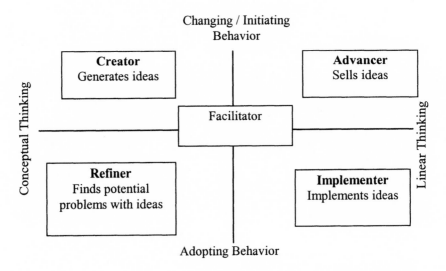

The <u>Creator</u> pattern draws upon the components of initiating behavior and conceptual thinking. An individual preferring this pattern is most comfortable with the role of generating fresh, original concepts and ideas. Creators are not afraid of taking risks and enjoy identifying problems and exploring solutions.

The <u>Advancer</u> pattern draws upon the components of initiating behavior and linear thought. An individual preferring this pattern recognizes new opportunities, is most comfortable with the role of moving ideas forward and derives satisfaction from the process of selling the idea and removing roadblocks to its success.

The <u>Refiner</u> pattern draws upon the components of adopting behavior and conceptual thought and challenges new concepts and ideas. A refiner is comfortable in the role of "devil's advocate," causing others to examine the idea closely, and think the idea through thoroughly before implementing it.

The <u>Implementer</u> pattern draws upon the components of adopting behavior and linear thought. An individual who prefers this pattern lays the groundwork for implementation, checks for executional flaws, manages the detailed tasks of getting the job done in a quality way.

A fifth pattern, <u>Facilitator</u>, is derived from low scores for all dimensions, indicating a flexible, consensus-building team member who is adept at adapting to other people, assumes the tendencies and strengths of other patterns, when necessary and appropriate, and helps the group move in new directions.

IDEA MANAGEMENT: TRANSFORMING IDEAS INTO REALITY

Idea management refers to the concept that an idea must go beyond generation, through a transformational process, to become a reality. Useful ideas must be separated from the impractical, they must be implemented with a measure of discipline and technique, in a way that others can understand and use them. Figure 5-3 diagrams a model that relates to the concept of idea management, moving ideas from the creation stage to a finished product that can be evaluated for usefulness[16].

The Dimensions of Team Innovation model provides a process for ideas to advance within a team, with hand-offs to the most suitable team member at the appropriate time.

Figure 5-3. Idea Management: How ideas are transformed from raw ideas to new and usable products, processes, or services

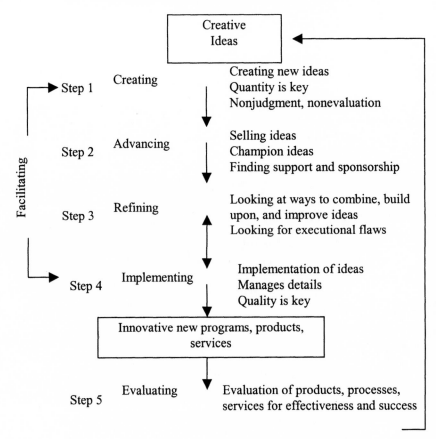

The process begins with the creation of ideas, best suited for those with the Creator pattern. Once ideas are generated, the Advancer sees the possibilities of these ideas and begins a marketing strategy, moving the innovation process forward by serving as champions and key proponents and promoters of the ideas. The Refiner is best suited for analyzing the ideas and identifying potential loopholes and problems, suggesting revisions, and proposing alternative solutions. The Refiner may hand back the plans to Advancers or Creators before handing off tasks to the Implementer. The Implementer develops the basic implementation plan, and pulls things together to successfully see the idea transformed into a product. The Facilitator takes on the role of moderator, as well as adapting to different roles as needed. An analogy of this process is a relay race, where runners pass the baton at the appropriate moment. Teams relay ideas to the most appropriate individual at appropriate times, and in doing so, becoming more effective in their innovative process (Fahden, 1993).

The first determinant of an innovative team is to have a blend of roles or patterns on the team. A team with a heavy emphasis on Creators and few Refiners would have difficulty moving ideas from conception to reality. Or a team with many Refiners and Executors and fewer Creators and Advancers would have difficulty generating fresh and new ideas.

Once there is a blend of patterns on the team, collaborative efforts occur in the hand-off of ideas. Team members know when and how to turn to others and hand-off an idea or task to those best suited. Katzenbach and Smith (1993) refer to this as "a common approach . . . how they will work together to accomplish their purpose. Team members must agree on who will do particular jobs."

The Team Innovation Model, or one like it, is a way for organization development practitioners to assist teams in becoming more creative and innovative. All teams engage in some type of problem solving. Understanding the various roles team members prefer and are most comfortable with increases team effectiveness.

ORGANIZATIONAL FACTORS THAT IMPACT CREATIVITY AND INNOVATION

Amabile (1997) and her associates, in the Componential Theory of Organizational Creativity and Innovation, propose that elements of the work environment will impact individuals' creativity, and that the creativity produced by individuals and teams of individuals serves as a primary source of innovation within the organization. The social (work) environment influences creativity by influencing individual components; the impact on task motivation has the most immediate and direct. Their research has resulted in a distinction of three major elements of the work environment that affect creativity and innovation: organizational motivation to innovate, resources, and management practices.

Organizational Motivation to Innovate—basic orientation of the organization toward innovation, as well as supports for creativity and innovation throughout the organization. Most important are: a value placed on creativity and innovation, orientation toward risk, sense of pride in the organization's members and enthusiasm about what they are capable of doing, an offensive strategy of taking the lead toward the future.

Organization-wide supports for innovation include mechanisms for developing new ideas; open, active communication of information and ideas; reward and recognition for creative work; fair evaluation of work, including work that might be perceived as a "failure;" absence of political "turf battles," and destructive criticism and competition; reduction in strict controls by upper management, and excess of formal structures and procedures.

Resources—things the organization has available to aid work in the domain targeted for innovation, including time for producing novel work, people with necessary expertise, funds allocated to this work domain, material resources, systems and processes for work in the domain, relevant information, and availability of training.

Management Practices—at all levels, but particularly important at the level of individual departments and projects. Includes ability to clearly set overall project goals while allowing procedural autonomy, clear planning and feedback, good communications between supervisor and the work group, enthusiastic support for the work of individuals as well as the entire group.

Management practices that support creativity include the ability to establish effective work groups that represent a diversity of skills, are made up of individuals who trust and communicate well with each other, constructively challenge each other's ideas, are mutually supportive, and are committed to the work they are doing.

The encouragement of creative factors helps organizational members cultivate a spirit of enthusiasm and sense of significance (Bleedorn, 1993 among others). Table 5-1 lists ways in which an organization can enable or stifle creative and innovative performance. Dimensions that are examined are organizational culture, motivation, social and group dynamics, evaluation, reward, encouragement and recognition, problem solving, work environment, and humor[17].

Table 5-1. Enablers and Barriers to Creative and Innovative Performance in Organizations

Organizational Dimension	Positive Factors (Enablers)	Negative Factors (Barriers)
Culture	Encouragement of innovative, new ideas; encouragement of risk-taking; stimulates creative thinking; maximizes interpersonal relationships; invests in new products; flexible work environment and structure; orientation toward playfulness; tolerance for ambiguity; assumption that change is good.	Discouragement of employees from thinking "outside the box"; rigid environment; discouragement of risk-taking; serious atmosphere; lack of interest in true quality; intolerance for chaos and ambiguity; short term outlook; assumption that change is bad.
Motivation	Promotes intrinsic motivations such as self-esteem, learning, self-actualization; encourages people to work on projects that fully utilize their talents and that they are interested in; encourages people to work with colleagues of similar interests.	Promotes and fosters extrinsic motivations such as salary, benefits, and security.
Social and group dynamics	Promotes and fosters group interactions to stimulate creative thinking; allows for a mixture of individual and group work; recognizes group dynamics; promotes synergy; promotes a trusting environment; promotes diversity.	Promotes and fosters peer pressure and individual competition; forces all work to be done in groups or teams; pressure to conform.
Evaluation	Recognizes that evaluation can have a negative effect on creative performance, i.e., the boss in the room during a group	Fosters negative external evaluation, such as rewards and deadlines.

	brainstorming session, and undermine creativity; however, recognizes that external evaluation can have positive effects when it is work-focused and constructive; fosters constructive feedback on projects.	
Reward	Recognizes that reward can have a negative impact on creative performance and can be demotivating; fosters desired rewards, i.e., ability to attend a conference and present work; recognizes that people choose more heuristic path to solving problems when not being rewarded (allows for pure enjoyment of the task.)	Rewards all tasks, creating an environment in which non-rewarded conditions become non-productive and which can decrease the enjoyment of the task; creates a competitive environment; people choose less heuristic path to solving problems when being rewarded.
Encouragement and recognition	Encourages and recognizes creative performance; promotes peer review; psychological safety in which people are recognized for their talents; recognizes that failure in work can provide valuable information.	Discourages creative performance among majority of employees; does not recognize innovative ideas; no or inappropriate incentives for creativity and innovation.
Problem solving	Open-ended viewpoint (multiple alternatives); see problems as opportunities; ability to know which problems to pursue and those best suited to work the problems; balance of idea-generators and implementers in the problem-solving process.	Closed-ended viewpoint (one correct answer); inability to properly define problems; inability to screen multiple ideas and select a good one to pursue; too many or too few idea generators, not enough idea implementers; time, budget, and other resource constraints.

Work environment	Less extrinsic constraints; little interference with work; support for innovation from high levels of organization; technical resources; flexible work schedules; bright, colorful workspace in which "decorating" is encouraged; psychological freedom in which people are free to express, think, to be whatever is most true for themselves; quiet alone time.	Close supervision; rigid work patterns and routines; preoccupation with order and tradition; over-reliance on ineffective algorithms; discouragement of play; dull and rigid workspace; outdated technology and tools; workspace that is noisy, crowded, and confining; schedules that are too hectic to allow time for thinking and ideas to "incubate."
Humor	Encourages humor and play, laughter, games, contests, stories, tasteful jokes and cartoons.	Discourages humor and playfulness.

LEADING CREATIVITY

Creative leaders make certain assumptions that facilitate creativity and innovation to occur, including (Knowles, 1983):

- Creative leaders take an essentially positive assumption about human nature; they have faith in people, offer them challenging opportunities, and delegate responsibility to them. This, in turn, fosters an atmosphere in which people perceive the locus of control to reside within themselves, allowing them to be more creative and productive, and feel their unique potential is being utilized.
- Creative leaders accept as a law of human nature that people feel a commitment to a decision in proportion to the extent that they feel they have participated in it. They involve their clients, workers, or students in every step of the planning process, from assessing needs, formulating goals, designing lines of action, carrying out activities, and evaluating results.
- Creative leaders believe in and use the power of self-fulfilling prophecy. They understand that people tend to live up to others' expectations of them.
- Creative leaders highly value individuality. They sense that people perform at a higher level when they are operating on the basis of their unique strengths, talents, interests, and goals than when they are trying to conform to some imposed stereotype. Creative leaders see the purpose of all life

activities, e.g., work, learning, recreation, and civic participation, as enablers of achieving full and unique potential.

- Creative leaders stimulate and reward creativity. They understand that in a world of constant and accelerating change, creativity is a basic requirement for the survival of individuals, organizations, and societies. They exemplify creativity in their own behavior and provide an environment that encourages and rewards innovation in others. They make it legitimate for people to experiment, and treat failures as opportunities to learn rather than as acts to be punished.

- Creative leaders are committed to a process of continuous change and are skillful in managing change. They understand the difference between static and innovative organizations, are well grounded in the theory of planned change, and skillful in selecting the most appropriate and effective strategies to bring about change.

- Creative leaders emphasize internal motivators over external motivators. They understand the importance of satisfiers (motivators) such as achievement, a sense of pride in one's work, advancement, and growth.

- Creative leaders encourage people to be self-directing. They sense intuitively that a universal characteristic of the maturation process is movement from a state of dependency toward states of increasing self-directedness.

LEARNING AND CHANGE GO HAND IN HAND

Organization development practitioners are actively engaged in the process of creating learning organizations. Understanding why and how organizational members engage in the learning process is integral to success in facilitating an environment that captures the talent and passion for learning.

The environment can be shaped to increase and enhance learning and creative performance. Organizations can learn to foster a continuous learning, and creative environment. The overlap of organizational learning and innovation might provide the understanding for 1) how learning (innovation) is induced, 2) how to design organizations which are productive of innovations (learning), and 3) how to change an innovation (or learning) resistant organization into an innovation (or learning) producing organization.

IDEA GENERATION AND BRAINSTORMING

One of the most widely used processes in the group or team problem-solving state is brainstorming. Brainstorming sessions are designed to capture the synergy of the group. Devised by Alex Osborn (1963) in advertising as a technique to stimulate small groups of knowledgeable, industry-savvy individuals to come up with product names, new uses for clients' tired products, and fresh ways to position established products, it has become a tool with many applications in virtually all industries, any situation where people feel the need to get their creative juices flowing to address problems and opportunities.

Basic Method	Rules of Conduct
Preparation/Orientation The purpose of the session is stated; the process is outlined. A question is posed to the group to generate ideas. **Idea-Generation** Rapid-fire idea-generation period is conducted, in which ideas are captured by a scribe on a board or easel. It is important to avoid judgment or clarification at this stage, allow ideas to flow. Timeframe is dependent upon topic and question, typically lasting from 30-45 minutes. Facilitator mediates the process, encouraging group to continue with idea-generation until time is up. **Clarification and Evaluation** Unclear ideas are clarified, duplicates are eliminated, ideas are combined when appropriate. A discussion of ideas is conducted, lasting 45-60 minutes. Ideas are prioritized and categorized. A vote on ideas can be taken, or categories can be refined and studied and specific recommendations made. **Follow-up** Someone is designated to receive additional ideas that participants generate after the session. This person also reports on the group's best ideas to the problem owner if that person is not present at the session.	**No Criticism** No evaluation or criticism allowed during the idea-generating phase. The goal is to have a plethora of possibilities open for discussion, not to refine a single consensus solution. **Freewheeling** Freewheeling is encouraged: participants are encouraged to blurt out whatever wild or strange or seemingly mundane ideas that come to mind. Participants are told that what seems crazy or impractical at first may contain the seed of a great solution. **Quantity** The purpose of idea-generation is to generate lots of ideas, the more ideas generated, the more likely a creative solution to the topic. **Compare and Improve** The facilitator's role is to encourage participants to build on ideas (piggybacking or hitchhiking) and to look for ways to combine two or more ideas that have already been offered and recorded.

The value of brainstorming sessions include 1) generating useful and potentially profitable ideas; 2) finding solutions to difficult problems; and 3) generating a sense of participation and engagement. These sessions, however, sometimes have less than favorable results, due to limiting boundaries superficially imposed on the situation. One such factor, evaluation, is imposed by the presence of the "boss" during the brainstorming session, which introduces the perceived judgment of that person on ideas considered unusual[18].

Negative comments, or "killer phrases" during the idea generation phase of brainstorming act as idea stoppers (Clark, 1980, p. 18). Such phrases as "we've tried that before and it didn't work," "They won't buy that?," and "yeah, but . . ." permeate organizations and reduce the creative and innovative process.

Peer pressure can also inhibit innovative and off-the-wall ideas from emerging, the same peer pressure that kept us from giving answers in grade school for fear of being made fun of (i.e., teacher's pet.) While the rules of brainstorming call for non-judgmental acceptance of all ideas, the political climate in the room can emit silent judging.

Additionally, gender, racial and cultural differences affect the way we respond to brainstorming sessions. If I am the only woman in an all male group, I may feel inhibited from submitting my ideas, particularly if they are different from the dominant ideas being generated[19]. Likewise, if I am of a different ethnic group from the majority, I may feel uneasy with putting forth my ideas. For example, Western (Anglo, male) culture encourages men to speak out, while other cultures (e.g., Asian) do not.

One additional consideration with idea generation is the timeframe. Within brainstorming sessions, a restricted timeframe is used as a mechanism to force ideas. However, not everyone is a fast thinker, some people require time to think about a topic before discussing thoughts or generating ideas.

While the brainstorming process may generate a large number of possible solutions to a problem, the quantity does not guarantee that the group will adopt the best or most creative solution (Hoffman, 1965). Ideas are the raw material for the process of innovation, which starts with an idea and proceeds through stages of making that idea concrete, practical and profitable.

BRAINWRITING: AN ALTERNATIVE TO CLASSICAL BRAINSTORMING[20]

Purpose: Free inhibited participants; minimize intimidation during idea-generation phase.

Brainwriting Pool	Method 6-3-5
Participants write 4 ideas on sheet of paper or large note card. Participant places sheet in middle of table (the pool) in exchange for another participant's sheet. Reads ideas recorded on this sheet and adds any ideas of their own. Returns sheet to pool and draws another sheet when in need of further inspiration. Session lasts 30-45 minutes. Idea sheets are collected, recorded on some medium for all to see, and clarification/evaluation phase begins.	Same as brainwriting pool, with exception that 6 participants have 5 minutes to write 3 ideas on sheet of paper. At each 5 minute interval, sheets are passed to the person on your left, and participants add ideas to sheet. Process continues until all sheets get back to original owner (30 minutes). Ideas are recorded for all to see, and clarification/evaluation phase begins.
Pin-Cards	**Gallery Method**
Participants given a stack of colored cards and write one idea per card. As ideas are recorded, lay cards down next to the person on immediate right. When in need of stimulation and inspiration, participant draws cards that have been passed on, recording new ideas to blank cards. Process continues for 20 minutes. Cards are collected, sorted into categories and pinned to large board. Duplications are eliminated and clarification/evaluation phase begins.	Sheets of flip-chart paper are hung on walls of room. Each participant writes his ideas on one sheet. After 15 minutes, group takes a 15 minute break, during which participants walk around room, reading other ideas. After the break, participants return to their own sheet and add additional ideas. After the second round, a consolidation and evaluation phase begins.

14 WAYS TO FIRE UP YOUR CREATIVITY[21]

1. Think of yourself as a creative genius. We have been trained or told perhaps we are not creative by people who put creativity on a pedestal and think it is only for a select few.

2. Listen to your inner voice. The subconscious mind is often at work solving problems when the conscious mind is doing something else, like sleeping, or playing. Learn to pay attention to the subconscious mind. Keep a notepad or tape recorder by your bedside to capture your dreams.

3. Change your rhythm. Staying within your comfort zone does not promote fresh thinking. For example, if you are a linear thinker, try *drawing* your problem, this engages the right side of the brain, which promotes images, concepts and intuition. Turn your ideas into motion pictures in your mind.

4. Change your scene. A different environment may promote new ways of looking at old things. Take a walk in the park or at the beach. Take a weekend at the mountains.

5. Develop a process for creative problem-solving. Creativity requires a good amount of preparation and stimulation, as well as times of diversion and intellectual rest. First, gather as many ideas as possible, stimulate your mind by saturating it with ideas and information. Then, after you have gorged yourself for a while on this information feast, just relax and wait, while you do something different.

6. Sharpen your sense of problem assessment. Practice asking questions, and develop curiosity about how and why things go wrong. Listen to others, jot down ideas about how things can be improved. Keep an ideas notebook. Ask questions and develop sensitivity to problems festering below the surface. Don't always accept at face value the presenting problem. Broaden or narrow the problem in order to consider a wider range of possibilities. Get others' input into the problem.

7. Find the second (or third) "right" answer. We are conditioned to look at only one right answer. Once you've hit on the first right idea, ask yourself, "How can we find something better or different?"

8. Learn to play the violin or other musical instrument. This activity puts you into a different context and forces you outside your comfort zone.

9. Argue the other side. It is helpful to periodically scrutinize your beliefs, and look at the other side.

10. Believe that a solution is possible. Also believe that you will find it. Accept that it may take time, but that every step you take in the process will take you closer to it.

11. Try numerous brainstorming techniques, alone and with others.

12. Turn your ideas into actions. Put your ideas into practice, see what works and what doesn't.

13. Create an illustrated discovery journal. Gather images of how you would like to see the "problem solved." Meditate on these visual images; it can lead to revealing insights.

14. Engage in appreciative inquiry. Ask questions that uncover what works well and what you would wish to happen.

TEAM INNOVATION EFFECTIVENESS SURVEY[22]

Purpose. This survey is designed to take a snapshot of your team's current situation, as seen through the eyes of team members. The items on the survey gauge team members' feelings and perceptions about the teams' innovation process. Team Innovation is defined as the process used in by a team in order to generate new ideas and transform them into usable products, programs, or services

Directions: For each of the following items, circle the one number that best describes the extent to which you agree or disagree with the item. Work as fast as you can, and do not spend too much time on any one statement. Your first reaction is likely to be your most accurate.

Scale:

1	2	3	4
Strongly Disagree	Disagree	Agree	Strongly Agree

1. Team members seek solutions to problems.	1 2 3 4
2. Team members listen to one another when problem solving.	1 2 3 4
3. I feel my ideas and suggestions will be supported within my team.	1 2 3 4
4. My team uses creative problem-solving to solve unstructured problems.	1 2 3 4
5. My team is willing to implement solutions that we come up with.	1 2 3 4
Total Problem Solving score:	_____
6. New ideas are encouraged and openly discussed regularly.	1 2 3 4
7. My ideas are listened to by other team members.	1 2 3 4
8. Team members suspend judgment of ideas during brainstorming.	1 2 3 4
9. The team uses a process in which ideas are evaluated for their usefulness.	1 2 3 4
10. Within my team there is a clear distribution of responsibilities for moving from idea generation to turning those ideas into usable products.	1 2 3 4

Total Idea Management score:				
11. My team has an identified innovation process.	1	2	3	4
12. My team utilizes the skills of each individual in the innovation process.	1	2	3	4
13. I understand my role in the innovation process within this team.	1	2	3	4
14. The team accepts risk as a condition of growth and change.	1	2	3	4
15. The team has identified the individual strengths of team members in the innovation process.	1	2	3	4
Total Innovation Process Score:				

Interpretation: A range of 16-20 represents a perceived high level of efficiency in the dimension. A range of 11-15 represents a moderate level of efficiency in the dimension. A range of 5-10 represents a low level of efficiency in the dimension.

ENDNOTES

[1] This section draws from The Fifth Discipline by Peter M. Senge, copyright © 1990 by Peter M. Senge. Used by permission of Doubleday, a division of Random House, Inc.

[2] See Senge, P. M. (1990). *The Fifth Discipline: The Art & Practice of The Learning Organization.* New York: Currency Doubleday; and Senge, P.; Kleiner, A.; Roberts, C.; Ross, R.; Roth, G.; & Smith, B. (1999). *The Dance of Change: The Challenges of Sustaining Momentum in Learning Organizations.* New York: Currency Doubleday.

[3] See Amabile, T. (1983). *Social Psychology of Creativity.* New York: Springer-Verlag; and Amabile, T. M. (1996). *Creativity in Context: Update to the Social Psychology of Creativity.* Boulder, CO: Westview Press.

[4] This model draws from the work of Amabile, Woodman, Sawyer & Griffin, Van Gundy, Kirton, Fahden and Namakkal, as well as numerous others who have contributed to our understanding of individual, group, and organizational factors that impact creativity and innovation in organizational settings.

[5] e.g., Knowles, M. (1990). *The Adult Learner: A Neglected Species.* Houston, TX: Gulf Publishing Company; Senge, P. 1990). *The Fifth Discipline.* New York: Doubleday.

[6] Adapted from Knowles, M. (1990). *The Adult Learner: A Neglected Species.* Houston, TX: Gulf Publishing Company, p. 103; and Kanter, R. M. (1983). *The Change Masters: Innovation for Productivity in the American Corporation.* New York: Simon and Schuster.

[7] Adapted from Knowles, M. (1990). *The Adult Learner: A Neglected Species.* Houston, TX: Gulf Publishing Company, p. 103; and Kanter, R. M. (1983). *The Change Masters: Innovation for Productivity in the American Corporation.* New York: Simon and Schuster.

[8] See Morgan, G. (1993). *Imaginization: The Art of Creative Management.* Newbury Park, CA: Sage Publications; and Wheatley, M. & Kellner-Rogers, M. (1996). *A Simpler Way.* San Francisco: Berrett-Koehler.

[9] See Amabile, T. (1997). Motivating Creativity in Organizations. *California Management Review,* 40(1), 39-58; and Amabile, T. M., Conti, R., Coon, H., Lazenby, J., & Herron, M. (1996). Assessing the Work Environment for Creativity. *Academy of Management Journal,* 39(5), 1154-1184.

[10] See Albrecht (1987). *The Creative Corporation.* Homewood, ILL: Dow Jones-Irwin, p. 74; Amabile, T. (1997). Motivating Creativity in Organizations. *California Management Review,* 40(1), 39-58; and Amabile, T. M., Conti, R., Coon, H., Lazenby, J., & Herron, M. (1996). Assessing the Work Environment for Creativity. *Academy of Management Journal,* 39(5), 1154-1184; Van Gundy, A. (1984). *Managing Group Creativity.* New York: American Management Association, p. 106-114.

[11] see Osborn, A. (1963). *Applied Imagination,* 3rd ed. New York: Charles Scribner's Sons; Parnes, S. J. (1987). The Creative Studies Project. In S. G. Isaksen (Ed.) *Frontiers of Creativity Research: Beyond the Basics.* Buffalo, NY: Bearly Limited, pp. 156-188; Van Gundy, A. (1987). Organizational Creativity and Innovation. In S. G. Isaksen (Ed.) *Frontiers of Creativity Research: Beyond the Basics.* Buffalo, NY: Bearly Limited, pp. 358-370.

[12] Jackson, J. C. (1995). *Dimensions of Innovation: An Examination of the Factors of Personal Style and Idea Management in the Team Innovation Process.* Unpublished doctoral dissertation, Santa Barbara, CA: The Fielding Graduate Institute.

[13] For example, see Grossman, S. R., Rodgers, B. E., & Moore, B. R. (1988). *Innovation, Inc.* Plano, TX: Wordware Publishing, Inc.; Kirton, M. J. (1976). Adaptors and Innovators: A Description and Measure. *Journal of Applied Psychology.* 61, 622-629; Kirton, M. J. (1987). Adaptors and Innovators: Cognitive Style and Personality. In S. G. Isaksen (Ed.) *Frontiers of Creativity Research: Beyond the Basics.* Buffalo, NY: Bearly Limited, pp. 282-304; Van Gundy, A. (1984). *Managing Group Creativity.* New York: American Management Association; and Van Gundy, A. (1987). Organizational Creativity and Innovation. In S. G. Isaksen (Ed.) *Frontiers of Creativity Research: Beyond the Basics.* Buffalo, NY: Bearly Limited, pp. 358-370.

[14] I have changed this term from "Executor" to "Implementer" for asthetic purposes.

[15] Inscape Publishing, Inc. (2001). *Team Dimensions Profile®.* http://www.inscapepublishing.com; Inscape Publishing, Inc. (2001). *Innovate with C.A.R.E. Profile Facilitator's Kit.* http://www.inscapepublishing.com; and Fahden, A. (1993). *Innovation on Demand.* Minneapolis, MN: The Illiterati.

[16] Adapted from the work of Fahden and Namakkal with this author's inclusion of the Evaluating Component.

[17] Draws from Amabile, T. (1983). *Social Psychology of Creativity.* New York: Springer-Verlag; Amabile, T. M. (1996). *Creativity in Context: Update to the Social Psychology of Creativity.* Boulder, CO: Westview Press; Bleedorn, B. (1993). Toward an Integration of Creative and Critical Thinking. *American Behavioral Scientist*, 37(1), 10-19; Knowles, M. (1990). *The Adult Learner: A Neglected Species.* Houston, TX: Gulf Publishing Company; Morgan, G. (1993). *Imaginization: The Art of Creative Management.* Newbury Park, CA: Sage Publications; Roger, C. (1961). *On Becoming a Person.* Boston: Houghton Mifflin; Smith, N. I., & Ainsworth, M. (1989). *Managing for Innovation.* London: Mercury Books Division of W. H. Allen & Co. Plc.; and Sonnenberg, F. K. (1991, August). Cultivating Creativity. *Executive Excellence.* 8(8), 13-14.

[18] See Amabile, T. (1983). *Social Psychology of Creativity.* New York: Springer-Verlag; and Amabile, T. M. (1996). *Creativity in Context: Update to the Social Psychology of Creativity.* Boulder, CO: Westview Press.

[19] See Belenky, M. F.; Clinchy, B. M.; Goldberger, N. R.; & Tarule, J. M. (1986). *Women's Ways of Knowing.* New York: Basic Books; and Gilligan, C. (1982). *In A Different Voice.* Cambridge, MA: Harvard University Press.

[20] There are many alternatives to traditional brainstorming including: Braincalming, Osborn-Parnes Creative Problem Solving Program, Crawford Slip Method, Nominal Group Technique, Storyboarding, Synetics, Lions Den, Six Thinking Hats, and Mindmapping.

[21] Adapted from numerous sources including those listed in this chapter.

[22] Jackson, J. C. (1995). *Dimensions of Innovation: An Examination of the Factors of Personal Style and Idea Management in the Team Innovation Process.* Unpublished doctoral dissertation, Santa Barbara, CA: The Fielding Graduate Institute.

CHAPTER 6:
DYNAMICS OF ORGANIZATIONAL CHANGE

INVESTIGATION OF A CHANGE[1]

Purpose
This exercise is intended to help you improve your grasp, insight and understanding of the human processes by which changes are made in organizations. It will also help you see how a change in one department or area affects other areas.

Directions
Think of a specific change carried out in a particular organization you are familiar with. It is ideal if you have first hand experience of the change. Try to find a change that is recent enough to be fresh in your memory. The change need not be earth shattering or organization-wide. A change affecting a single group is sufficient for the purpose of this exercise.

Your task is (a) to think about the information you have on the change, especially the human processes by which it was made, i.e., who did what with and/or to whom, and when, in the course of the change; and (b) to analyze the information thoroughly. Pay particular attention to:

1. Causes and perceptions: What were the causes of the change? Who/what precipitated it? Who perceived what problem?
2. Problem-solving and decision making process: In what way was the change decided on and implemented? Who decided on it? Who was involved? How/Why?
3. What areas of the organization were affected by this change? In what ways were they affected? Were they part of the problem-solving and decision making process (see b)?
4. Outcome: Did the attempted change work? Was the change accepted, resisted or rejected by the people affected by it? How did they react/behave?

Prepare a careful, systematic description of the change, for verbal presentation to other people, in terms of causes, human processes and outcomes. You should try to explain why the change attained the level of success or failure it did.

Change is the metaphysics of our age.
Warren Bennis

Change is probably the most ubiquitous element of modern life. At every level - global, societal, organizational, and personal - we are witness to continuous and continual changes. We are faced with adapting to changes occurring around us, to evaluating the planned changes of which we become aware. Before we can become accustomed to changes already occurring, we are forced to respond to the exhortations of those who are advocating even more changes!

Organizations today are facing a wide range of social, economic, political, and technological changes. On the social side, there is a greater concern with the public image of the organization's behavior, for example, how an organization deals with toxic waste. While it has always been a problem, environmentalists are pressuring organizations to deal with their impact on society. Another social issue is the vast change in the workforce, more dual career families, with half of the working population being women. This calls for a need to change the way in which we organize our places of employment, including such considerations as flexible working hours and an increase in the professionalism of part-time, contract work, or other alternative work routines.

The worker of the 21st century is very different from one of even a decade ago. There is an increased demand for choice, having a voice in decisions concerning the goals and objectives of the organization, as well as how the job gets done. With an increase of "knowledge workers", there is an increase in the degree of autonomy in the method and form of work. Organizations have learned that they will not retain certain types of workers if they do not respond to the new demands. Creating balance between work, family, and leisure is a social change, as more workers are choosing to "downshift" and select alternative careers. Even with economic shifts, there is an increased concern with the quality of life.

Economic pressures on organizations are requiring change. Downsizing, mergers, reorganizations typically require different methods of operation, and affect people in a multitude of ways. Globalization is requiring us to rethink our boundaries.

Technology has moved us from a manufacturing/industrial era to the information age. This calls for a shift in the focus of workers, including retraining the workforce to new technology, as well as a shift in location, where one works. With such technologies as computing, fax machines, and telecommunications, workers no longer need to physically be located at a place of employment, and there is an increase of people who work from their homes. Technology has allowed entire work units to work from different physical locations; indeed the virtual office is one wave of the future that is with us now.

THE NATURE OF PLANNED CHANGE

> Starting a change journey without knowing where one is heading is
> called the Christopher Columbus School of Management because
> when he set out, he did not know where he was going, when he got
> there, he did not know where he was, and when he returned, he did
> not know where he had been. (Imai and Heymans, 1999)

Organization development (OD) efforts are directed at bringing about
planned change within an organization to increase the effectiveness of that
organization. Organizations can use organization development to more readily
solve problems, to learn from experience, to adapt to changes, and to influence
future changes. Kurt Lewin and others offer us a variety of lens through which
to view the phases of change that occur in people and organizations.

Organizational leaders are searching for more relevant and effective ways of
accomplishing their work with a sense of quality, mission and productive, long-
term results. At the same time individuals are seeking increased responsibility,
creative challenge, higher levels of performance and purpose in their work.
Today, more than ever before, leaders, managers and employees are questioning
how best to integrate their skills for enhancing the effectiveness of people,
organizations, communities and the world.

THE PROACTIVE CHALLENGE

The old reactive behavioral policies and programs that describe how people
and systems work are of less relevance today than ever before. These reactive
approaches harbor assumptions that stifle the potential for innovation and
creativity. As McGregor (1960) taught us many years ago, managers and
organizations base their actions on implicit or latent theories and assumptions.
As leaders, we must assess our personal views and assumptions that we make of
others, and examine those that lead to win-lose thinking and dead-end self-
fulfilling prophecies.

Whether conscious or not, many of these negative/reactive assumptions
guide our expectations and eventually our behavior, reinforcing the results that
we planted in our minds earlier in the cycle. This observation has many parallels
in organizational thinking and practice. In contrast, proactive assumptions
suggest more healthy and dynamic possibilities that are applicable at any level of
personal behavior or system effectiveness. Differences are listed in Table 6-1.

The signals are clear that the old world is dramatically different from today,
and a new paradigm is underway, in which new assumptions and creative
responses are demanded. A more comprehensive model is needed, one that
includes concern with the most unique dimensions of the individual and a vision
of system possibilities. The challenge today is for organizations to involve the
entire system in order to utilize the collective creative capabilities for constant
learning and innovation.

Table 6-1. Reactive versus Proactive Assumptions About Organizational Change

Reactive Assumptions	Proactive Assumptions
• Managers (or teachers) who think workers (or students) are ignorant or lazy, will act upon this assumption and get the results they expect (self-fulfilling prophecy).	• We must adopt a philosophy that views success, wellness and productive living as an integrated, and gradual process of improvement. Practical and effective outcomes will emerge from the efforts of building a solid foundation of continuous learning.
• There is no need to respond to issues until they become major problems or someone in charge becomes aware that something is wrong -- "if it ain't broke, don't fix it".	• We learn to anticipate and sense issues before they become problems, erupt into crisis, or overwhelm our abilities to respond effectively -- "attend to it constantly, even before it breaks down".
• All problems can be broken down into logically arranged, component pieces and solved independent of each other, as long as we use rational and logical problem-solving methods.	• All problems *can't* be reduced to logical pieces of a puzzle and solved independently of each other. Rational problem-solving methods should be complemented with creative, innovative, and systems thinking.
• We can blame our failures on others and events beyond our control. We can shift responsibility to "those we work for".	• We must take responsibility for our own destiny, anticipate and examine behaviors, values and trends that might negatively impact us or organizations in the future.
• Innovation is abrupt and drastic change to the normal mode of operations, requiring large investments in new technology, equipment, and time.	• We must stay ahead of change by managing it and not ignore signals which indicate that something is even slightly wrong, even when it appears to most people that everything is perfect.

Innovation is the generation, acceptance and implementation of new ideas, processes, products or services. People are innovators. People are the main ingredients to the success of a corporation. How the corporation utilizes its human resources is the key to innovation, organizational growth, organizational strength, and organizational success. Change, therefore, is a key component to an organization wishing to remain competitive and innovative.

UNDERSTANDING PLANNED CHANGE

We could adapt one of several strategies in dealing with change: 1) we can ignore or deny the reality of what is happening around us; 2) we can reactively adjust to changes after the impact has devastated our ability to adequately cope; or 3) we can proactively anticipate some of the negative impact and focus on using our knowledge of the positive dimensions of change to devise practical strategies.

Obviously the goal for strategic leaders is to move as quickly as possible from denial to the utilization of planned change as a business strategy. Timing is an important factor in change. We often satisfice, rather than optimize, because of the constraints of time, and the impossibility of deciding the best alternative. The key is to recognize that change, like learning, is continuous.

Change is meaningful because it is subjectively determined and felt. People perceive the impact of change in their own emotional way. This ability is limited by their fears, low self-esteem, lack of education, inability to distinguish good information from bad, and the failure to understand human nature. Thus, we need to increase our understanding of the human dimensions of change. We must learn about how individuals emotionally interpret proposed changes to determine whether they will embrace them or resist them. To do this, change agents (leaders, managers, consultants) must begin by becoming more empathetic towards individuals involved with change.

Among others, three things are needed for making organizational change more effective: empathy, clear communications, and involvement. It is crucial to learn more about employees and understand some of the barriers that will prevent a partnership in change between leaders and followers. Additionally, it is crucial to develop systems thinking, understanding the underlying cultural assumptions that keep individuals rooted in non-productive behavioral patterns.

Change is often difficult to categorize and measure because it defies any complex modeling of cause and effect, indeed it is often seen as both, and separating them isn't easy. Change effects are often not perceived immediately because the time lag between the initiation of change (cause) and perception of change (feeling or seeing) impacts the effects. When anticipating a new event or action and the expected effect is delayed, we are feeling the impact of this time lag.

Change is value-based, as it impacts and even expresses our most important priorities. It is difficult to quantify this value precisely because it depends upon our perception and other experiential skills, including maturity, job experiences, and even personality.

Clear communications in the change process is crucial to reducing the resistance to change. Individuals are limited by fear of change and other barriers. Change agents must manage and facilitate change to reduce those barriers.

Change is complex, and we must resist the temptation to simplify it. Taking into consideration that many individuals are not readily adaptable to major change, we must involve them in the change process, empower them to assist in the change, no matter how small. A change such as moving a worker's desk from one location to another without her consultation could be viewed as minor, and the temptation might be to treat it as such. This change affects the worker involved, however, and she might not see it as minor. She will undoubtedly have valuable input into the change process, and should be empowered to participate in the change.

INTERDEPENDENCIES OF ORGANIZATIONAL COMPONENTS

Organizations are a system of complex, interconnected components, and change in one element influences the others. As mentioned in Chapter 2, there are six organizational components that interact with and affect each other, as shown in Figure 2-3.

Change is holistic; change in one area affects and influences the others. While not all changes affect the entire system at the same level of intensity, effective OD work calls for awareness of the interactions. Organization development uses a systems approach to change and organizational transformation. Figure 6-1 shows how varying levels of interdependence among system components affect change.[2]

An example is rearranging an office. This takes a small effort; most change in an independent setting is relatively simple. However, most change today has some level of interdependence. For example, most offices are wired with cable, making the rearrangement more complex, and requiring participation of many people. Another example is asking an organizational member to do something in a new way, only to be met with what could be perceived as resistance. Without a systems perspective, you cannot see the interconnections between this employee and her supervisor, organizational structure, policies, performance appraisal systems, personal habits, cultures, and so on. What looks like resistance is the need to engage numerous components in the system to allow the employee to move in a new direction. Organizational change and transformation is much the same. Recognizing interdependencies between system components is critical to introducing change within an organization.

Figure 6-1. Creating Change in Systems of Varying Interdependence

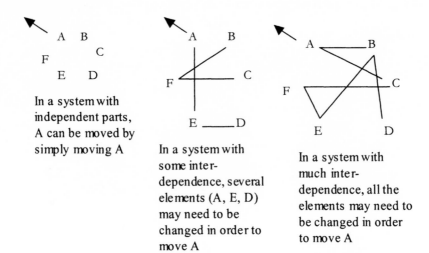

In a system with
independent parts,
A can be moved by
simply moving A

In a system with
some inter-
dependence, several
elements (A, E, D)
may need to be
changed in order to
move A

In a system with
much inter-
dependence, all the
elements may need to
be changed in order
to move A

ELIMINATION OF UNNECESSARY INTERDEPENDENCIES

In addition to recognition and inclusion of interdependencies in planning for change, we also need to look for unnecessary interdependencies, those in existence out of habit and no longer relevant. Often arrived at out of frustration, asking such questions as these are helpful:

Why does Department A need to send out a report to Department B? Does Department B need the information? What do they do with the information? Is there a better way to report this information? How often does Department B need and act on the information?

Why do divisions/departments have to check with corporate HR before making a job offer over $50,000? Does corporate HR need to be involved? If a legitimate reason exists, is $50,000 too low a cutoff point?

Through Action Research (described in the next chapter) organization development practitioners can uncover these unnecessary interdependencies and work towards refining or eliminating them.

MULTI-FRAME APPROACH TO CHANGE

Some managers try to produce major change by redesigning formal structures, only to find people unable or unwilling to carry out new responsibilities. Others import new people or retrain old ones, only to find new ideas get rejected. Managers who anticipate that new roles require new skills and vice-versa have a greater likelihood of success. However, change also alters power relationships and undermines existing agreements and pacts. It intrudes upon deeply rooted cultural norms and ritual behavior. Bolman and Deal (1999) suggest four frames that are essential to understanding organizational change. Each frame highlights a different set of barriers and strategies for change processes.

Table 6-2. Reframing Organizational Change

Frame	Barriers to Change	Essential Strategies
Human Resource—focus on needs and skills	Anxiety, uncertainty. People feel incompetent and needy.	Training to develop new skills. Participation and involvement. Psychological support.
Structural—focus on alignment and clarity	Loss of clarity and stability. Confusion, chaos.	Communicating, realigning, and renegotiating formal patterns and policies.
Political—focus on conflict	Disempowerment. Conflict between winners and losers.	Create arenas where issues can be renegotiated and new coalitions formed.
Symbolic—focus on meaning and purpose	Loss of meaning and purpose. Clinging to the past.	Create transition rituals: mourn the past, celebrate the future.

Human Resource Frame. From a human resource perspective, people have good reason to resist change—feelings of anxiety and incompetence caused by changes that undermine existing knowledge and skill, undercutting ability to perform with confidence and success. This creates resistance or even sabotage of the change, or compliance in public while covertly not supporting the change. Training can enhance individual skills and increase confidence.

Structural Frame. Training doesn't do much good if the structure isn't in alignment with the new initiative. Structure provides clarity, predictability, and security. Formal roles prescribe how work is to be performed. Policies and operating procedures synchronize diverse efforts into well-coordinated programs. Formal distribution of authority clarifies who is in charge, when, and over what. Change efforts must anticipate structural issues and work to realign roles and responsibilities. This can be done informally, or in a more formal restructuring.

Political Frame. From a political perspective, conflict in change situations is natural, and when well-managed, an essential source of energy, creativity, and clarity. The key is creating processes of negotiation and bargaining where settlements and agreements can be hammered out. Successful change requires the ability to frame issues, build coalitions, and establish an environment in which disagreements can be forged into workable pacts.

Symbolic Frame. Symbols create and carry meaning. When a symbol is destroyed or vanishes, people experience emotions of loss. For example, we harbor a sense of loss when a computer replaces old procedures, or a leader is replaced with a new one. This sense of loss typically triggers two conflicting responses: keep things as they were, replay the past, or ignore the loss and rush busily into the future. Individuals can get stuck in either response or vacillate between the two. Loss is an unavoidable by-product of change; as change accelerates, people get caught up in endless cycles of unresolved grief.

From the symbolic perspective, ritual is the essential companion to significant change. Transition rituals initiate a sequence of steps that helps people let go of the past, deal with the pain of the present, and move into a meaningful future. (See discussion of the phases of transition in Chapter 4.)

TWO STRATEGIES: PARTICIPATIVE AND DIRECTIVE CHANGE

Hersey and Blanchard describe participative change as being implemented when new knowledge is made available to the individual or group. It is hoped that the group will accept the data and will develop a positive attitude and commitment in the direction of the desired change. Directed change, on the other hand, is when the change cycle begins by change being imposed on the organization and organizational members by some external force, such as higher management, the community, or new laws. Table 6-3 examines the two.[3]

Participative change is best used when the organization is an open environment, people are willing to examine problems and seek solutions and take responsibility for implementing changes into the organization, and organizational leadership is supportive of this kind of atmosphere.

Table 6-3. Participative versus Directive Change

Participative Change	Directive Change
New knowledge is made available. Desired that the group will accept the data and develop a positive attitude and commitment to the change.	Change is imposed from an external force, such as executive management or new law.
Driven by informal leadership (personal power).	Driven by formal leadership (position power).
Appropriate when motivation level is high, when people seek responsibility, want to achieve, have a degree of knowledge and experience that may	Appropriate when motivation level is low, low ambition, people are dependent, not seeking responsibility, prefer direction (low readiness level).

add to implementing the change (high readiness level).	
Once change is accepted it tends to be long lasting.	Tends to last only as long as the leader remains in position of power.
High level of commitment to implementation.	Low level of commitment -- often results in animosity, hostility, and behavior to undermine and overthrow the decision.
Slower implementation process (could take years).	Quicker implementation process (can be immediate).
Effective strategy to use if restraining forces outweigh the driving forces.	Effectively used if driving forces far outweigh restraining forces.

Directive change is appropriate when the workforce is low in competence (referring to ability to do the job; job task or specific and/or knowledge and skill level, including information, education, experience, transferable skills and knowledge), and there is a low level of commitment (referring to motivation and desire to do the job, interest, excitement, or enthusiasm they have to get ahead or to do a good job, as well as self-confidence that they can perform the task well). Directive change is also appropriate in emergency situations.

ORGANIZATIONAL DESIGN AND THE IMPACT ON ORGANIZATIONAL CHANGE

Organizational structural factors affect change both positively and negatively, and heavily impact the success of an organizational effectiveness initiative. One such factor is organizational design. A hierarchical structure, such as that found in traditional large bureaucratic organizations, places people in small, specialized compartments and forms a hierarchy of functions and responsibilities. This structure inhibits effective change and innovation as it

- does not allow for open communications among the layers of hierarchy ($\uparrow\downarrow$)
- does not allow for open communications between the components ($\leftrightarrow$)

In order for organizations to be successful, they must have flexible structures that enable them to be highly responsive to customer requirements and adaptive to changes in the competitive environment. These new organizations must be leaner, have fewer layers, and be able to engage in transnational and nontraditional alliances and mergers (Bennis, 1993.) A web-like organizational design, depicted in Figure 6-2, embraces a more fluid structure and design, with sharing of information, allowing for information to flow freely among all the components.

Figure 6-2. Web-like Organizational Design

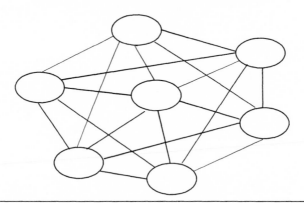

Within this type of organizational structure, leadership is dispersed according to knowledge and skills, allowing flexibility and the ability to respond quickly, and allocate resources as needed. It is a particularly useful model for facilitating organizational change.[4]

Significant change requires the *engagement* of all people affected by the change. As mentioned earlier in this chapter, and throughout the book, when "change is done to" people, there is a higher risk of resistance. When people affected by the change are part of the decision-making and planning process, there is less likelihood of resistance. Additionally, the "end users" of the change initiative probably have excellent ideas for how to plan for success, as they are oftentimes closest to the problem. The "end users", in turn, are able to act as internal change agents with others in the organization.

One way to achieve this engagement is through consensus decision-making. This process allows all parties involved to feel their voice has been heard, culminating in a decision that all can *live with*. While consensus is not a panacea of techniques to overcome resistance to change, it is a process that moves towards a more successful implementation.

Open systems design is an important factor in enabling and enhancing large-scale change efforts within organizational settings. Open system organizations are by nature open to internal and external influences, i.e., organizational members, external customers, and the community. The open systems design facilitates a participative environment in which a hierarchy does not bound communications. The atmosphere is one in which organizational members are encouraged to experiment, learn from errors, utilize all resources, tolerate ambiguity. The structure is more like a cluster of temporary tasks forces, functional linkages, and broad role definitions. The open system is open to and encourages change.

ORGANIZATIONAL CULTURE AND THE IMPACT ON ORGANIZATIONAL CHANGE

Organizational culture refers to norms of behavior and shared values among organizational members. Norms of behavior are common or pervasive ways of acting that are found in a group, that persist because group members tend to behave in ways that teach these practices to new members. Shared values are important concerns and goals shared by most of the people in a group that tend to shape group behavior and often persist over time when group membership changes. In large organizations, you will find corporate culture affects everyone, while certain behaviors and values are specific to subunits.

Culture has a powerful influence on behavior, even though it is nearly invisible, making it difficult to address directly. Shared values, less apparent and more deeply ingrained in culture, are more difficult to change than norms of behavior.

Artifacts exist that are manifestations of shared values and underlying assumptions. Things such as the organizations architecture, office layout, dress code, and status symbols portray a picture of the underlying values. It is important to identify which values support the organizational change effort, and those that will hinder the organization from reaching organizational goals[5].

In transformation, any planned changes that are not anchored firmly in the organizational culture, is likely to fail. Organizational members will likely regress to existing norms of group behavior and shared values. In some transformations, the core of the old culture is compatible with the new visions, but behaviors need to change. It is important to recognize what will be kept and what needs to change. Some ways to support changing the culture include[6]:

- Seek out and publicize performance improvements that are linked to new practices.
- Engage in dialogue about the history of the organization and its culture, how this culture had served the firm well, but why it is no longer helpful.
- Offer those who are not willing to make the transformation to the new culture other opportunities, i.e., early retirement.
- Work hard to convince anyone who has embraced the new culture to stay.
- Hire selectively according to new norms and values. Use new employee orientations to compellingly show recruits what the organization really cares about.
- Promote those who demonstrate results through the new practices; move them into influential and visible positions.
- Tell vivid stories over and over about the new organization, what it does, and why it succeeds.
- Make absolutely sure you have the continuity of behavior and results that help a new culture grow.

Culture change comes with time. It is not something easily manipulated, because it is deeply ingrained and nearly invisible. Culture changes only after you have successfully altered people's actions, after the new behavior produces some group benefit for a period of time, and after people see the connection between the new actions and the performance improvement.[7]

IMPLICATIONS FOR FACILITATING ORGANIZATIONAL CHANGE

We have learned through experience that our approach to organizational life in uncertain times requires more than one narrow approach. It is necessary to assume a systems perspective for integrating ideas regarding quality of work life, technology, structure, leadership, and ways of motivating and rewarding people. We must continually seek ways to tap into the creative and innovative nature of people, and find new opportunities for developing organizational members.

More importantly, our organizations need effective, proactive programs for employee health promotion, such as work-family balance, and human resource development, such as creative problem solving, effective communications strategies, risk taking, and empowerment through collaboration. In addition, organizations must develop improved awareness of the critical forces that operate to limit their true potential: old metaphors, models, frozen attitudes, and incompetent systems. This is challenging because individuals will go to great lengths to protect their beliefs, even when faced with data that shows a problem.

One critical factor of change efforts is the focus: Is it on an individual? Team? Department? Organization? Change at each of these levels requires different interventions, yet they have two things in common. First, the individual, team or department is one unit of a *system*. There is interdependency, a change affects the entire system. And secondly, each consists of *people*.

A common complaint among training and development specialists is that organizations send individuals to training sessions but provide no follow-up support for that individual. The problem occurs when the *changed* individual or team enters the *unchanged* organization. The individual or team, receiving little or no reinforcement of their developmental experience, quickly becomes frustrated with the realization that they cannot create *real* and *sustaining* change, either within their own behavior or that of the team or organization. Individual change efforts such as executive development programs may be good at creating individual renewal and the mindset required to help lead change efforts, but an individual, exclusive of the system, cannot sustain organizational change.

Another critical aspect for leadership consideration is the tendency to rebuild the organization and "start anew." Bennis warns us that failing to appreciate the importance of the organization of the people who are already in it is a classic managerial mistake. Change agents often fall prone to a disregard of the existing organization (history), and in doing so, create chaos, disrupt continuity, and alienate key resources (Bennis, 1993).

At the onset of a planned change effort, the minimum one should take into consideration is:

- Clarity about the goals and objectives of the change; what the future state looks like.
- The likely impact of the change on the organizational unit as well as the entire system.
- An assessment of whom in the organizational unit will be affected by the change, how, and to what degree.
- Prediction of the reactions of individuals who will be affected by or called on to implement the change.

Some helpful tips are listed here as a beginning to the discussion of facilitating a large-scale change effort.

- Use people-centered behaviors, be supportive, and help those affected by the change.
- Provide the rationale for change. Provide an opportunity for discussion of the implications and consequences. Provide visions of opportunity.
- Explain the problem thoroughly. Build acceptance of the change into the process. Listen carefully before making any decisions. Gain input from all parties involved in the change.
- Pilot test the intervention prior to going full scale. This provides you with an opportunity to work out any details or flaws, and test to see if you are going to achieve the desired effect.
- Involve organizational members in the decision making and change effort. Remember that those who are closest to the problem probably have the best ideas for fixing it.
- Continuously monitor and evaluate the change initiative.

Now that we have discussed the dynamics of planned organizational change, we turn our attention to "tools" available for facilitating the change process. But first, read the "case study" offered on the next page. What is the key lesson?

What Happened To That TQM Binder?

You've been asked to meet with a client that has implemented a Total Quality Management (TQM) system but found it "not working". The organization creates and produces marketing gizmos, like the kind you find inside cereal boxes. It's a small company of approximately 50 people, all located at one site. Your contact is the Human Resource Manager, Steve. Steve was recently promoted to HR from his previous office manager position. He has no HR training, but has attended a few seminars.

Upon initial discussions, you discover that the organization had gone through a week of training, and everyone had been equipped with large binders with slick multi-colored pages describing the many processes involved in TQM. During the course of meeting people, you find the TQM binders sitting on their bookshelves. You learn that organizational members have quickly returned to their old way of doing things. You also discover there had been no follow-up to the training. The consultant who provided the training is no longer involved with the client.

You ask Steve why the training was conducted and he informs you that the president of the company, Jerry, had met a consultant at a party who told him about the program. Jerry talked to his VPs about it and they agreed to have the consultant come in to discuss the program. The consultant, being a good salesperson, convinced them that they had a need for the program.

When you ask Steve how they had planned for the TQM process to be implemented, he responds, "We set dates for the employees to go through a day of training, with everyone completing training within one week. The week proceeded well, no glitches, everyone showed up for training as scheduled."

Initially, the executives were optimistic about the program and its ability to meet their needs to address problems. During the week after the training, everyone was talking about how interesting it was, what a good trainer the consultant was, how much information they now had in their binders. These kinds of discussions began to wane, however, when everyday issues had to be dealt with; and within a very short period of time, no one mentioned the training and the binders became dust collectors.

Steve said that management felt it was the "worker's inability to get with the new program" that was the current problem. They felt that the training was sufficient. After all, they had paid big bucks for that expertise!

In talking to both the managers and the employees, you learn that during the training, they were introduced to such tools as a basic problem-solving process. However, people weren't using it because they felt it was too time-consuming. Yet they disclose that there is need for a consistent method of addressing problems.

Many dollars had been spent on this TQM program, and it was highly unsuccessful. The consultant came in and shared his expertise with organizational members. At the end of the week, he left the company feeling quite satisfied that he had successfully completed this project. And now you have been called in to help them solve the problem. You are an organization development consultant. You can help this organization.

1. How can OD help this organization?
2. What did the organizational executives do right? Wrong?
3. What did the consultant do right? Wrong?
4. What would you do now?
5. Is more training the answer?

ENDNOTES:

[1] Adapted from Roy McLennan. (1989). *Managing Organizational Change, 1ˢᵗ ed.* . Englewood Cliffs, NJ: Prentice-Hall, p. 103. Reprinted by permission of Pearson Education, In., Upper Saddle River, NJ.

[2] Adapted from Kotter, J. P. (1996). *Leading Change.* Boston, MA: Harvard Business School Press, p. 155; and Kotter, J. P. (2002). *The Heart of Change.* Harvard Business School Press, p. 137.

[3] Adapted from Paul Hersey and Kenneth Blanchard. (1993). *Management of Organizational Behavior.* 6th ed. Englewood Cliffs, NJ: Prentice Hall, pp. 374-375

[4] See Helgesen, S. (1993). *The Web of Inclusion.* New York: Doubleday. Helgesen does not specify an organizational design; this is my interpretation. Frances Hesselbein also describes her organization chart as a series of concentric circles. See Hesselbein, F. (2002). *Hesselbein on Leadership.* San Francisco, CA: Jossey-Bass.

[5] See Edgar H. Schein. (1992). *Organizational Culture and Leadership,* 2nd ed. San Francisco, CA: Jossey-Bass Publishers.

[6] See Kotter, J. P. (1996). *Leading Change.* Boston, MA: Harvard Business School Press, p. 155; Kotter, J. P. (2002). *The Heart of Change.* Harvard Business School Press, p. 177.

[7] See Kotter, J. P. (1996). *Leading Change.* Boston, MA: Harvard Business School Press, p. 155; Kotter, J. P. 2002. *The Heart of Change.* Harvard Business School Press, p. 156.

CHAPTER 7:

APPROACHES TO ORGANIZATIONAL CHANGE

FORCE-FIELD ANALYSIS: PART I

Objectives:
1.   To improve your analytical skills for addressing complex situations
2.   To assist you in understanding how force-field analysis can be used in facilitating change

Directions:
1.   Think about a situation that you are currently struggling with, perhaps a decision you are in the process of contemplating. This situation can be personal or work-related. The main criteria are that (1) there is a problem or opportunity that indicate a need for change, and (2) there are pros and cons related to any decision you make.
2.   Respond to the following questions by writing answers below:
   a.   Describe the situation as it now exists (*current state*).
   b.   Describe how you would like to see the situation, how you would like it to be (*desired state*).
   c.   Identify factors that are presently helping to move things in the desired direction (*driving forces*).
   d.   Identify factors that are presently keeping the situation in its current state, things that are holding back moving toward the desired direction (*restraining forces*).
3.   Try to be as specific as possible in relation to your situation. You should attempt to be *exhaustive* in your listing of both restraining and driving forces. List as many as you can think of.

a. Current State: _____
_____
_____

b. Desired State: _____
_____
_____

c. Factors pushing towards the change (Things that support the change)

"Driving Forces"

_____
_____
_____
_____
_____
_____

d. Factors pushing away from the change (Things that support the status quo)

"Restraining Forces"

_____
_____
_____
_____
_____
_____

Since the beginning, the field of organization development has offered practitioners a variety of approaches to organizational change. Two, *Action Research* and *Survey Research and Feedback*, became the foundational methodologies for the practice of organization development.

A key contributor was Kurt Lewin, a social psychologist whose field theory and conceptualization about group dynamics, change processes, and action research profoundly influenced the field of organization development. Lewin and his colleagues applied action research to such areas as improving intergroup relations, community relations projects, leadership training, the study of resistance of change. Lewin (1951) promoted the concept of "no action without research, and no research without action."

In this chapter, we explore basic "tools" available to change agents. Approaches frequently useful to organization development practitioners include action research and force-field analysis, as well as data collecting methodologies. Traditional approaches to change include basic problem solving models. Contemporary approaches to facilitating organizational change involve getting the whole system engaged in the process. Two methodologies that do this, Preferred Futuring and Appreciative Inquiry, are presented as alternatives to traditional problem solving.[1]

ACTION RESEARCH

The most fundamental approach to organization development and change is action research, which focuses on planned change as a cyclical process, as shown in Figure 7-1. It involves collaboration between organizational members and organizational development practitioners. Action research is a systematic method of data collection and feedback, action, and evaluation based on further data collection. It is a method that combines *learning* and *doing*—learning about the dynamics of organizational change (research), and doing or implementing change efforts (action).

Even though action research is not unique to OD, French and Bell (1999) define it as a cornerstone of organization development, a

> process of systematically collecting research data about an on-going system relative to some objective, goal, or need of that system; feeding these data back into the system; taking actions by altering selected variables within the system based both on the data and on hypotheses; and evaluating the results of actions by collecting more data.

Figure 7-1. Action Research Model for Organization Development

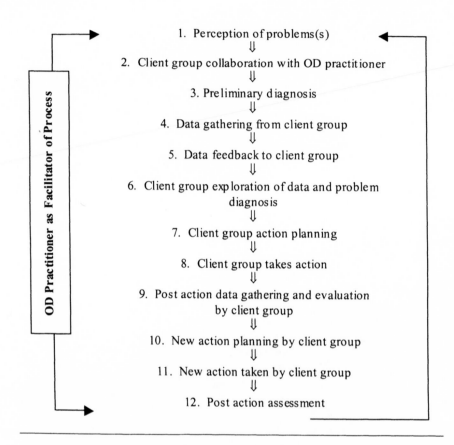

The action research process begins with *problem perception*, when someone realizes that the organization has one or more problems and persuades others in the organization that a change is required and the services of an organization development practitioner or other change agent is necessary.

A *preliminary diagnosis* is made of the problem. To support this and provide further explanation, data is collected within the client organization by the OD practitioner, in collaboration with the client group. All relevant data are shared with the client during the *feedback phase*. The client group, in turn, explores the data, developing possible courses of action, selects and plans the action to be taken. The change initiative (*action*) is implemented. After the action has taken place, there is another data gathering phase, a *rediagnosis* of the situation, after which *further action* is planned and taken. Once again, there is *post action assessment.* This process repeats itself until the problem is resolved. Throughout the process, the OD practitioner acts as facilitator of the process.

Basic characteristics of action research include (Bryant, 1979):

- It is a *group* process that involves the *participation* of all parties (or at least their representatives) as members of an action research team.

- It is based on a *collaborative relationship* between the interested parties in the organization and independent resource people who do not function as conventional "experts" but rather contribute advice on methods of scientific experimentation and group processes, such as OD practitioners.

- It requires a *consensus* amongst the interested parties before attempting the implementation of any experimental changes.

- It requires the *involvement of the participants in monitoring and evaluating* the effects of any change, with the provision that the situation can be returned to its original state, if the change produces undesired results.

- It assumes that *organizational life is a shared experience* in which people are interdependent for their survival and success and that the commitment of action research resource people is to the organization as a whole and not to any sectional interest group (i.e., management, supervision, union, or workforce.)

- It assumes that, at the individual level, *most people can change* and, under the right conditions, will change, if they want to.

Action research focuses on continuous diagnosis and feedback, which enables organizational members to be alert to and assume a proactive position regarding potential problems and opportunities. Action research also allows organizational members to take an active role in the change initiative as it occurs, with feedback occurring throughout the process. Action research yields both change and new knowledge: change occurs from actions taken, and new knowledge occurs from examining the results of the actions. Each step is an intervention. The client organization learns how to diagnose problems, discover what works, what does not work, and why.

Action research is aimed at both increasing an organization's effectiveness and developing new knowledge that can be applied to other settings. It is a useful tool for examining the organization's need and readiness for change, and provides a basic framework for introducing change into organizational settings.

DATA COLLECTION

As stated earlier, the organization development process begins with a felt need for action and change, a "problem" or "opportunity." No matter what the perception is, the energy to fix the problem drives resources committed to change. The initial role of the OD practitioner is to assist organizational leaders with appropriate analysis of the perceived problem. To establish a collaborative effort (and ensure support of eventual change processes), those potentially affected by the intended change need to be included.

The OD practitioner uses many methodologies for investigating the problem, including administering survey questionnaires; conducting interviews; employing observational techniques; using company data such as absenteeism, turnover, production levels; asking organizational members to generate on-the-spot data. From these data, much can be gleaned about elements governing organizational life:

- Behavior (individual, subsystem, and system)
- Interpersonal and intergroup relations
- Patterns and frequency of contact between individuals and groups
- Role behavior and interdependence (ways in which individuals and groups define their roles)
- Structure and process of problem solving and decision making
- Organizational structure
- Ways in which planned changes are (or not) executed
- Attitudes and perceptions

Three basic methods of collecting data are survey feedback, interviews, and focus groups.

SURVEY FEEDBACK

Survey feedback began at the Survey Research Center at the University of Michigan. Rensis Likert's dissertation, *A Technique for the Measurement of Attitudes*, became a classic study that developed the widely used five-point Likert scale. He and his colleagues perfected the survey process that became known as survey feedback.

Surveys have become widely used in organizations as a means of collecting data on a variety of issues. Survey feedback is a systematic method of collecting data from an organization, feeding these data back to groups within the organization, and asking these groups to use the information as a basis for planning and taking corrective action. The survey feedback method is itself a change intervention, as group members learn and process such organizational factors as the sample of measures listed below:

- Organizational climate: Communication flow; emphasis on human resources; decision-making practices; influence and control; coordination; job challenge; job reward; emphasis on cooperation.
- Supervisor/Management/Leadership: managerial support; goal emphasis; work facilitation; team building; collaboration.
- Peer relationships: peer support; peer team building.
- End results: group functioning; worker and customer satisfaction; goal integration.

Several steps are involved in survey feedback:

1. Initial planning involves top-level management and key individuals representing the various constituencies involved in the survey feedback process.

2. A questionnaire (standard or customized) is administered to all (or relevant) organizational members.

3. An analysis of the data and results with tabulations at the group and organizational level.

4. Feedback of data and results to key executive team and functional teams, usually beginning with the top management team and flowing down to successive levels of the organization. The feedback mechanism includes: each manager receiving results from his/or work team; sharing these results with the whole work team; everyone sees the results for the organization as a whole.

5. Team leaders/managers meet with team members to interpret data as it relates to team and plan steps for action.

The purpose of survey feedback includes: developing an understanding of the organizational problems; improving working relationships; and identifying forces for and against change, or determine areas where more research is needed. Advantages of this method of data collection include: it is based on data; it directly involves organizational members; it provides information about what to change and in which priority, as well as driving and restraining forces; it focuses change toward the larger system, not individuals.

NOTE: One must take extreme care and caution in the development of a survey questionnaire in the attempt to get valuable data. Many people avoid completing a survey truthfully for any number of reasons, such as not wanting to admit their imperfections or errors, fear of retribution, or the 'halo effect', where we respond to a survey based on our most immediate experiences.

A limitation of survey feedback is that it uncovers surface data only; it doesn't diagnose the underlying drivers of behavior. For example, surveys could show that people are frustrated, as well as the surface causes of the frustration. They won't show, however, the systems perspective, all the interconnected pieces that create and maintain the system that causes and perpetuates the frustration.

However, given these limitations, survey feedback is an economical and quick method of gathering data, and when used with other data gathering methods, such as interview and/or focus groups, provides useful information. Survey feedback used within the framework of action research will uncover the connected-ness of data.

INTERVIEWS

Another way to gather data about an organization is through the technique of interviewing. The purpose of an interview is to explore ways in which the organization can be more effective. The interviewing process typically uncovers both positive and negative opinions and sentiments about a wide range of topics.

Advantages of the interview method of data collection include it's flexibility over the survey method, and the fact that it provides two-way communication, thereby permitting the interviewer to learn more about the problems, challenges, and limitations of the organization than responses to a survey questionnaire would uncover. Questions posed by the interviewer should help the interviewee express whatever is on his or her mind about the organization.

As with data collection through surveys, information from interviews is fed back into the system through the action research process. For both methods, anonymity is important to gain "good" data. It needs to be established upfront how the information will be used, for what purpose, and how the privacy of the interviewee will be maintained.

Information from interviews can be presented verbatim or thematically. Presenting the data verbatim runs the risk of an unorganized, confusing data dump. It also does not protect the privacy of interviewees. Themes emerge from data, and allow the data to be presented in an organized fashion, easily summarized, and hence easier to grasp.

As with survey questionnaires, there are certain "risks" attached to interviews. A good interview often takes one or two hours, and can therefore consume a lot of time. Interviews can often turn up more information of a personal nature, which may be rejected by the client group or seen as extraneous to the project at hand. If the information is highly critical of a manager or highly valued group member, the data may become threatening and thereby rejected. The messenger (interviewer) may also be attacked, as in, "don't shoot the messenger."

Even with these potential risks, however, interviews add a richness to data collected via survey questionnaires.

FOCUS GROUPS

A third way of data collection is through the use of focus groups. Focus groups are unstructured, free-flowing discussions with a small group of people. Not a rigid, highly constructed session, its flexible format encourages open discussion of issues.

The focus group allows for *depth* of data to emerge. Focus group discussions provide an opportunity to probe respondent feelings and beliefs in a way not possible through less personal, written survey methods and can be used to assess reactions or solicit information about behavioral or productivity changes.

Primary advantages of focus groups are that they are relatively brief, easy to conduct, quickly analyzed, and inexpensive. There is a synergism that results from the combined effort of the group that produces a wider range of information. There are disadvantages, including the fact that the small group does not necessarily represent the whole organization or system, and therefore cannot take the place of quantitative research. Focus groups also need a trained facilitator who will not allow a single voice to dominate the discussion. Combined with survey questionnaires and interviews, the focus group method provides a depth of data in the data collection phase.

Data alone, are not enough. We need a way of analyzing the data in terms of the intended change. One way is through force field analysis.

FORCE FIELD ANALYSIS

A basic "tool" for interpreting data is force-field analysis. In planning for change, it is advantageous to identify those conditions that will help or hinder the change initiative. Force-field analysis, developed by Kurt Lewin, is one of the most beneficial frameworks for analyzing data, both factual and emotional[2].

Lewin suggested that in the development of change strategies, one should view the present situation, or *status quo*, as being maintained by certain conditions or forces. *Driving forces* are those that push for change, while *restraining forces* are those that are obstacles to changing the situation. In any given situation, and at any given time, forces are in operation to maintain a balance or equilibrium. For example, a sales team's productivity remains fairly stable (status quo) because the forces pushing towards higher sales productivity equal forces pushing towards lower sales productivity, as depicted by equal arrows in Figure 7-2. Thus, a particular phase of organizational life is viewed as quasi-stationary, maintained by dynamic balance of opposing forces.

Figure 7-2. Restraining and Driving Forces Create Quasi-Stationary Equilibrium

↓ ↓ ↓   **Restraining Forces towards Lower Productivity** ↓ ↓ ↓
(maintain status quo)

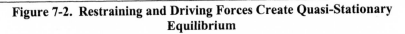

↑ ↑ ↑   **Driving Forces towards Higher Productivity**   ↑ ↑ ↑
(strive for change)

Through force field analysis, not only are driving and restraining forces identified, but also weighting is given to each force. This places value of each force in terms of its ability to impact the change. For example, while the cost to provide sales training (restraint) may be given a weight of "5", the loss of business to competition (driver) may be weighted as a "10", thereby placing heavier importance on the driving factor than the hindering. Increasing or decreasing either of the forces or a combination of both, will allow change to occur, as depicted by unequal arrows in Figure 7-3.

Figure 7-3. Driving Forces Create Change

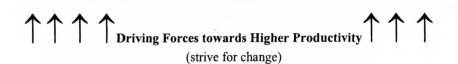

↓ ↓   **Restraining Forces towards Lower Productivity** ↓   ↓
(maintain status quo)

↑ ↑ ↑ ↑**Driving Forces towards Higher Productivity** ↑ ↑ ↑
(strive for change)

Force-field analysis is used to enhance understanding of the complexities of a situation through a series of steps.

Step 1. Decide upon the problem situation and completely describe the current state. What is the status quo? What is the current state? Why do you want it changed?

Step 2. Carefully and complete describe the desired state. Where do you want to be? What is the desired state?

Step 3. Identify the forces and factors operating in the current force field. Identify the driving forces pushing in the direction of the desired state. Identify restraining forces pushing away from the desired state. It is critical that this step provide a thorough and exhaustive picture of why things are as they are.

Step 4. Examine the forces. Which ones are strong, which are weak? Which forces are susceptible to influence, which are not? Which forces are under your control, which are not? (Important individual forces could themselves be analyzed through force-field analysis in order to better understand them.) Assign a weight to each force.

Step 5. Employ strategies for moving the equilibrium from the current state to the desired state. This includes selecting important adaptable restraining forces and developing action plans to remove them from the field of forces, or move them to the driving forces. As restraining forces are removed, the equilibrium shifts toward the desired state. New driving forces may be proposed and action plans developed to implement them.

Step 6. Implement the action plans developed in the previous step. This should cause the desired state to be realized.

Step 7. Describe what actions must be taken to *stabilize the equilibrium* in the desired state and implement these actions (see Change Process Model described in Chapter 4).

STRATEGIES FOR REDUCING RESTRAINING FORCES[3]

1. Education and communication: Communicate information concerning the *what* and *why* involved in the change program to all organization members. Show *advantages* and *rewards* of the change.
2. Create and communicate a *vision* of the future state: Show how the change will incorporate pieces of the present state and take the organization into the future.
3. *Participation* of members in the change initiative: Involve organizational members in the planning for and implementation of change.
4. Acknowledge *endings*: Recognize that the organization will go through a period of "mourning" the way things were.
5. Facilitation and *support*: Support and reward those who are embracing the change.
6. Create a climate conducive to communications: Allow organizational members to feel free to express their concerns; develop a climate of trust.
7. *Negotiation* and agreement: Negotiate with potential resisters i.e., increase an employee's pension benefits in exchange for early retirement, or transfer employees to other divisions rather than laying them off.
8. Leadership: All leaders *model the way*. Build "grass-roots" leadership to support the change.
9. Reward systems: *reward* organizational members for embracing the change i.e., profit-sharing, or knowledge-based pay.
10. Explicit and implicit *coercion*: While threats are not a positive and desired alternative, some people may not be willing to make the change. These individuals need to understand their alternatives, i.e., losing their jobs or being transferred to other areas of the organization.

Force-field analysis is excellent for diagnosing change situations. It allows the identification of factors that affect or are impacted by the situation, assess the value of each factor, and identifies strategies for reducing restraining forces while maximizing driving forces. It is particularly powerful when used as a team intervention; group analysis typically yield a more comprehensive understanding of what is happening and what must be done to correct it.

In order to facilitate a systems approach to planned change, use force field analysis with individual groups analyzing a particular problem, and then, as a whole group, review the results, looking for interconnections and linkages. This will likely uncover a variety of perspectives, data that can be used to look for underlying root problems.

Force field analysis works well within the process of action research, particularly during diagnosis and evaluation phases. Combining force field analysis with the change process model, allows us to visualize the change process, as depicted in Figure 7-4.

Figure 7-4. Force Field Analysis and Process of Change

Restraining Forces: Inhibiting Change

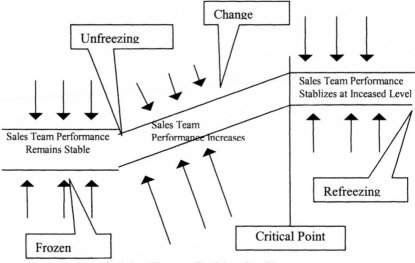

Driving Forces: Pushing for Change

While in the frozen state, the sales team is unaware of a need for change; there are no perceived problems with their performance. Increased competition, for example, creates a need for change, moving the team to a conscious need to alter their sales process. Through an assessment of driving and restraining forces, and the use of strategies to reduce restraining forces, the team experiences a change in performance. Organizational support is provided through the change process beyond the critical point, and the team stabilizes performance at a higher level.

PROBLEM SOLVING APPROACH TO FACILITATING CHANGE

One of the basic "tools" that a team utilizes is a model for identifying and analyzing problems and coming up with solutions to resolve these problems. It is surprising how many teams do not have an explicit model for problem solving, rather use a "hit and miss" method. Without a process, it is likely that the "solution" addresses a surface level issue, leaving the underlying problem unaddressed.

A problem could be described as a discrepancy between current conditions and desired outcomes. Problems are not necessarily negative (e.g., low employee morale), and can be seen as opportunities (e.g., an identified need for a new process for handling customer inquiries.) Problems are solved by developing goals or objectives which, when achieved, reduce the discrepancy or gap between the ideal and reality. Problem solving strategies utilize a wide variety of information to both set and achieve goals.

The problem solving process includes two dimensions of *problem analysis* and *decision making*. Problem analysis is the identification of those factors or forces that prevent goal attainment. Decision making is the process of determining goals and action strategies for reaching those goals. Organizational and strategic planning depends upon the processes of identifying significant problems, setting realistic goals and objectives, diagnosing the forces and influences that impact the problem, and suggesting how a specific set of interventions can solve or lessen the problem.

Problem solving is a strategic process, as it includes rethinking old ideas, and focusing on the premise of trying to do the right things, not simply doing things right. Details for the steps of a basic problem solving process are described below. While this may appear to be straight-forward, people, especially when rushed or facing tight deadlines, often sidestep some of these steps and end up simply putting a Band-Aid on the real issue. This works in the short term, but the real problem arises again at some future point, often in a more deteriorated state.

1. Assess the situation. What is occurring that indicates a problem? What evidence do we have that something is wrong? What information do we need? How does this situation relate to our other priorities? Have we had this situation before? How was it handled? What have we learned so far about this situation? Who needs to participate in this process, i.e., what is the relationship of this situation to the system?

2. Identify and analyze the problem. What is the actual problem or deficit condition? What is desired that is not happening? What is happening in terms of who is involved, where, when, what, and how much? What objective measures, variables or indicators can we use to identify the extent of the problem? What past and present forces or influences have created the problem situation? Analyze the context and payoffs or benefits of past decisions impacting problem. Do a force field analysis. How is this problem related to the organizational system?

3. Define goals and objectives of the desired state. What are the desired outcomes or results? What is the criteria or measures for judging when we are meeting or falling short of our goals and objectives? What resources are available to assist us? Focus on the ends, not means or strategies.

4. Generate alternative strategies to meet the desired state. Fantasize freely about potential solutions. Share your thoughts with others and compare solutions to uncover patterns. Synthesize a list of items that appear to have some organic or logical connection. Each combination should be defined by a description of the strategy to be used.

5. Select the best strategy to meet the goals and objectives of the desired state. Select a strategy by determining the criteria and assigning a cost/benefit value. Do the selected strategies look as though they will meet the desired goals of the desired state?

6. Identify potential problems with the selected strategy. What, potentially, will get in the way of achieving our goals and objectives? How important are these to our success? What can we do to work with these hindering forces? What, potentially, will assist us in achieving our goals and objectives? How can we maximize these driving forces? Will the current organizational structure and culture facilitate the desired state?

7. Test selected strategies. Test strategy in order to reveal additional potential problems or clarify commitment to carry out the strategy. Are you getting the desired results? Are you able to handle the problems identified in #6?

8. Write a plan to carry out the strategy organization-wide. List all tasks necessary to carry out strategy. Rank order tasks. Assign primary responsibilities and deadlines.

9. Implement and evaluate the plan. Follow the plan to implement the strategy. Be persistent - understand that errors and failures are normal. Evaluate and revise your plan according to data gathered regarding its successes and failures.

The basic problem solving process provides steps to identify and resolve organizational problems or opportunities. It is important to remember that while following a linear model is helpful as a guideline, it is also necessary to be creative in your process.

CREATIVE APPROACH TO PROBLEM SOLVING

Creative problem solving requires that we utilize both critical (evaluative, analytical, linear thinking) and imaginative (generalizing, visualizing, abstracting, intuiting) functions. Creative problem solving can be defined as the generation (creation) and evaluation (judgment) of information; thus both tasks must be synthesized in a mutually reinforcing manner. However, excessive judgment during times of idea generation can hinder creative ideas, information, and goal setting (this was discussed in Chapter 5: Organizational Learning and Creativity.) In addition to the linear, rational process, utilize intuitive processes such as:

• In describing and reformulating the problem, brainstorm freely, avoid censorship of ideas. Focus on relationship of problem to larger system.

• When establishing criteria or strategy for problem resolution, brainstorm to search for new arrangements and explore ignored alternatives. Don't allow judgment to intercept this process.

• In seeking alternatives, cultivate intuitive choices; use opening up techniques to bring more sublimated data to the surface. Asking "what if . . ." is powerful! Use "lessons learned" to guide thinking.

- Visualize and check feelings to see if decided upon alternative feels intuitively right. Divergent and contradictory ideas can be valuable.
- Be aware of negative feelings and gut awareness of issues and concerns. Don't ignore internal feelings that something is not quite right with the tentative solution(s).
- Monitor feelings and intuitions throughout the process. Remain self aware.[4]

During the process of creative problem solving, the critical function must be suspended and the imaginative function stimulated. Premature judgment must be avoided before numerous ideas are explored. However, during latter stages of the problem solving process, evaluation and judgment are certainly necessary; critical and creative functions must be made to complement and support each other. See Chapter 5 for a description of roles team members play during the problem solving process.

Problem solving processes are necessary tools for teams and organizations; they provide a framework for closing the gap between current performance and desired performance. Typically, problem solving is event-based; it results when there is a perception that something is wrong. However, classical problem-solving methods do not explicitly involve the whole system. Therefore the solution may not be the best one available. Problem solving used within the framework of action research will support a systems approach.

GROUP APPROACHES TO FACILITATING CHANGE

Problem solving is a methodology for addressing small-scale developmental change. Traditional problem solving does not explicitly engage the whole system in the process. Contemporary organizational change work includes a "whole system" approach to facilitating change, where all organizational members are actively engaged. Based on such classical frameworks as Planned Change[5] and Large Scale Technology[6], contemporary models include Preferred Futuring, Whole-Scale Change, Open Space Technology, The Conference Model, and Gemba Kaizen[7].

When facilitating large-scale change and transformation, the object is to get the whole system involved in the process. Stakeholders are not merely represented, but participate in and are directly engaged. As a result, they are more committed to its outcomes.

I've chosen two methodologies to present in overview fashion: Preferred Futuring and Appreciative Inquiry. I've chosen these because they shift the focus from "problems to be fixed" to "possibilities for the future", representing a critical shift in organization development thinking. Both methods engage organizational members in the process of shaping the future of the organization.

PREFERRED FUTURING[8]

Developed by Larry Lippitt and based on the work of his father, Ron Lippitt and colleagues, Preferred Futuring™ helps teams, organizations, or communities construct the future they want and mobilize the energy to reach it. This methodology was one of the first to enable organizations to think in terms of "whole systems." Groups establish a common understanding of who they are, what success looks like, and create plans to achieve success. Preferred Futuring is a business strategy, a process, and a philosophical approach to change.

Unlike traditional problem solving models that focus on problems, Preferred Futuring focuses on potential, tapping into the notion that organizational members can proactively create and therefore be responsible for their future. A model is used to diagnose the need for Preferred Futuring:

$C = D \times V \times F > R$
*(C)*hange $= (D)$issatisfaction x (V)ision x (F)irst step $> (R)$esistance

Within this model, change is dependent on four factors:

- *Dissatisfaction* with the current situation, expressed as complaints and the belief that nothing can be done. Dissatisfaction must be transformed into motivation for change.
- A clear, detailed, and agreed-upon *vision* of the future, a picture that organizational members align with and focus their energy on to accomplish. The vision is a collective picture of a future that all stakeholders agree upon and passionately want.
- Action plans with concrete, agreed-upon *steps* for moving from vision to implementation and specific results.
- *Resistance to change* is reduced when people let go of the dissatisfaction, are able to see the future and determine the organization's direction and its implications for their work, connect passion with energy that is focused on planning and confronting specific resistors.

If any factor of (D), (V), or (F) are missing, the product (R) is zero. Resistance remains greater than the desire for change. If people are stuck in dissatisfaction, there is no vision or first steps. Preferred Futuring is designed to move thinking beyond dissatisfaction to envisioning a desired future state. There are eight basic steps to Preferred Futuring:

1. **History**: create a common sense of history and current vision.
2. **Current state**: establish what is working and what is not, what business we are in, and who our customers are.
3. **Values and Beliefs**: establish a common understanding of values and beliefs as they relate to goals and objectives.
4. **Strategic Trends/Developments**: conduct a strategic assessment of trends that may impact us.
5. **Vision**: determine a common, clear, and specific picture of success, including measurable criteria.

6. **Strategic Action, Goals, and Roadblocks**: translate the vision into common, specific, actionable strategic objectives
7. **Action Plans**: develop specific action plans with responsibilities and timelines.
8. **Follow-Up Support**: develop follow-up structures that include milestone checks and celebrations and strategies for sustaining success.

These steps can be the basis for a three-day event with an organization's top 500 leaders or a nine-month process with a city of 500,000. Participants can be top leaders, the whole organization, or a community of hundreds of thousands. Participants share their stories in small groups and during large-group reports. Implementation is done by functional, cross-functional, and cross-level groups.[9]

Preferred Futuring is more effective if leadership is willing to partner with the rest of the system. This shift in power and authority can be uncomfortable for both leaders and others. The method of Preferred Futuring enables both to partner and discover the benefits of tapping into the talent of all members of the organization. It works because it capitalizes on the diversity within the system. When diverse truths are combined, a greater truth is constructed. Also, when people have an exciting and concrete vision of the future, they let go, allowing old ways to end and new ones to begin. The transformation feels less risky. Preferred Futuring provides an alternative to the problem solving approach, as shown in Table 7-1[10].

Table 7-1. Problem Solving versus Preferred Futuring

Problem Solving	Preferred Futuring
Blaming increases and responsibility-taking decreases.	An air of honesty and realism, even catharsis, creates constructive dissatisfaction, replacing defeatism and blaming.
Depression and despair increase, reducing cooperation and teamwork.	Tremendous excitement, hope, and optimism generate more cooperation and teamwork.
Shorter-term goals focus on reducing pain or fixing immediate problems.	More "stretch," breakthrough, and longer-range goals and solutions are developed.
Decreased motivation results from generating a large, prioritized list of problems.	High motivation results from moving toward something attractive rather than away from something painful and to be avoided.
Attributing causes to factors that are outside the group's sphere of influence or control decreases a sense of power and increased sense of helplessness.	High levels of energy and empowerment carry over into implementation and action taking.

The difference manifests itself in higher levels of energy among organizational members who see possibilities for determining their future. Another approach that encourages looking at possibilities is Appreciative Inquiry.

APPRECIATIVE INQUIRY[11]

Most people and organizations are constrained by the *perception* that their resources, and hence their horizons, are limited. This perception -- that we must "face reality"—is a great constraint on human imagination, vision and creativity.

Appreciative inquiry begins with a different set of assumptions. It begins with the belief that we have a *choice,* that we can consciously choose what we "see" and act upon. In both the personal and social realms, we can choose to focus on problems, needs and deficits—the traditional problem-solving approach. Or we can choose to see possibilities, capabilities and assets—the basis of appreciative inquiry.

Appreciative inquiry (AI) is a philosophy of knowing, a methodology for managing change, an approach to leadership and human development; it is

> . . . the cooperative search for the best in people, their organizations, and the world around them. It involves systematic discovery of what gives a system "life" when it is most effective and capable . . . AI involves the art and practice of asking questions that strengthen a system's capacity to heighten positive potential . . .[12]

As a practical philosophy, Appreciative Inquiry invites organizational members to search for and ask about what is energizing and life-enhancing—it explores hopes and dreams for the future. It is a process that involves creating an environment organizational members want to live in. Assumptions of AI include:

- In every human system, something works.
- What we focus on, and the language we use, becomes our reality.
- Reality is created in the moment and there are multiple realities. It is important to value differences.
- The act of asking questions influences the group in some way.
- People have more confidence and comfort to move to an unknown future when they carry forward parts of the past.
- What we carry forward should be what is best about the past.

Appreciative Inquiry involves the art and practice of asking questions that strengthen a system's capacity to heighten positive potential, questions such as:

- Describe a high-point experience in your organization, a time when you have been most alive and engaged.
- Describe what it is that you most value about yourself, your work, and your organization.

- What are the core factors that give life to your organization, without which the organization would not be the same?
- What three wishes do you have to enhance the health and vitality of your organization?

These questions evoke possibility thinking and, like Preferred Futuring, switch the focus from problems (what is wrong that we need to fix) to what is right that we can use as we move toward the desired future state. There are five principles of Appreciative Inquiry that must be regarded as essential for the application of AI to be truly effective:

- **The Constructionist Principle**: Human knowledge and organizational destiny are interwoven. To be effective, we must understand organizations as living, human constructions.
- **The Principle of Simultaneity**: Inquiry and change are not separate moments but are simultaneous.
- **The Poetic Principle**: Human organizations are like open books. The story of the system is constantly being co-authored, and it is open to infinite interpretations.
- **The Anticipatory Principle**: Our positive images of the future lead our positive actions—this is the increasingly energizing basis and presumption of Appreciative Inquiry.
- **Positive Principle**: Building and sustaining momentum for change requires large amounts of positive outlook and social bonding—things like hope, excitement, inspiration, caring, camaraderie, sense of urgent purpose, and sheer joy in creating something meaningful together. The more positive the question asked, the more long-lasting and successful the change effort.

The appreciative inquiry process includes four dimensions, as shown in Figure 7-5: 1) *Discovery*—appreciation of what gives life to the organization, the best of what is; 2) *Dream*—envisioning what might be, what the world is calling for; 3) *Design*—co-constructing what should be, the ideal future; and 4) *Destiny/Delivery*—how to empower, learn, and adjust/improvise; sustaining the change[13].

The cycle can occur with any number of people in any given timeframe. One method, the AI Summit is a large-scale meeting process that focuses on discovering and developing the organization's positive change core and designing it into strategic business processes. Participation in the Summit is diverse by design and includes all the organization's stakeholders. It is generally four days long; however, each Summit is a unique design based on the challenges of the organization and industry involved. Table 7-2 depicts the common aspects of successful AI Summits[14].

The core of AI is the *appreciative interview*. Stemming from a fundamentally affirmative focus, these interviews uncover what gives life to an organization, when at its best. Personal and organizational high points, what people value, and what they hope and wish for to enhance the organization's social, economic, and environmental vitality are revealed in the interviews.

Table 7-2. The AI Cycle and the AI Summit

Day—Cycle	Focus	Participants . . .
1—Discovery **Appreciating**	Mobilize a systemic or system wide inquiry into a positive change core	Engage in appreciative interviews and storytelling. Reflect on interview highlights.
2—Dream **Envisioning impact**	Envision the organization's greatest potential for positive influence and impact in the world	Review themes of interviews. Create and present possibility statements.
3—Design **Co-constructing**	Craft an organization in which the positive change core is boldly alive in all strategies, processes, systems, decisions, and collaborations	Identify high-impact design elements and create an organization design. Draft provocative propositions (design statements) incorporating the positive change core.
4—Destiny/Delivery **Sustaining**	Invite action inspired by the days of discovery, dream, and design	Publicly declare intended actions and ask for support. Self-selected groups plan next steps. Implementation of planned actions.

Appreciative inquiry works best when an organization wants greater cooperation across functional lines, greater employee commitment and responsibility, and faster cycle time. AI provides a process that engages people in interviews across functional lines, involves organizational members in making decisions and determining the process, in a quick timeframe. AI provides an alternative to traditional problem solving, as shown in Table 7-3[15].

The basic assumption of appreciative inquiry creates the opportunity for organizational learning and creativity to occur. By focusing on what's *right*, rather than what's wrong with an organization, an individual or even a society, AI accesses the kind of energy that can be transformative. Having that kind of energy to work with gives organizational members the confidence to develop and pursue a new image of the future.

Table 7-3. Focus and Assumptions of Problem Solving and Appreciative Inquiry

Problem Solving	Appreciative Inquiry
Identify Problem ↓	Appreciate "What is" (What gives life)? ↓
Conduct Root Cause Analysis ↓	Imagine "What Might Be" ↓
Brainstorm and Analyze Solutions ↓	Determine "What Should Be" ↓
Develop Action Plans ↓	Create "What Will Be" ↓
Basic Assumption: An organization is a problem to be solved	Basic Assumption: An organization is a solution/mystery to be embraced

THERE'S LOTS MORE FOR YOUR INVESTIGATION...

The items presented in this chapter provide foundational approaches to organization development and change. From the traditional Force Field Analysis to the more contemporary approach of Appreciative Inquiry, the basic OD framework rests upon Action Research. While not meant to be an exhaustive presentation of all methodologies available to the OD practitioner, this chapter, hopefully, stimulates you towards further investigation.

RELATED READING: KURT LEWIN[16]

One of Lewin's earliest and most significant studies came as a result of a commission from the US government to see what he could do to change the buying, cooking, and eating habits of American housewives during World War II. To help the war effort, government agents encouraged women to buy and use more of the visceral organs and less of the muscle cuts of beef.

Officials explained the facts and logically presented the driving forces—patriotism, availability, economy, and nutrition—to motivate and encourage housewives to buy, cook and serve the visceral cuts of beef to their families. However, they underestimated the restraining forces. Not used to eating tongue, heart, and kidney, the women didn't know how to buy such products, how to serve them, how to cook them. They feared their families would respond negatively.

These housewives resisted change until they started meeting together and gaining an understanding of the nature of the problem. When they really got involved in the nature of the problem they gradually loosened up, "unfroze" their perceptions, broadened their thinking, and seriously considered alternatives. As they came to understand how their change of diet could help the war effort, and as they expressed themselves fully—without fear of being censured, embarrassed, or ridiculed about their fears and doubts—many actually changed their buying and eating habits.

Lewin and the government learned an important lesson: When people become involved in the problem, they become significantly and sincerely committed to coming up with solutions to the problem.

FORCE FIELD ANALYSIS: PART II

Return to the activity at the beginning of this chapter. Respond to the following questions.

1.   If I consider the present state of the problem as a temporary balance of opposing forces, the following would be on my list of forces *driving* toward change: (Fill in the spaces to the right of the letters. Leave spaces to the left blank for now.)

_____   a. _____

_____   b. _____

_____   c. _____

_____   d. _____

_____   e. _____

_____   f. _____

_____   g. _____

_____   h. _____

2.   The following would be on my list of forces *restraining* change:

_____   a. _____

_____   b. _____

_____   c. _____

_____   d. _____

_____   e. _____

_____   f. _____

_____   g. _____

_____   h. _____

3.   In the spaces to the left of the letters in item 1, rate the driving forces
        from 1 to 5.

        1. It has *almost nothing* to do with the drive toward change in the
        problem.
        2. It has *relatively little* to do with the drive toward change in the
        problem.
        3. It is of *moderate importance* in the drive toward change in the
        problem.
        4. It is an *important factor* in the drive toward change in the problem.
        5. It is a *major factor* in the drive toward change in the problem.

4.   In the spaces to the left of the letters in item 2, rate the forces
        restraining change, using the number scale in item 3.

5.   Select two or more restraining forces from list and then outline a
        strategy for reducing their potency. (See list of potential strategies for
        reducing resistance earlier in this chapter.)

APPRECIATE WHAT IS AND IMAGINE WHAT COULD BE

Think of an organization you are closely involved in. Perhaps it is your place of employment, or a civic organization where you provide volunteer work, or your school. More than likely you see problems that need to be solved—most organizations are not perfect. You have probably spent time thinking and talking to others about these problems and how you would solve them if you were "in charge."

The purpose of this activity is to switch your thinking from problems to possibilities. Respond to the following questions. Give this some time—don't be tempted to pass it by or rush through responding. Give each question thoughtful consideration.

1. Describe a high-point experience in your organization, a time when you have been most alive and engaged.

2. Without being modest, tell me what is it that you most value about yourself, your work, and your organization.

3. What are the core factors that give life to your organization, without which the organization would not be the same?

4. What three wishes do you have to enhance the health and vitality of your organization?

Now, go and find someone else to ask these questions of. Together, discuss your responses. Focus on possibilities. Dare to dream the future!

ENDNOTES

[1] Please note that this chapter is not exhaustive in the models available to change facilitators. One resource that is helpful is Holman, E., & Devane, T. (1999). *The Change Handbook: Group Methods for Shaping the Future*. San Francisco: Berrett-Koehler Publishers, Inc.

[2] Lewin, K. (1951). *Field Theory in Social Science*. New York: Harper; and Lewin, K. (1958). Group decision and social change. In E. E. Macoby, T. M. Newcomb, & E. L. Hartley (Eds.), *Readings in Social Psychology*. New York: Holt, Rinehart & Winston, pp. 197-211.

[3] Adapted from Don Harvey & Donald R. Brown. (2001). *An Experiential Approach to Organization Development* 6th Ed. New Jersey: Prentice Hall, pp. 172-177.

[4] See Malcolm Gladwell (2005). *Blink: The power of thinking without thinking*. New York: Little, Brown and Company for further discussion on intuition.

[5] Lippitt, R., Watson, J, and Wetley, B. (1958). *The Dynamics of Planned Change*. New York: Harcourt, Brace & World.

[6] Beckhard, R. (1975). Strategies for large system change. In K. Benne, L. Bradford, J. Gibb & R. Lippitt (Eds.), *Laboratory method of changing and learning*. Palo Alto, CA: Science and Behavior Books; and Lippitt, R. (1983). Future before you plan. In R. A. Ritvo & A. G. Sargent (Eds.), *The NTL managers' handbook*. Arlington, VA: NTL Institute.

[7] For a good description of whole system approaches to change, see Holman, E., & Devane, T. (1999). *The Change Handbook: Group Methods for Shaping the Future*. San Francisco: Berrett-Koehler Publishers, Inc.

[8] Lippitt, L. L. (1999). Preferred Futuring™: The Power to Change Whole Systems of Any Size. In P. Holman, & T. Devane (Eds.), *The Change Handbook: Group Methods for Shaping the Future*. San Francisco: Berrett-Koehler Publishers, Inc., pp. 159-174.

[9] ibid, p. 164 and 167.

[10] ibid, p. 171-172.

[11] See Cooperrider, D. L., & Whitney, D. (1999). Appreciative Inquiry: A Positive Revolution in Change. In P. Holman, & T. Devane (Eds.), *The Change Handbook: Group Methods for Shaping the Future*. San Francisco: Berrett-Koehler Publishers, Inc., pp. 245-261; Hall, J., & Hammond, S. "What is Appreciative Inquiry?" www.thinbook.com; Mohr, B. (2001). Appreciative Inquiry: Igniting Transformative Action. *The Systems Thinker*, 12(1) at www.pegasuscommunications.com; and AI Commons website at http://appreciativeinquiry.cwru.edu/.

[12] Cooperrider, D. L., & Whitney, D. (1999). Appreciative Inquiry: A Positive Revolution in Change. In P. Holman, & T. Devane (Eds.), *The Change Handbook: Group Methods for Shaping the Future*. San Francisco: Berrett-Koehler Publishers, Inc., pp. 245-261.

[13] ibid, p. 249.

[14] ibid, p. 249-250.

[15] ibid, p. 255.

[16] Source: Stephen R. Covey. (1992). *Principle-Centered Leadership*. New York: Simon & Schuster, p. 221.

CHAPTER 8:
THE PROCESS OF ORGANIZATIONAL CHANGE

"WHAT ARE WE DOING THIS FOR?"

QUESTIONS FOR PLANNING THE TRANSFORMATION FOCUS[1]

Purpose: Articulating the reasons for change.

Who: Members of a pilot group looking at potential change initiatives.

Time: Several hours.   Allow time for people to talk through the reasoning behind their answers to these questions, especially when there is disagreement.

Questions:

1.   Why is the change urgent? Are we driven by external forces? By a crisis? Or by our collective desire to create something together? Why might this effort actually matter? (See next activity to support determining the driving cause for change.)

2.   Who wants it to happen? Who (in or out of the group) has set change as a priority? Are there clearly defined sponsors of the change effort? Are we aware of their needs and the pressures they feel? What might be the reasoning behind their requests?

3.   What results do we want to produce? What, specifically, is the change we are seeking? If the change takes place, what will that get us? How will our efforts benefit our customers?

4.   How will we change? What kinds of new capabilities will we need to develop? And how will we develop them? Which aspects of our current work and practices will be affected by the change? What challenges do we expect to face? And how could we prepare for them?

5.   Who will be involved? Will the change initiative mean new activities for everyone in this group? Should other people (inside or outside the group) be included?

6.   Where is our support? In the organization at large, what is the reputation of our group, and of our sponsors? Will that help or hinder us?

7.   What do I, personally, have to do? When will the change initiative begin? What steps do I need to take, in which domain? What do I hope to learn? What skills and capabilities would I like to gain? And what do I want to do first?

DETERMINING WHAT IS DRIVING THE CHANGE[2]

Purpose: Examine a variety of factors that drive organizational change to determine what is driving the current change.

Directions: Have individuals examine these factors and create their own list. Facilitate a group discussion, looking at each of the factors. Look for commonalities.

Environmental Forces	
Marketplace Requirements for Success	
Business Imperatives	
Operational Imperatives	
Cultural Imperatives	
Leader/Employee Behavior	
Leader/Employee Mindset	

So, you are about to embark on a journey of change. Where do you begin? When I began working as an organizational change agent, I didn't have a model to follow. Indeed, I didn't even think of myself as a change agent. My job was to introduce our clients to new technology, using a management model for selling, planning, and implementing this technology. This model vaguely resembled a change model, but did not address the human side of change, and paid little attention to the *process* of change.

Models of planned change help us plan for not only the *content* of a change initiative, but also the *process*. Planned change models take into consideration the various aspects of the change process, from addressing the driving and restraining forces, understanding the personal change process, to a systematic plan for introducing and evaluating change in an organizational setting.

Many authors provide a systematic process to manage organizational change or transformation. For example, Kotter (1996) presents an eight-stage change process based on the premise that "major change will not happen easily for a long list of reasons . . . to be effective, a method designed to alter strategies, reengineer processes, or improve quality must address these barriers and address them well." Table 8-1 lists errors common to organizational efforts and their consequences.

Table 8-1. Common Errors of Organizational Change and Consequences

Common Errors	Consequences
• Allowing too much complacency • Failing to create a sufficiently powerful guiding coalition • Underestimating the power of vision • Under-communicating the vision by a factor of 10 (or 100 or even 1,000) • Permitting obstacles to block the new vision • Failing to create short-term wins • Declaring victory too soon • Neglecting to anchor changes firmly in the corporate culture	• New strategies aren't implemented well • Acquisitions don't achieve expected synergies • Reengineering takes too long and costs too much • Downsizing doesn't get costs under control • Quality programs don't delivery hoped-for results

Based on these common errors, Kotter (1996, 2002) proposes an eight-step progressive process, or flow of major change.

1. **Establish a Sense of Urgency**. Through an examination of the market and competitive realities, identify crisis, potential crisis, or other major

opportunities. People start telling each other, "Let's go, we need to change things!"

2. **Create the Guiding Coalition**. Put together a group with enough power to lead the change, and get the group to work together like a team.

3. **Develop a Vision and Strategy**. The guiding team develops the right vision and strategy for the change effort.

4. **Communicate the Change Vision**. Use every vehicle possible to constantly communicate the new vision and strategies. The guiding team role models the behavior expected of others. People begin to buy into the change, and this shows in their behavior.

5. **Empower Broad-Based Action**. Reduce or remove obstacles, change systems and structures that undermine the change vision, encourage risk taking and nontraditional ideas, activities, and actions, allow people to feel able to act on the vision.

6. **Create Short-term Wins**. Plan for visible improvements in performance and create those wins. Momentum builds as people try to fulfill the vision, while fewer and fewer resist change. Visibly recognize and reward people who make the wins possible.

7. **Consolidate Gains and Produce More Change**. Use increased credibility to change all systems, structures, and policies that don't fit the transformation vision. Hire, promote, and develop people who can implement the change vision. Reinvigorate the process with new projects, themes, and change agents. Don't let up! Allow people to make wave after wave of changes until the vision is fulfilled.

8. **Anchor New Approaches in the Culture—make it stick**. Create better performance through customer- and productivity-oriented behavior, more and better leadership, and more effective management. Articulate the connections between new behaviors and organizational success. Develop means to ensure leadership development and succession.

The first four steps help defrost a hardened status quo, while phases five to seven introduce many new practices. The last stage grounds the changes in the corporate culture and helps make them stick. Successful change of any magnitude goes through all eight stages, usually in the sequence shown. Although you may operate in multiple phases at once, skipping even a single step or getting too far ahead without a solid base almost always creates problems.

ORGANIZATIONAL CHANGE PROCESS

Similarly, the Organization Change Process is a method of facilitating and managing the change process, a plan for initiating change into organizational settings. It is designed to provide a *roadmap* of the change process. It works for all types of change, from small- to large-scale, as the process is the same, albeit different time frames, people involved, etc.

The Organization Change Process (OCP) takes an organization from the initial stages of forming change teams, to creating a vision for the future state, to planning for, and implementing a change intervention. It provides guidelines for each step of the process, and uses action research for continual monitoring and feedback.

The timeframe for the process would be dependent upon the intensity and extent of the change initiative. A large-scale transformational change, such as changing the leadership philosophy and culture can take upwards of five years or more. A smaller-scale change, such as upgrading and enhancing a specific process, would take less time. However, each step of the process is beneficial for all magnitudes of change within an organization, as it is systems-oriented, and takes into consideration how a change in one organizational subset affects the rest of the system.

I have borrowed from many sources for this model. The OCP operationalizes the basic concepts and assumptions of organization development. The process begins with a perceived problem or opportunity, a perceived need for change. Transition teams are established, teams that will guide and facilitate the change process. An analysis of the current state and desired future state form the basis for the vision of the future. This vision is communicated throughout the organization in an attempt to build enthusiasm and commitment on the part of organizational members and other stakeholders. The transition teams plan and organize the change initiative(s). These initiatives, the actual change itself, are implemented, adjustments are made as shown necessary through evaluation methods. The change is stabilized and becomes the new culture of the organization. The entire process is monitored and guided by Action Research.

STAGE 1. THE OPPORTUNITY

Goal of this stage: *Create a sense of urgency among relevant people, a critical mass of people who will see the need to undertake a change initiative in order to pursue an opportunity.*

A realtor friend once told me she never uses the term "problem," she sees every problem as an opportunity. She is quite successful because of this attitude, helping her clients overcome the barriers to home ownership, creating happy clients who recommend their friends to her and who return to her when it is time to move again. I have specifically used the term opportunity here, rather than the standard terminology at this stage of "problem identification" because of the difference in attitude it suggests.

Through continual environmental scanning, organizational leaders see what is ahead, what's facing the organization. It could be a problem brewing below the surface, or a new opportunity about to present itself. The key is to proactively pursue opportunities, not wait for problems to appear. Often, by the time a problem has presented itself, it is too late to maximize the opportunity, and necessary to react in a less than effective method. Through reading, surveys, interviews, and so on, we identify major trends likely to affect the organization.

Traditional organization development held that organizations were full of problems to be solved, and used survey feedback, for example, to uncover gaps between current and desired states. Contemporary thinking in the field of organization development and change looks more at opportunities to examine ways in which organizational members can work together with more shared authority to create a desired future state. In addition to Preferred Futuring and Appreciative Inquiry discussed in the last chapter, Search Conference[3] and Future Search[4] are other methods available to develop a shared learning process, operationalize systems thinking, and enable people to experience connections to a larger whole.

Things to consider at this stage:

- What is our business/mission?
- Who is our customer?
- What does the customer value?
- What are our results?
- What new demands will we face?
- What will be different about our customers?
- Who will be our new customers?
- What can we do that will make the biggest difference?
- What is the one thing that we must do for anything else to happen?
- Who are the relevant people needed to build awareness of this opportunity?
- By what means do we create a sense of urgency?

This stage equates to Kotter's creating a sense of urgency, where the organization examines the market, identifies crisis, potential crises, or major opportunities. In an earlier chapter, we discussed the "unfreezing stage," where the organization becomes aware of the need for some type of change.

Senge (1999), in acknowledging that profound change requires investment of time, energy, and resources, suggests creating an initial core pilot group, genuinely committed to new organizational purposes, methods, and working environments. The most important change initiatives have these qualities:

- They are connected with real work goals and processes;
- they are connected with improving performance;
- they involve people who have the power to take action regarding these goals;
- they seek to balance action and reflection, connecting inquiry and experimentation;
- they afford people an increased amount of "white space": opportunities for people to think and reflect without pressure to make decisions;
- they are intended to increase people's capacity, individually and collectively; and

- they focus on learning about learning, in settings that matter.

STAGE 2. THE TRANSITION TEAMS

Goal of this stage: *Connect groups of people with the desire, ability, and power to lead the change initiative. Build a leadership corps.*

Once you have revisited your mission and discovered areas for change initiatives, form teams that will be responsible for leading, facilitating, and implementing the change initiatives. The first, **Strategic Transition Team** (STT), is designed to guide the organization towards a future vision. Members of this team need to have credibility, skills, connections, reputations, and formal authority to provide leadership in this effort. The team learns how to act with trust and emotional commitment, they *feel* the sense of urgency. The STT has representation from all major components of the system (including external components if appropriate.) At a minimum, the STT consists of members from each of the departments that will be affected by the change initiative. The role this team plays involves creating and communicating the vision of the future state, providing guidance and direction for the change initiative process, sponsoring the change, and modeling the way.

In addition to the Strategic Transition Team, a second team is formed. The **Action Research Team** (ART) consists of individuals that are closest to the heart of the opportunity or problem at question. This team is responsible for working closely with the Strategic Transition Team to accurately assess the current state and provide valuable input into the future state. Data collection and analysis is this team's major contribution. The ART plays a key role in planning and implementation of change initiatives at the end-user or grassroots level. This team is empowered to move the organization towards its future state. They, therefore, need full access to organizational resources.

Implementation Teams (IT) are established, if necessary, as the change initiative is ready to be implemented. Their primary responsibility is for actual implementation at the team and department level.

Bennis (1993) suggests we recruit for these teams with scrupulous honesty about the projected changes, timeframes, and their commitment to the change process. Important components to consider in forming transition teams are:

- Each team needs to have members that represent all the sections of the organization that will be impacted by the change initiative.
- Team members should be respected members of the community, who are positioned to gain trust of those they interact with.
- At least one member of the Strategic Transition Team should be a liaison to the Action Research Team, and one member of the Action Research Team should sit on the Strategic Transition Team. Additionally, one member of each Implementation Team should have access to the Action Research Team. This provides the "linking pin" that connects all components of the system to the whole organization, as shown in Figure 8-1.

- A strategy needs to be established for inter- and intra-team communications. This would include meeting schedules and establishing who attends which meetings, as well as a strategy for keeping each group informed.
- Team building activities should be used to assist teams in becoming highly functioning.   Team processes should be implemented to maximize effectiveness of the team interactions.

Figure 8-1. Linking Pins of Transition Teams

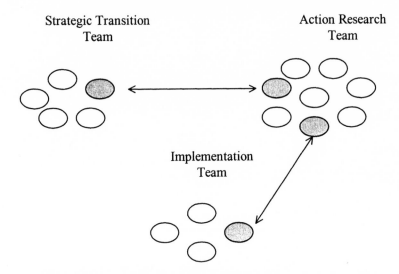

In addition to forming transition teams, this stage calls for enlisting the support of a **change consultant**. The discussion of external versus internal and process versus content expertise was discussed earlier in Chapter 3.

Things to consider in this stage in developing teams:

- Who are the critical leaders best suited to sponsor, support, and model the change?
- Who are the people closest to the problem? They will be instrumental in assessing the driving and hindering forces related to the change, as well as providing valuable important input to the vision of the future state.
- Who are the people that will be instrumental in the implementation phase? Are key members of the informal organization chart represented?
- Do the teams need external representation (i.e., suppliers, customers) as well?
- Once teams are established, who should be the linking pins to other teams?
- What kind of activities need to take place to create high-functioning teams? What skills do they need? What resources do they need? Do they have access to needed resources?

- What kind of training is required for each of the teams? What tools do they need to be effective?
- What forms of inter- and intra-team communications will the teams use? What is the frequency of interactions?
- What do we need in terms of facilitating the change process? Do we contract with an individual from within the organization, i.e., Human Resources or Organization Development? Do we contract with someone from outside of the organization, i.e., a consultant with a specific area of expertise? Do we need support with the process of the change and/or the technical component?
- How will the consultant interact with the change process teams?
- If the consultant is external to the organization, to whom will this person "report?"

BUILD A LEADERSHIP CORPS

Change and transformation often requires moving people out of their organizational boxes into flexible, fluid management systems. It is critical for people to learn new skills, expand positions, to ban the hierarchy that keeps people boxed into old ways of thinking and behaving. Transformation calls for building a leadership corps (Hesselbein, 2002), developing a plan for the leadership of the organization, and involves as much time, energy, and rigor as the strategic change itself.

Things to consider in building a leadership corps:

- What are our leadership strengths?
- What are the areas to be strengthened?
- Are we leading from the front? Do we anticipate change and articulate shared aspirations, or simply react to crises?
- How do we deploy our leaders, our teams, and our people to further the mission and achieve our goals?
- Do we use job expansion, job rotation, and opportunities for development in innovative ways to release the energies of people and increase job satisfaction?
- Do our leaders see themselves as the embodiment of the mission, values, and beliefs of the organization?
- How can we sharpen communication skills and attitudes—knowing communication is not merely saying something, it is being heard?
- Are we building today the richly diverse, inclusive, cohesive organization that our vision and mission and the future demand?

The answers to these questions help create effective teams, allocate appropriate resources, and develop energetic leaders in response to powerful goals and objectives.

STAGE 3. THE VISION FOR THE FUTURE

Goal at this stage: *Create a compelling vision of the future; a vision based on what already gives life to the organization, as well as future dreams for the organization.*

Working with organizational members, the transition teams create a sensible, clear, simple vision of the future or desired state. This vision is designed to paint the picture of what is possible, and to capture the hearts and minds of stakeholders. The Action Research Team is primarily responsible for collecting and analyzing data that will define the current state within the organization. The Strategic Transition Team is primarily responsible for defining the future or desired state. In addition, the transition teams outline, in broad terms, strategies for moving the organization toward that vision. (Detailed plans and budgets will come later.) Appropriate strategies in this stage include data collection and analysis, and forms of future visioning, such as Preferred Futuring, and Appreciative Inquiry (described in Chapter 7.)

STEP 1: DEFINE CURRENT STATE

The first step in creating a vision for the future is to understand where you are currently, to clearly define and analyze the current state. The important focus here is to understand what is working and what is not; assessing the present state in terms of strengths, weaknesses, opportunities, and threats.

One approach is to describe the problem or opportunity statement. Gather information regarding the performance of the organization and deterrents to desired performance levels. In this stage, care must be taken not to confuse symptoms with underlying root causes. Concentrate on the real problem(s). Attempt to understand the root underlying causes of such problems as absenteeism, poor quality, or deteriorating relationships. While these are manifestations of the problem, look for underlying causes. Examine the organizational culture or structure that keeps the organization from being as effective as possible and from moving to the future state.

Another approach is to use the 4-D Method of Appreciative Inquiry. Examine what gives life to the organization (what is working well), envision what might be (dreams for the future of the organization).

The Action Research Team has primary responsibility for this step, facilitated by the change consultant. Data is gathered, analyzed, and fed back to the Strategic Transition Team. Data gathering procedures include survey feedback, appreciative inquiry, questionnaires, interviews, company documents, observation, and focus groups. Both quantitative and qualitative data are useful in accurately assessing the real issues.

Things to consider while defining the current state:

- What information do we need? Where can we get this information?
- Where are we now?
- What's working? What do we do well?

- What's not working? What do we need to improve upon?
- What practices, processes, policies are in place to keep us from being the best we can be?
- What core factors define us as an organization?
- What desires do organizational members have for the future of this organization?
- What suggestions do organizational members have for moving this organization to the next level (or specifically to address the opportunity/problem?)

A helpful technique is to have a variety of teams and levels of the organization go through this exercise. A comparison of data collected could uncover issues and concerns, as well as offer helpful hints to underlying root causes of problems. For example, it could prove to be quite useful information if the STT defines the current state in very different terms from non-management organizational members.

STEP 2: DEFINE FUTURE STATE

Using data gathered to define the current state allows the transition teams to look to the future. Assessing where the organization needs to go in order to remain competitive and promote growth is the key activity in this stage. Describing how things will look in the future is critical to formulating a strategy and vision for any change initiative.

Things to consider while defining the future state:

- What information do we need to determine the future state? Where can we get this information?
- Where do we want to go as an organization?
- Where do we need to be in order to remain competitive and promote growth?
- How will we respond to the changing environment?
- What will the organization look like in its desired future state?
- Do we understand the underlying root causes of existing problems?
- Do we clearly understand how the problems are manifested?
- What change initiatives will address the root causes of organizational problems and opportunities?
- What will behavior look like in the desired future state?
- What behavior needs to change in order for us to reach our desired state?
- How will the future state define us as an organization?
- What vision will organizational members align with and focus their energy on to accomplish?
- Who are the obvious champions for the desired state?

STEP 3: CREATE THE VISION OF THE FUTURE

Once you have clearly described and assessed the current state, and described the future state, the task is to engage in assessing what needs to happen in order to move the organization ahead. Select appropriate change objectives based on an accurate assessment of the present state and the gap between what is current and what is desired. Define these change objectives clearly and specifically, in both behavioral and quantitative terms, so that they are appropriate to and consistent with the organization.

A critical aspect is to determine the implications of the gap between the current and future state, what Anderson and Anderson refer to as "impact analysis." The impact analysis assesses both organizational and human impacts, providing essential information for building a good change plan and reducing human trauma. The impact analysis reveals what aspects of the old state serve the new state and can be carried forward; what aspects of the old state will need to be dismantled or dropped; and what will need to be created from scratch to fit the needs of the new state. This will help determine exactly what will need to change and what will not need to change (Anderson & Anderson, 2001).

At this stage, it is critical to engage all areas of the organization that will be affected by the change. Avoid later implementation problems by including relevant voices in the process of determining how to get to the desired future state.

Seek alternate solutions. Use a variety of methodologies to seek ideas to improve, eliminate, combine, and develop new processes. It is critical to avoid judgment and seek a free flow of ideas. It is also important not to focus on *how* the change will be implemented, but more importantly on *what* is desired for the future of the organization. Implementation concerns are addressed later in the process. Once ideas have been generated, clarified, and refined, the transition teams outline the future in broad terms.

It is also helpful to select a "winning project" to work on, one that is associated with a high probability of success and one that will provide some "quick wins". This allows a potentially high, quick return, and opens doors to other opportunities as a result of early success.

Things to consider while creating the vision for the future:

- What alternatives do we have for getting to the future state?
- Have we included the voice from all sections of the organization that will be affected?
- Which alternative seems best at this point?
- What is ideal?
- What can we keep from the current state that will aid us in reaching the future?

- What exactly needs to change? Behaviorally? Practices, processes, policies?
- Have we formed a clear, concise vision statement?
- How committed are we to move towards the desired future state?
- Are we willing to make tough decisions?
- How will we incorporate what is already working well into the future state?
- What potential resistors are we likely to encounter?

STAGE 4. COMMUNICATE THE VISION

Goal: *Generate interest, induce understanding of the need for change, develop commitment, capture the hearts of organizational members, and generate energy within the community; build a shared vision.*

At this stage, the Strategic Transition Team communicates the vision in simple, heartfelt messages sent through many channels. People need to understand what the desired future state looks like. Create a picture of that through words, actions, and symbols. Remembering the old adage "actions speak louder than words," the transition teams begin to "model the way" by embodying the behaviors called for in the desired future state. Use metaphors, analogies, and examples, a verbal picture is worth a thousand words. Repetition is key, particularly when the channels are varied.

Along with the vision, you need to communicate the strategy for reaching the desired state. A successful, long-term change or organization development initiative begins with and is guided by a conscientiously and deliberately planned strategy. This strategy is a comprehensive plan based on a thorough analysis of organizational needs and goals designed to bring about specific changes, and to ensure that appropriate steps are taken to maintain these changes. The strategy should specify primary as well as alternative interventions and take into consideration the power and influence dynamics of the organization. The strategy should communicate *how* the organization is going to go about engaging in the process of change.

All transition teams play a crucial role in this stage. The Strategic Transition Team communicates the vision. They begin the process by modeling the way, demonstrating behaviors that are consistent with the future vision. Action Research Teams and Implementation Teams garner support for the change at the grassroots level by focusing on the importance of the vision and the role each individual plays in moving the organization towards its future state.

You cannot give too much information at this stage. Understanding the various aspects of resistance to change, the more clear and specific the communications are at this stage, the more the organization can reduce that resistance. It is better to acknowledge that all answers are not known than to withhold information, allowing the informal communications, such as the grapevine, to provide inaccurate information.

All organizational members need to see and feel their personal role in achieving the new vision. Be clear about expectations of everyone in making the change successful.

Establish open dialogue about the change effort. Use feedback of those involved. Providing opportunity for people to voice their opinions and raise their objections can 1) clarify the objection, 2) raise valid points which may otherwise have gone unnoticed, and 3) reveal the real and potential barriers to achieving success. Keep communications consistent, both in information and timing. Build a trusting work climate by eliminating (or at least addressing) rumors and keeping the lines of communication open. Try to alleviate people's fears about the proposed changes.

Timing is critical. It is amazing how quickly rumors spread. It is critical to positively set the stage for the impending change initiative. Allowing the rumor mill to spread the news prior to organizational executives will damage the process, causing harm that may be irreparable. It is best to formally communicate the strategy for change before the informal word spreads.

Things to consider when communicating the vision:

- What will the changed organization look like? How can we describe it so that organizational members can "see" the vision? How can we describe it so that organizational members can "feel" the vision?
- How do we describe the need for change? How do we identify the current state, problem, or opportunity?
- How can we best describe the strategy for moving toward the future state?
- How do we best describe the benefits of this future state to organizational stakeholders?
- How do we describe any potential risk?
- What form(s) should this communication take?
- Who should participate in the communications process?
- What is the best timing for the various communications?
- What follow up communications are best?
- Are the transition teams beginning to model the way?

STAGE 5. PLAN THE CHANGE INITIATIVE

Goal: *Empower people to act on the vision by removing obstacles and barriers. Plan for the implementation of the change initiative within the organization. Pilot test the change.*

Now that the change initiative has been described and communicated, the work of planning begins. This includes assessing readiness for change, preparing a detailed implementation plan, and conducting a pilot test. All transition teams are actively engaged in the planning for change stage. The STT focuses primarily on organizational structure, policies, and practices that will enable the change initiative, looking for barriers that will get in the way. The

ART focuses primarily on gathering and analyzing data related to driving and hindering forces towards the intended change. The IT focuses primarily on planning for the change initiative at the team and/or department level.

It is recommended that the plan include two parallel and separate structures; one that keeps the operation running effectively and one that oversees the change. This is an extremely effective approach to change.

STEP 1:   ASSESSING READINESS AND CAPACITY FOR CHANGE

The first step of planning for change is to determine the organization's readiness and capacity to implement the change strategy. This will allow you to determine where to start the change and which interventions to use. Use action research to collect data from all areas affected by the change strategy. Use such tools as force-field analysis to uncover driving and restraining forces, and examine ways to maximize the supportive forces and reduce the hindering forces.

Assess the organizational culture and its ability to integrate the proposed change. Appraise the organizational structure in terms of how it will facilitate the change. Evaluate leadership and management processes for its ability to model, support, and synthesize the change. Evaluate resources required to support the change, such as money, knowledge, people, and technology.

Determine which groups and individuals are most likely to resist the change. Seek ways to work with them to reduce the resistance. Engage them in the process. Remember that resistance can come from all levels of the organization, including management.

Consider effects on the working environment and group habits. Consider such issues as breaking up congenial workgroups, disrupting commuting schedules and car pools, or group composition. Try to assure that the change affecting one group has a positive effect on other groups or allied systems.

Things to consider in assessing readiness and capacity for change:

- How will we maintain the current business practices while planning for and implementing the change initiative?
- What resources do we need to make this change happen? What resources do we have available? Where can we get the resources we don't have?
- How will the change be perceived?
- What are the driving forces? How can we maximize these?
- What are the hindering forces? How can we minimize these?
- Who (or what groups) will be most likely to embrace the change? Who (or what groups) will be most likely to resist the change?
- How can we support organizational members through this process?
- What do we need to do in order to reduce resistance?
- Are we willing to make tough decisions about those who aren't willing to make the change?

- Is the current organization structure capable of integrating the change? Do we need to consider a different structure, such as moving away from a hierarchical pyramid to a circular structure?
- Is the organizational culture flexible enough to integrate the change?
- Are organizational leaders ready for change?
- Are the leadership and management processes flexible enough to integrate the change?
- How will managers, at all levels, be supported through this process?
- Are we willing to make tough decisions about managers who won't or can't support the change?
- What is a realistic timeframe for implementing the change?
- What time of the year is best for implementation? What time of the year do we want to avoid implementing the change initiative?

STEP 2: CHANGE IMPLEMENTATION PLAN

With a good understanding (you can never assess every possible facet of the change process), you are in position to develop a plan for reaching the change objectives. Determine which intervention(s) to use, where to begin, who will be involved at each phase of the change process, how much time is required, how the effort will be monitored. This plan should be in specific detail, and include all action items as well as a timeline for the implementation. Individuals and teams responsible for each action item should also be listed.

Involve all individuals who will be impacted by the change in this planning process. People need to understand the need for the change and be given the opportunity to gain the confidence that management is not going to "do them wrong." When people are part of the decision making and planning process, they will adapt to changes more readily.

Select a starting place for the change initiative. Examine the total organization to determine its key subsystems and personnel. Focus on those groups that will exert the greatest impact on organizational performance and individuals who influence the direction of the organization. Look for sections of the organization that are most enthusiastic about the change; they will create the "quick wins" so important to generating enthusiasm and support throughout the rest of the organization.

The Importance of Quick Wins[5]

Major change takes times, sometimes lots of time. Zealous believers will often stay the course no matter what happens. Most of the rest of us expect to see convincing evidence that all the effort is paying off. Nonbelievers have even higher standards of proof. They want to see clear data indicating that the changes are working and that the change process isn't absorbing so many resources in the short term as to endanger the organization.

Quick short-term wins have the benefit of providing evidence that the change is working. There are three characteristics of short-term wins:

1. It's visible; large numbers of people can see for themselves whether the result is real or just hype.
2. It's unambiguous; there can be little argument that it's a win.
3. It's clearly related to the change effort

When a reengineering effort promises that the first cost reductions will come in twelve months and they occur as predicted, that's a win. When a reorganization early in a transformation reduces the first phase of the new-product development cycle from ten to three months, that's a win.

In small companies or in small units of an organization, the first results are often needed in half a year. In large organizations, some unambiguous wins are required by eighteen months. Regardless of size, this means that you will be operating in multiple stages of change and transformation at once. Quick performance improvements help transformation in several ways:

- They provide evidence that the sacrifices are worth it. Wins greatly help justify the short-term costs involved.
- They reward change agents with a pat on the back. After a lot of hard work, positive feedback builds morale and motivation.
- They help fine-tune vision and strategies. Short-term wins give the transformation team concrete data on the viability of their idea and plan.
- They undermine cynics and self-serving resisters. Clear performance improvements make it difficult for people to block needed change.
- They keep bosses on board by providing those higher in the hierarchy with evidence that the transformation is on track.
- They speak to powerful players whose support you need and do not yet have.
- They build momentum, turning neutrals into supporters, reluctant supporters into active helpers, etc.

Without sufficient wins that are visible, timely, unambiguous, and meaningful to others, change efforts inevitably run into serious problems. The more the wins speak to employee issues, concerns, and values, the more they help the process. Valued achievements connect to people at a deeper level, and a deeper level can change behavior that is generally very difficult to change.

Things to consider in change implementation planning:

- Who needs to be involved in the planning process?
- What methods of implementation should we use? Should the change begin in one department and cascade out to the rest of the organization? At the top and cascade down? Or should the change happen all at once throughout the organization?
- What actions need to happen to implement this change?
- Who should be responsible for each action?
- What timeframe should be attached to each action?

- Do we have the necessary resources for the action items to happen?

STEP 3: PILOT TEST

It is important to test implementation through a *pilot* project. This is especially important when the change initiative is organization-wide. Initiate the change within a limited area of the organization. This "test" allows you to assess the implementation strategy and plan. Very importantly, it allows an initial evaluation of the results of the change intervention. Because it is on a small scale, adjustments can more easily be made than if the intervention was implemented throughout the entire organization. A pilot test also provides an opportunity for quick wins, helps establish support and credibility for the change intervention, and helps gain momentum.

Given that, it is important to be selective in your choice of targeted pilot test area. Criteria to consider includes:

- An area where you can achieve visible, meaningful, and unambiguous progress quickly.
- An area that is enthusiastic about the change initiative.
- An area that is aligned with the principles of organization development.
- An area where it will be relatively easy to implement the change.
- An area that has a powerful person or group whose help you need to generate enthusiasm and overcome critics.

Things to consider for planning the pilot test:

- Where is the best place to begin?
- Who is most supportive to the intended change?
- Where can we get a "quick win?"
- Who has shown initial enthusiasm and support for the change?
- What support will we give to the pilot test?
- What types of data do we need to assess the change initiative plan and make any needed adjustments?
- How well recognize success during the pilot test stage?

STEP 4: PLAN FOR ROLLOUT AND TRANSITION

Prepare for the rollout of the change initiative to the rest of the organization, or sections that are involved in this change effort. Using evaluative data from the pilot test, plan the schedule for rollout. Use increased credibility to change the systems, structures, and policies that do not support the vision (Kotter, 1996)

As discussed in Chapter 4, Bridges (1991) suggests a transition process that we, as individuals and as organizations, undergo during change. (See Related Reading at end of this chapter). Develop a plan for the celebration of endings, to allow people to celebrate what was and welcome what is to be. Remember that new starts are frightening to those who sense that this new beginning is the end of their careers.

An important component of the Change Initiative Plan is the measurement and evaluation of methods and processes. The plan should specifically state how the change intervention will be monitored, measures and what criteria for evaluation will be used. If a pre-post measurement is used, criteria for success needs to be clearly described and outlined.

Establish specific goals for organizational members to measure performance before, during, and after the change initiative has been implemented. Establish a plan for checking progress, providing feedback and coaching, and providing rewards and recognition.

Things to consider in planning for rollout:

- How will we implement the change initiative throughout the rest of the organization (or affected departments)?
- What exactly is ending?
- How can we celebrate the endings?
- How will we support the neutral zone?
- How will we get people enthused about this change?
- How do we get people involved and supportive of the change?
- How do we plan to address resistance to change?
- How will we know the change initiative is successful? Be specific.
- What forms of monitoring need to occur?
- What should be measured prior to the change initiative?
- What should be measured during the implementation?
- With what frequency should results be measured?
- How will we provide reinforcement to the change once it is underway?

STAGE 6. TAKE ACTION

Goal: *Implement the change initiative throughout the organization (or specific departments.) Create quick wins.*

It is now time to implement the change initiative according to the plan. With the implementation phase comes the need for heavy support in terms of resources and time. Continuous monitoring and evaluation needs to occur during this phase. The implementation plan also needs monitoring and any necessary adjustments made.

The Strategic Transition Team plays a critical role in this phase. They model the way for the change, provide heavy support, and recognize successes. They look for and praise those who have immediate success. They celebrate all steps that lead towards the desired vision, no matter how small. They look for pockets of success within the organization.

The Action Research Team and Implementation Teams are also critical to the success of implementation. They assume primary responsibility for implementation. Communications with each other and the STT are important.

These teams build a critical mass, developing strong commitment to the change initiative.

CELEBRATE EARLY WINS

Publicize the early wins through whatever means possible.   This will generate enthusiasm, especially for the "fence sitters" who have not become fully engaged in the change initiative.   The more the wins speak to organizational members, both personally and professionally, the more they want to contribute to further success.   The more visible, unambiguous, and meaningful, the better.

MONITOR, MEASURE, REINFORCE, REFINE, EVALUATE

Once the change initiative is underway, the challenge is to keep the process rolling.   This requires a dual focus: on the organization as a whole, and the people who are involved with the change.   In this stage, performance standards are addressed, as well as an analysis of how much and how well the change is implemented.

Continual follow up and evaluation are important to the success of the change initiative, measuring results, and making modifications as needed in order to achieve maximum success.   Don't settle for rhetorical change; make sure that what is being measured (quantitative and qualitative) represents reality.

Keep an eye on the present while looking to the future.   Don't loose focus on other important projects going on within the organization; at the same time, keep the focus on this change initiative until it is firmly established in the organization.

Things to consider while taking action:

- How is the plan working?
- Is everyone doing what they are responsible for?
- Are we meeting our targets in terms of securing resources and implementing the change?
- Does the plan need adjusting or customizing for any specific group or department?
- Are we monitoring the implementation closely?
- Are there areas that require extra support and are they getting it?
- Where is the implementation going well?
- Are we providing recognition for the individuals driving this success?
- Are we publicizing and celebrating the successes?
- Are we on target in terms of reaching our desired results?
- Are we keeping focus on this project while not loosing sight of other important projects?

STAGE 7. STABILIZE THE CHANGE

Goal: *Keep momentum going.   Nurture the new culture.   Integrate the change into the culture of the organization.*

As pointed out in the Change Process Model (Chapter 4), there is a critical stage during the change process where it is important to keep people from naturally reverting back to previous ways of doing things. To make change stick, change leaders throughout organizations nurture the new culture. This new culture develops through consistency of successful action over a sufficient period of time (Kotter, 2002).

Stabilizing change (refreezing) requires heavy organizational support. For transformation to occur, and the desired future vision to become reality, the change needs to be stabilized. Provide recognition to the people who maintain the new and different ways of doing things, especially when under pressure. Provide support to those who need it.

Things to consider while stabilizing change:

- In what ways has the culture of the organization changed?
- Has the change initiative become integrated into the way people act and do their jobs?
- Have we articulated how the change (new behaviors) has led to increased organizational success?
- Are we providing support to reinforce the change and keep the momentum going?
- Do organizational members feel good about the change? And their role in creating it?
- Are we providing recognition for those who have successfully made the transition?
- Are we using hiring and promotion opportunities in alignment with the new vision?
- Are we "refreezing" in new behaviors? Are organizational members beginning to behave in new ways without thinking about it?
- Does it feel as though we have reached our desired state?
- Have we achieved our "dream?"

Most major change initiatives are made up of a number of smaller projects that also tend to go through the staged process. So at any time, you might be halfway through the overall effort, finished with a few of smaller pieces, and just beginning other projects.

IMPLICATIONS FOR FACILITATING ORGANIZATIONAL CHANGE

To optimize the effectiveness of organizational change, the following basic principles need to be considered.

- For a large-scale change initiative, start with a winning project. Select a project that is associated with a high probability of success and small chance of failure. This provides a potentially high, quick return, and opens doors to other opportunities as a result of early success.

- Determine how to keep dual processes going—current business practice and the change initiative.
- Involve all organizational members in planning for change as appropriate to the change initiative. People need to understand the change and be given the opportunity to take part in the planning process or decision making. In doing so, they will likely adapt to the changes more readily.
- Involve employees at the implementation stage. Allow employees to have a voice and decision in how the change is to be operationalized at their level.
- Keep open dialogue about the change effort, from beginning to end. Share as much information as possible at all times. Remember that people can usually handle "bad news" and would rather deal with it upfront, rather than being surprised later on.
- Make stakeholders aware of the changes that are to take place and the expected outcome, addressing the benefits to them and how they will "play" in the changed state.
- Build a trusting work climate. Try to eliminate rumors and mistrust by keeping the lines of communication open. Try to alleviate their fears about the proposed changes.
- Ensure an early experience of successful change. When implementing the change, praise those who have had immediate successes, those who have helped make the change successful. Celebrate all steps that lead towards the desired state, no matter how small.
- Find a spark of enthusiasm and fan it. As Gareth Morgan (1993, p. 47) says, "Look for every seed of enthusiasm, and try to build pockets of success."
- Build a critical mass. Develop a strong and increasing body that is committed to the change.
- Quickly stabilize the change. Support those who individuals who maintain the new and different. Build the changed state into the organizational culture.

RELATED READINGS:

MANAGING TRANSITIONS[6]

In an earlier chapter on personal change, we examined William Bridges stages of transitions: ending, neutral zone, and new beginning. The application of this model to organizational change suggests the following and is predicated on four principles:

Purpose: Sell the problem;

Picture: Shared vision of the outcome;

Plan: Shared scenario for getting there; and

Part: What everyone can do to get there.

To manage endings:

- ❑ "Sell the problem" without denigrating the past.
- ❑ Allow people to understand what is over and what is not.
- ❑ Look for ways to soften the impact and protect people's interests.
- ❑ Allow people to feel that their losses are seen and acknowledged.
- ❑ Treat the past with respect.
- ❑ Use symbolic events to mark a clean break with "the way things were."
- ❑ Understand and accept grieving, and don't confuse it with bad morale or unacceptable behavior.
- ❑ Show how endings ensure continuity and organizational survival.

To manage the neutral zone:

- ❑ Use temporary solutions to neutral zone problems, including transition monitoring teams[7].
- ❑ Stay connected and show your concern for people.
- ❑ Use the neutral zone time creatively, both personally and organizationally; encourage creative solutions to problems.
- ❑ Use short-range goals to aim toward and establish check points along the way toward longer-term outcomes that you are seeking.
- ❑ (Re)build trust and make it safe to take risks.
- ❑ Help affected people to rethink their career plans.

To facilitate new beginnings:

- ❑ Explain the basic purpose behind the desired outcome and paint a picture of how the future state will look and feel.
- ❑ Fine tune the implementation plan using input from transition monitoring teams.
- ❑ Translate all changes into new behaviors and attitudes that will be needed to make them work.
- ❑ Update the reward structure so that you aren't rewarding old behaviors and attitudes.
- ❑ Focus on and publicize the early successes achieved by the changes.
- ❑ Build in the resources and structures that will be needed to make transition less disruptive.

CONDITIONS FOR CHANGE ASSESSMENT[8]

The difference between successful changes and those that don't work has nothing to do with the quality of the idea. It is the human side of planning and implementation strategies that usually marks the difference between success and failure. Consider a current major change, such as reorganization, reengineering, a merger, quality improvement effort, or the application of a new software system, and answer the following statements about the change management plan. (Respond from the viewpoint of manager or change agent.)

Your change management plan:	
1. Identifies all parties who have a stake in the outcome.	❑ Yes ❑ Somewhat ❑ No
2. Includes a way to get all stakeholders involved in the planning and implementation. If it is unrealistic to get all individual parties involved, a significant cross-section (including a diagonal slice of the organization) is encouraged to take part in planning.	❑ Yes ❑ Somewhat ❑ No
3. Allows you to keep your long-range goal in mind throughout the process, even when it might be tempting to get immersed in the details of the project or overwhelmed by the resistance.	❑ Yes ❑ Somewhat ❑ No
4. Provides ways to monitor the extent to which support is building or waning.	❑ Yes ❑ Somewhat ❑ No
5. Provides context for the change to stakeholders. Answers such questions as: What is the business reason for change? What are the conditions that led up to this change?	❑ Yes ❑ Somewhat ❑ No
6. Includes ways to keep the doors of communication open throughout the planning and implementation of the change.	❑ Yes ❑ Somewhat ❑ No
7. Includes multiple ways to get beneath the surface and hear what people really think about these changes.	❑ Yes ❑ Somewhat ❑ No
8. Lets people know that you've heard their concerns and value their input.	❑ Yes ❑ Somewhat ❑ No
9. Allows you to be influenced by their views.	❑ Yes ❑ Somewhat ❑ No
10. Gives people timely and candid information about the change.	❑ Yes ❑ Somewhat ❑ No

11. Allows you to get hot issues out in the open and stay within your own comfort zone.	❑ Yes ❑ Somewhat ❑ No
12. Provides a way for you to clearly state why you think this is an important issue and any recommendations you have developed. Addresses the question of "what's in it for me (or the group I represent)?"	❑ Yes ❑ Somewhat ❑ No
13. Offers a way for all the interested parties to communicate what's in it—and not in it—for them.	❑ Yes ❑ Somewhat ❑ No
14. Includes ways to try and pull together disparate interests in a mutually beneficial solution that meets most of the needs of most of the stakeholders.	❑ Yes ❑ Somewhat ❑ No
15. You believe the change management plan is sound and will work.	❑ Yes ❑ Somewhat ❑ No

Scoring

14-15	Yes Answers	Your change management plan is probably quite sound.
11-13	Somewhat Answers	You are at some risk. You may be overlooking some key aspects of ways to build support for change.
0-10	No Answers	This change is at great risk of failing.

Reflection

1. Where is your plan strong? How can you maximize these elements?

2. Where is your plan weak? What can be done to bolster the weak areas?

3. Develop a specific action plan for incorporating strategies to reduce resistance to change in your planned change initiative (also see Chapter 9).

ENDNOTES

[1] Adapted from The Dance of Change by Peter M. Senge, Kleiner, Roberts and Ross, copyright © 1999 by Peter Senge, Art Kleiner, Charlotte Roberts and Richard Ross. Used by permission of Doubleday, a division of Random House, Inc.

[2] Anderson, L. A., & Anderson, D. (2001). *The Change Leader's Roadmap*. Jossey Bass Pfeiffer: A Wiley Company, p. 43.

[3] See Emery, M., & Devane, T. (1999). Search Conference. In P. Holman, & T. Devane (Eds.), *The Change Handbook: Group Methods for Shaping the Future*. San Francisco: Berrett-Koehler Publishers, Inc., pp. 25-41.

[4] See Weisbord, M., & Janoff, S. (1999). In P. Holman, & T. Devane (Eds.), *The Change Handbook: Group Methods for Shaping the Future*. San Francisco: Berrett-Koehler Publishers, Inc., pp. 43-57.

[5] This section was adapted from John P. Kotter and Dan S. Cohen. (2002). *The Heart of Change: Real-Life Stories of How People Change Their Organizations*. Boston, MA: Harvard Business School Press, pp. 125-141; and John P. Kotter. (1996). *Leading Change*. Boston, MA: Harvard Business School Press, pp. 117-124.

[6] Adapted from William Bridges & Associates. (2002). *Leading Transition: Dealing Successfully with the Human Side of Change*. City of Anaheim Management Meeting, February 7, 2002; and Bridges, W. (1991). *Managing Transitions: Making the Most of Change*. Reading, MA: Addison-Wesley Publishing Company.

[7] A Transition Monitoring Team is a group of 7 to 12 people chosen from a wide cross section of the organization, who meet every 2 weeks with the goal of demonstrating that the organization wants to know how things are going for the employees, acting as a focus group to review plans before they are announced, and providing point of ready access to the organization's grapevine to correct misinformation and counter rumors.

[8] Adapted from Maurer, R. (2003). *Conditions for Change Assessment*. http://www.beyondresistance.com. Downloaded 6/16/03.

CHAPTER 9:

LEADING ORGANIZATIONAL CHANGE

LEADERSHIP HALL OF FAME

List your five most respected leaders, from public life and personal experience. Next to each mention two or three KEY QUALITIES that you find critical to his/her success.

1. _____   _____

                                                   _____

                                                   _____

2. _____   _____

                                                   _____

                                                   _____

3. _____   _____

                                                   _____

                                                   _____

4. _____   _____

                                                   _____

                                                   _____

5. _____   _____

                                                   _____

                                                   _____

Now write down the qualities you listed MOST OFTEN in descending order. These are keys to *why* you respect these leaders, and what sort of leader *you* respect.

1. _____   6. _____

2. _____   7. _____

3. _____   8. _____

4. _____   9. _____

5. _____   10. _____

Now, write down your definition of leadership

_____

_____

_____

_____

Much is written about leaders and change. Indeed, leadership is about change, moving an organization ahead into the future. Much is also written about organization development and change, and the role of the OD consultant/specialist assisting organizational leaders through change initiatives. Less is written about the type of leaders and leadership required to facilitate real change. What is required of a leader who wants to effectively initiate and sustain change and transformation? What style of leadership is best suited for facilitating this process? What is the relationship between leadership and the organization development process? How can leaders help reduce resistance to change?

LEADERSHIP AND MANAGEMENT IN ORGANIZATIONAL CHANGE

Leadership is the art and science of influencing behavior in people in order to accomplish goals, both personal and organizational. Leaders must face both outward to read the signs of pivotal changes and trends around them, as well as facing inward to empower and energize the organization and organizational members with vision and purpose. Burns (1978, p. 18) has defined leadership as being:

> when persons with certain motives and purposes mobilize . . .
> institutional, political, psychological, and other resources so as to
> arouse, engage, and satisfy the motives of followers.

Leadership is the heart and blood of any organization: it pumps vitality into the task and team processes of reading and responding to the challenges that rapid change requires. Leaders set the organizational direction with clear purposes and mobilize organizational resources for attaining often divergent goals. Many leadership experts contend that good leaders manage through their follower's point of view.

Traditional thought was that leaders were simply good managers. Contemporary thinking views differences and contends that all leaders are not necessarily good managers, nor are all managers good leaders. For our purposes in examining leadership and change, I will use Rost's definitions of leadership and management because it is focused on change and because it distinguishes between the two. Rost (1993, p. 102) defines leadership as:

> . . . an influence relationship among leaders and followers who intend
> real changes that reflect their mutual purposes.

In comparison, Rost (1993, p. 145) defines management as:

> . . . an authority relationship between at least one manager and one
> subordinate who coordinate their activities to produce and sell
> particular goods and/or services.

The first distinction refers to the use of coercion by a manager over a subordinate, implied as part of top-down authority. Influence relationships are multi-directional; influence flows between leaders and other leaders and leaders and followers in both directions.

The second distinction implies position: managers and subordinates occupy separate and distinct positions. The opposing thought is that leaders and followers do not refer to position; indeed a "manager" can lead and follow, as can a "subordinate."

The third distinction involves the underlying premise or focus of the two. Managers are in a position to meet organizational goals through the production and selling of goods and/or services. Leaders set the direction of the organization through the intention of real change. Leaders and followers join forces to attempt to change something; while managers and subordinates join forces to produce a product.

The last distinction refers to the "common purposes developed over time as followers and leaders interact . . . about the changes they intend" (Rost, 1993, p. 151). This is different from a coordination of activities, which allows for independent goals in order to get the job done. These activities include such functions as staffing, decision-making, and planning, which are typically functions of management.

Rost's definition is closely related to general assumptions of organization development. One important note is that, in any change effort, both sets of activities, setting direction and meeting goals, are critical. The difference from a more traditional view of leadership is that leadership is not about position, and it is assumed that leadership can happen anywhere in the organization by anyone with ideas. In terms of facilitating change, it is also helpful to examine different functions that the "role of manager" and the "role of leader" play[1].

MANAGEMENT

Planning-budgeting, allocating resources; designed to produce orderly results to maintain the status quo.

Organizing, Staffing-create organizational and human systems that can implement plans as precisely and efficiently as possible; organizational design.

Controlling-problem solving, monitoring results; push people in the right direction; compare system behavior with plan and take action when a deviation is detected.

Leadership-Vision-setting a direction and course for the future; serves the interests of stakeholders; easily translated into strategy.

Alignment-communicate with all who can help or block implementation; empower people at all levels to initiate action; create coalitions; gain commitments.

Motivation-satisfy basic human needs such as achievement, sense of belonging, self-esteem, and recognition; inspiration.

From this perspective, leaders are responsible for setting the course for the organization to follow; creating and communicating the vision; empowering people to take action; motivating and getting people to want to follow the vision. Managers are responsible for getting the work done within the organization: planning, organizing, staffing, controlling. Both are crucial for real and intended change to occur. O'Toole (1996, p. xi) suggests,

> The task of a leader is to bring about constructive and necessary change; the responsibility of a leader is to bring about that change in a way that is responsive to the true and long-term needs of all constituencies; and the greatest source of power available to a leader is the trust that derives from faithfully serving followers.

It is well recognized that if organizations are to succeed, they need to cultivate and grow better leaders. People who not only can navigate the heavy seas of today's global business environment themselves, but who can inspire their colleagues to realize greater achievements than ever before. This not only applies to for-profit organizations, but also to non-profit, voluntary, and non-governmental organizations (NGOs). The search is on for more effective leadership strategies and philosophies.

Most writers and practitioners agree that while ideas for change are frequently initiated at lower levels of the organization, long-term, organization-wide change and transformation requires executive leadership initiative, support, modeling, and sustained focus. However, it is also acknowledged that the leader does not lead the change alone, and that most organizational transformation is not the sole work of a charismatic or heroic leader. Embedded within the definition of organization development is the assumption that the leader engages organizational members in moving the organization forward towards the desired future state, using action research methodology for facilitating change. Gone are the days in which we expect one leader to have all the answers. The empowerment of organizational members at all levels in the organization to initiate action is a major assumption of leading change.

As discussed, the role of management is to target objectives, budget for them, create plans to achieve objectives, organize for implementation, and control the process to keep it on track. Transformation does not involve leadership alone; good management is also essential. As Kotter points out, charismatic leaders are often poor managers, yet have a skill in convincing us that all we need to do is follow them, and the details will work themselves out.

In reality, a balance of leadership and management is required, as shown in Figure 9-1. Along with vision, managerial expertise is required: financial expertise, technical knowledge, strategic insight, and operational skill.

Figure 9-1. The Relationship of Leadership, Management, and Successful Transformation.

	Management	
++ Leadership	Transformation efforts can be successful for a while, but often fail after short-term results become erratic.	All highly successful transformation efforts combine good leadership with good management.
+	Transformation efforts go nowhere.	Short-term results are possible, especially through cost-cutting effort. But real transformation programs have trouble getting started and major, long-term change is rarely achieved.
	0 + ++	

Source: Kotter, J. P. (1996). *Leading Change*. Boston: Harvard Business School Press, p. 129-130.

TYPES OF LEADERSHIP

Senge et al (1999, p. 12) argue that little significant change can occur if it is driven from the top, claiming a top-down approach to change does not necessarily establish genuine commitment at all levels of the organization. Senge (1999, p. 45) argues "leaders are those people who 'walk ahead', people who are genuinely committed to deep change in themselves and in their organizations. They lead through developing new skills, capabilities, and understandings. And they come from many places within an organization." The types of leadership required leading change take on three forms:[2]

1. **Formal, executive leadership** is responsible for integrating, resourcing, and orchestrating the activities of the organization and various project teams. This form of leadership provides support for line leaders, in terms of championship, protection, and mentoring. Effective executive leaders build an environment for learning through articulating guiding ideas, conscious attention to a learning infrastructure, recognizing the need to change themselves (the executive team itself), and modeling the way in the gradual process of evolving norms and behaviors of a learning culture.

2. **Local line leaders** are individuals with significant business responsibility, heading organizational units that are large enough to be meaningful microcosms of the larger organization, and autonomy to be able to undertake meaningful change initiatives independent of the larger

organization. Their role is to sanction significant practical experiments, creating a sense of intrapreneurship, and to lead through their active participation in these experiments.

3. **Internal networkers,** or community builders, requires individual leadership in every team member that incorporates initiative, self-management capacity, readiness to make hard decisions, embodiment of organizational values, and a sense of business responsibility that was once limited to a few people at the top of the organization. These individuals are the "seed carriers" of the new culture, who can move freely about the organization to find other like-minded individuals who are predisposed to bringing about change, help out in organizational experiments, and aid in the diffusion of new learning.

GUIDING PRINCIPLES AND VALUES OF CHANGE LEADERS

> Moral and effective leaders listen to their followers *because* they respect them and *because* they honestly believe that the welfare of followers is the end of leadership (and not that followers are the means to the leader's goals). James O'Toole.

O'Toole's (1996, p. 9) quote may seem odd to add to a discussion of leadership in relation to organization development and change. However leadership is about ideas and values, understanding the differing and conflicting needs of followers, energizing followers to pursue a better end state than they thought possible, creating a values-based umbrella large enough to accommodate the various interests of followers, but focused enough to direct all their energies in pursuit of a common goal.

The primary role of the leader is to create effective followers; the task of the leader is to bring about constructive and necessary change; the responsibility of the leader is to bring about that change in a way that is responsive to the true and long-term needs of all constituencies; and the greatest source of power available to a leader is the trust that derives from faithfully serving followers. Emerging thought on leadership suggests that leaders must set aside what may be a natural instinct to lead by push and must instead adopt the "unnatural behavior of . . . leading by the pull of inspiring values."[3] In order to effect true change, one must inspires others to lead the transformation.

SERVANT LEADERSHIP

While not a new "model" of leadership, servant-leadership is gaining popularity in organizational thinking on how to be as a leader. Robert Greenleaf (1991, p. 7), the eminent source on servant-leadership as an organizational philosophy, defines it as [beginning] with the natural feeling that one wants to serve, to serve first. Then conscious choice brings one to aspire to lead. He is sharply different from one who is leader first . . . for such it will be a later choice to serve—after leadership is established.

The difference "manifests itself in the care taken by the servant-first to make sure that other people's highest priority needs are being served" (Greenleaf, 1991, p. 7.) He contrasts this to the leader-first as one who is perhaps driven to "assuage an unusual power drive or to acquire material possessions" (p. 7.) Individuals fall somewhere along the continuum of wanting to serve and wanting to lead. As with organization development, servant-leadership has certain distinguishing characteristics:[4]

1. **Listening**. Traditionally, leaders have been valued for their communication and decision making skills. Servant-leaders must reinforce these important skills by making a deep commitment to listening intently to others. Servant-leaders seek to identify and clarify the will of the group with a desire to understand what is said and not said. Listening also encompasses getting in touch with one's inner voice with reflection on what is being said.

2. **Empathy**. Servant-leaders strive to understand and empathize with others. People need to be accepted and recognized for their special and unique spirit. The servant-leader assumes the good intentions of others and does not reject them as people, even when forced to reject their behavior or performance.

3. **Healing**. A servant-leader understands that healing is a powerful force for transformation and integration. Greenleaf (1991) writes, "There is something subtle communicated to one who is being served and led, if implicit in the compact between the servant leader and led, is the understanding that the search for wholeness is something that they share" (p. 27). The servant-leader seizes the opportunity to help make self and others whole, addressing broken spirits and emotional hurts.

4. **Awareness**. General awareness, and especially self-awareness, strengthens the servant-leader. Making a commitment to foster awareness can be challenging, as Greenleaf (1991) says, "Able leaders are usually sharply awake and reasonably disturbed. They are not seekers of solace. They have their own inner security" (p. 20). Servant-leaders use awareness to understand issues involving ethics and values, viewing situations from an integrated, holistic position.

5. **Persuasion**. Servant-leaders seek to convince rather than coerce compliance. They rely on persuasion, rather than positional authority in making decisions. A servant-leader seeks to become effective at consensus building.

6. **Conceptualization**. Servant-leaders seek to survey their abilities to "dream great dreams," (Greenleaf, 1991, p. 9) the ability to look and think beyond day-to-day reality. The servant-leader nurtures others' capacity to work

outside their usual frame of thinking. They continually encourage others to share ideas, even when those ideas may seem a bit unusual.

7. **Foresight**. Greenleaf calls this the central ethic of leadership. The servant-leader, through foresight, is able to understand the lessons from the past, realities of the present, and the likely consequence of a decision for the future. The servant-leader honors intuition.

8. **Stewardship**. The servant-leader holds the organization in trust for the greater good of society, feels a deep sense of ownership in the success of others and the organization. The servant-leader shares responsibility for what the organization will become, and chooses service over self-interest.

9. **Commitment to the Growth of People**. Servant-leaders believe that people have intrinsic value beyond their employable skills. Servant-leaders are deeply committed to and foster the personal, spiritual, and professional growth of others in the organization. They take personal interest in the ideas and suggestions of others, and encourage worker involvement in decision-making.

10. **Building Community**. Understanding that the shift from local communities to large institutions as the primary shaper of human lives changed our perceptions and caused a certain sense of loss, servant-leaders seek to identify ways to build community within the organization. The servant-leader publicly commends and recognizes others for accomplishments achieved within and outside the workplace.

Greenleaf's metaphor of servant-as-leader is well connected to the guiding principles of the emerging and future field of organization development. Emerging thought suggests the leader does not act alone to create organizational vision; does not dictate that vision down into the organization; does not implement change simply for the sake of change. Emerging thought suggests the OD practitioner is no longer viewed as the content expert; rather the primary role of the OD practitioner is process facilitation, facilitating the client organization towards discovery of the processes that disable and/or enable their success. Greenleaf's "best test" (1991, p. 7) is one that fits well within this emerging OD framework:

> The best test . . . is: do those served grow as persons; do they, while being served, become healthier, wiser, freer, more autonomous, more likely themselves to become servants? And, what is the effect on the least privileged in society; will he benefit, or at least, will he not be further deprived?

This suggests involvement of those impacted by the decisions being made regarding the future of the organization. Leaders are encouraged to enable those led to grow and develop, to become active partners in the change process.

SERVANT-LEADERSHIP AND ORGANIZATIONAL STRUCTURE

> . . . caring for persons, the more able and the less able serving each
> other, is the rock upon which a good society is built . . . if a better
> society is to be built, one that is more just and more loving, one that
> provides greater creative opportunity for its people, then the most
> open course is to raise both the capacity to serve and the very
> performance as servant of existing major institutions by new
> regenerative forces operating within them (Greenleaf, 1976, p. 1).

As structure drives behavior, some consideration needs to be given to
organizational design, and its alignment to the previously mentioned guiding
values. Greenleaf discusses formal and informal organizational structure, the
latter responding more to leadership, resulting in "team effort and a network of
constructive interpersonal relationships that supports the total effort." (1976, p.
10) He refers to informal initiatives as the glue that holds "the formal structure
together and makes it function well;" (1976, p. 9) therefore acknowledging that
the combination of formal and informal structures gives an institution its
organizational strength. For optimal performance, a large institution needs
administration for order and consistency, and leadership so as to mitigate the
effects of administration on initiative and creativity and to build team effort to
give these qualities extraordinary encouragement (Greenleaf, 1976, p. 11). This
follows with the earlier discussion of leadership and management by Kotter,
Rost, and others.

Greenleaf, as one of the early challengers to traditional hierarchical design,
discusses two types of organizational structures, as depicted in Figures 9-2 and
9-3. The first is representative of the familiar pyramid found within most
organizations.

Figure 9-2. Traditional Hierarchical Organizational Structure

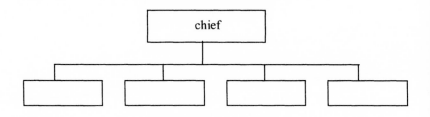

The second, based on the principle of primus inter pares or first among equals, suggests there is still a leader, but he is not chief. In Greenleaf's words, "It is important that the primus constantly tests and proves his leadership among a group of able peers" (1976, p. 11). He suggests that organizational success will only be met if more people are encouraged to serve as leaders, everywhere in the organization. He argued that the structure of equals with a primus will enable more leaders to grow and develop, supporting the concept of building a leadership corps.

Figure 9-3. Primus Inter Pares

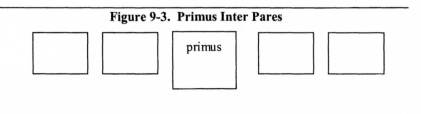

The stated purpose of organization development is to increase organizational effectiveness, and is most effective when linked to business strategy. Servant-leadership is being applied strategically in organizations of all types, replacing traditional hierarchical decision making with a servant-leader approach (Spears, 2002) What do companies that practice servant leadership have in common, and how do they resemble organization development principles? They focus on a long-term quality workforce through sustainable practices focused on the employee, the customer, the product, and the bottom line (Ruschman, 2002). There is a strong emphasis on such basic core values as: concern for and belief in people, valuing individual differences, honesty, building trusting relationships, fairness, responsible behavior, high standards of business ethics.

Greenleaf (1991) suggests, "An institution starts on a course toward people-building with leadership that has a firmly established context of people first.

With that, the right actions fall naturally into place" (p. 31). Relationships are cultivated between customers and employees. These relationships are strengthened by community outreach. Trust is another common theme; it is acknowledged that effective leaders generate trust.

Servant leadership offers new ways to capitalize on the knowledge and wisdom of all employees, thereby creating a learning organization. It allows for business strategies to be widely shared throughout the company rather than with only a few top executives, and it encourages individuals to grow from just doing a job into having fully engaged minds and hearts.

We have established that the role of the leader is to drive and facilitate organizational change. The servant-as-leader metaphor would suggest that a leader, best prepared to facilitate this change, is required to rethink basic underlying assumptions we hold about human capability and individual contribution; our beliefs and expectations regarding organizing human effort; how we value individual contribution; our beliefs about what and who is responsible for morale and motivation.

Greenleaf (1991, p. 9) asks the important question, "What are you trying to do?" The mark of a leader is that he or she is better than most at pointing the direction, showing the way for others. It doesn't matter how a goal is created, through group consensus or the leader acting on inspiration, the leader knows what the goal is and how to articulate it to others, providing certainty and purpose to others who may have difficulty in achieving it for themselves.

RESISTANCE TO CHANGE

When consulting with clients, I frequently experience what appears to be resistance to change. In the beginning of my consulting career, this was surprising to me, as I was bringing new technology to my clients, technology that would ultimately make their jobs easier and more challenging. I assumed clients would be pleased and excited about the opportunities to learn new ways of handling their everyday tasks. However, quite frequently what I observed was fear, anxiety, and in some cases absolute resistance. Only when I began to examine the social and human dynamics of change did I begin to understand this resistance.

One of my key discoveries was that when the organization *involved* the end users of this technology in the decision making, there was increased excitement about the project, less fear and anxiety, less resistance. These individuals played an important role in the success of the project, often significantly reducing the chaos associated with the change. On the other hand, when the ends users were not involved in the project upfront, rather brought in at the implementation phase, there was increased resistance, and far less enthusiasm about the change initiative.

As we saw in Chapter 4, some of us have a natural propensity towards change, while others experience it with more difficulty. For some, change carries the threat of uncertainty and loss of control; for others, it is an opportunity for challenge and growth. Facilitators of change must understand the human dynamics of change, the impact of the very people most needed for successful implementation of innovative efforts. First, let's examine the root cause of resistance to change.

ROOT CAUSE(S) OF RESISTANCE TO CHANGE

O'Toole (1996) offers several speculations about the root causes of resistance to change, including:

- **Homeostasis**: continual change is not a natural condition of life, resistance to change is a healthy human instinct.
- **Inertia**: when a large body is in motion, it takes considerable force to alter its course.
- **Satisfaction**: most people are perfectly content with the status quo, in fact, most people can't imagine any alternative to the status quo.
- **Lack of ripeness**: change occurs only when certain preconditions have been met; such conditions are rare and cannot be forced.
- **Fear**: humans have an innate fear of the unknown; we prefer to take our chances with the devil we know.
- **Self-interest**: change may be good for others or even for the system as a whole, but unless it is specifically good for us, we will resist it.
- **Lack of self-confidence**: change threatens our self-esteem; new conditions require of us fresh skills, abilities, attitudes, but we lack the confidence that we are up to the new challenges.
- **Future shock**: when people are overwhelmed by major changes, they hunker down and resist because the species is capable of only so much adaptation.
- **Futility**: since change is largely superficial, cosmetic, and hence illusory, why take part in the charade when we know that the power structure of society will remain unchanged?
- **Lack of knowledge**: we don't know how to change (or what to change); ignorance and faulty analysis get in the way of effective change.
- **Ego**: change requires that the powerful admit that they have been wrong.
- **Short-term thinking**: people can't defer gratification.
- **Myopia**: because we can't see beyond the tips of our noses, we can't see that change is in our broader self-interest.
- **Chauvinistic conditioning**: the way we do it is right; they are wrong; and if you are one of us and you advocate what they do, you are disloyal.
- **Fallacy of the exception**: change might work elsewhere, but we are different; in fact we can't learn anything from others unless their situation is exactly the same as ours.

- **Ideology**: because we each have different worldviews and inherently conflicting values, any plan for change will divide the community into adversarial camps.
- **Institutionalism**: individuals may change, but groups do not; indeed, the prime task of the organization is self-preservation and self-perpetuation.
- **The rectitude of the powerful**: the best and brightest have set us on the current course; who are we to question the wisdom of our leaders?
- **Determinism**: there is nothing anyone can do to bring about purposeful change; though change might occur, it is not the result of conscious human action.

As O'Toole points out, these hypotheses all seem to be correct, all are seen at play in society and organizations from time to time. Also, the lines of distinction between the various hypotheses are blurry; several of these factors may act in concert with one another. The conclusion is that *everything* in society seems to conspire against the receptivity to change. Fortunately, each fails the simplest test of logic: we can easily imagine an exception to each "rule."

RESISTANCE TO CHANGE IN ORGANIZATIONS

Resistance to change in organizations is based on a few basic factors: who brings about the change; what kind of change it is; what is the benefit to individual organizational members; the procedures for instituting change and transition; and the leadership attitude towards the change. Bridges proposes that *transition* is what causes stress in change and leads to potential resistance, especially if the transitional change is not well executed, resulting in: [5]

- Loss of identity and what is familiar.
- Disorientation and uncertainty; a feeling of being "left in the dark" and uncertainty about what is coming next.
- People possessing inadequate skills for functioning in the new state.
- People's lack of understanding of the need for change or the benefits of the new state.
- Homeostasis or inertia—people's natural resistance to learning new skills or behaviors.
- People's emotional pain or grief at the loss of the past.
- Poor planning and implementation of the change, which creates confusion and resentment.
- Unclear expectations about what will be required to succeed in the new state.
- Fear about being successful or capable in the new state.
- Inadequate support in the new state.

Bridges contends that it is the *transition* that people resist, not the change itself. We discussed strategies for managing transition and reducing resistance in Chapter 8. In her classic article "Managing the Human Side of Change", Rosabeth Moss Kanter (1985) listed the ten most common reasons managers encounter resistance to change. I've included an approach for dealing with each to expand our discussion of strategies for dealing with resistance to change.

Loss of control. Most people want and need to feel in control of the events around them. Change is exciting when it is initiated by us, threatening when done to us.

- Allow room for participation in the planning of change. Leave choices within the overall decision to change. Ownership counts in getting commitment to action.

Excess uncertainty. People need to know what the next step is going to be, where they will be as a result of the change. They want to have a comfort level with the impending change. Managers who do not share information face a great deal of resistance to change.

- Provide a clear picture of the change, a "vision" with details about the future state. Share information about the change strategy to the fullest extent possible. Divide a big change into more manageable and familiar steps; let people take small steps first.

Surprise, Surprise! Resistance occurs when changes are sprung on people without proper groundwork or preparation.

- Minimize surprises. Give people advance warning about new requirements. Allow for digestion of change requests, a chance to become accustomed to the idea of change before making a commitment.

The "Difference Effect". Change requires people to become conscious of, and to question, familiar routines and habits. Commitment to change is more likely to occur when the change is not presented as a wild difference, but rather as continuous, with tradition.

- Minimize or reduce the number of "differences" introduced by the change, leaving as many habits and routines as possible in place. Learn from history.

Loss of face. People are certain to resist, if accepting a change means admitting that the way things were done in the past was wrong. Commitment to change is ensured when past actions are put into perspective as the apparently right way to do it then, but now times are different.

- Show how the future state builds on the current or past state. Acknowledge individual's past contributions and ask for their support to build a future state. Show how circumstances have changed, requiring a new way of doing business. Repeatedly demonstrate your own commitment to the change.

Concerns about future competence. Sometimes people resist change because of personal concerns about their future ability to be effective after the change.

- Offer positive reinforcement for competence; let people know they can do it. Look for and reward pioneers, innovators, and early successes to serve as models.

- Provide sufficient training and education, as well as a chance to practice the new skills or actions. Make standards and requirements clear, tell people exactly what is expected of them in the future state.

Ripple effects. People may resist change for reasons connected to their own activities. The change may disrupt other kinds of plans or projects. The change may also negate promises the organization has previously made.

- Introduce change with flexibility and sensitivity. For example, if possible, allow people who have children to finish out the school year before relocating, or managers to finish an important project, or a department to go through a transition period before facing an abrupt change. Acknowledge that a change in one area will affect other areas; be supportive of people as they adjust to the new situation.

More work. Change means more work, requires more energy, more time, greater mental preoccupation. There is ample reason to resist change, if people do not want to put out the effort or feel they are already stretched to capacity.

- Help people find or feel compensated for the extra time and energy that change requires. Acknowledge that the change will more than likely take new effort initially, but that there will come a time when it becomes routine.

Past resentments. Anyone who has ever had a gripe against the organization is likely to resist change.

- Listen to and respond to old grievances that have been left unresolved. Try and involve these individuals in the planning for the change; perhaps the future state will resolve some of the past issues they have with the organization.

Sometimes the threat is real. Sometimes change does create winners and losers. Managing change well means recognizing its political realities.

- Avoid creating obvious "losers" from the change. However, if there are some, be honest with them, early on.
- Allow expressions of nostalgia and grief for the past; allow a period of ending. Then create excitement about the future.

Gareth Morgan (1993) suggests that "people are reluctant to relax their hold on existing reality unless they feel that they have somewhere to turn." An example of this can be seen in the difficulty with the effective implementation of empowerment or participative management. Many organizations have found managers to be resistant to these programs because they feel a loss of control through employee empowerment. Additionally, there are some employees who only want to "do their job", and are resistant to taking on increased decision making and responsibility. This empowerment is tough for both managers and employees, both faced with reluctance to letting go of their traditional roles. It is crucial for leaders to show how the impending change is beneficial to both them and to the future of the organization.

Peter Block (2001) urges us to avoid the phrase "overcoming resistance", that this suggests the use of data and logical arguments will convince the change participant not to be resistant. He suggests there is no way to talk clients out of their resistance, because resistance is an emotional process. Behind the resistance are certain feelings; you cannot talk people out of how they are feeling. A better strategy is to allow feelings to be expressed freely.

WHO IS THE RESISTOR: REFRAMING THE QUESTION

The central question posed by O'Toole (1996) is, "Why do would-be leaders resist embracing the very ideas that would motivate followers?" In reframing our thinking of followers resisting leaders, we examine why leaders fail to do the things necessary to overcome followers' natural resistance to change. He suggests leaders should listen to the true needs of followers; reframe issues in order to address those needs; and set aside their own ego in order to energize followers to achieve the high objectives that are in the best interest of both leaders and followers.

Leaders should reassure organizational members as clearly as possible about those areas that present no need for concern and those areas likely to see benefits, along with establishing realistic expectations about the pain and challenges that will occur. If decisions have already been made, for example, a major restructuring will occur, leaders should make clear that the sacrifice and pain will be shared across the organization and at all levels. Conversely, if extensive positive outcomes are expected, policies for sharing the gains should be clearly articulated (French and Bell, 1999).

PARADIGM SHIFT: ORGANIZATIONAL CHANGE BEGINS WITHIN THE LEADER

Many argue that the most compelling reason organization development efforts fail is because of leadership, or rather ineffective leadership. When change fails to occur as planned, the cause is almost always to be found at a deep level, rooted in the inappropriate behavior, beliefs, attitudes, and assumptions of leaders. Effective change begins when leaders effectively begin to change themselves.[6]

In leading transformational change, one must change one's frame of reference, such as worldview, beliefs about people, and view of management and leadership (Covey, 1992, p. 173). This has the ability to open up new insights, knowledge, and understanding, and allows us to see the situation in a totally new light. Senge et al (1999, p. 6) support this, saying,

> Sources of problems associated with failed change initiatives cannot be remedied by more expert advice, better consultants, or more committed managers. The sources lie in our basic ways of thinking. If these do not change, any new "input" will end up producing the same fundamentally unproductive types of actions.

Emerging thought on leading change provides a strong case for inclusion, suggesting that leaders who do not respect and trust their followers cannot lead them effectively into the future. Effective change leaders believe in and respect those led, including the people affected by the change in the change process. Therefore to effectively lead change and transformation, leaders are encouraged to follow these guidelines:[7]

- Scan the environment: through action research, identify major trends likely to affect the organization. Define the implications of those trends to provide essential background for planning change, i.e., sell the problem/opportunity.
- Revisit the mission on a regular basis: ask, What is our mission? Who is our customer? What does our customer value? What are our results? What is our plan?
- Ban the hierarchy; practice inclusive leadership extended over all stakeholders, enable organizational members to lead by sharing information, fostering a sense of community.
- Create a consistent system of rewards, structures, processes, and communication aligned with the desired future vision.
- Lead from the front, don't push from the rear; model desired behaviors.
- Commit to the principle of opportunity, allowing all followers the chance to make a greater contribution to the organization.
- Inspire a vision of continuous change, renewal, innovation, and learning.
- Adhere to the moral principle of respect for people.
- Celebrate and encourage divergent viewpoints.
- Manage paradox such as concern for both continuity and change, short- and long-term, accountability and freedom, planning and flexibility, leadership and participation.
- Energize a cadre of leaders, formal and informal, to lead change; create the space for all organizational members to lead.
- Practice personal mastery, commitment to continual learning from experience, through training, education, listening and learning from others. Continually expand competence; develop new skills and interests.
- Develop a service orientation, thoughtfulness and respect of others, partner with others.
- Exhibit positive energy; optimistic, positive, upbeat attitude.
- Believe in others. While being aware of others' weaknesses, realize that behavior and potential are two different things; believe in the unseen potential of all people; create a climate for growth and opportunity.
- See life as an adventure, have an internal sense of security, face new opportunities with enthusiasm.
- Practice synergism, building on strengths of self and others, positioning oneself to complement the weaknesses of others.

AND FINALLY...

I draw from Peter Senge (1999, pp. 55-56) for final remarks and suggestions to start with the basics in leading profound change. While nothing happens without commitment, initial commitment is almost always limited to a handful of people. Many "less committed" people may join and contribute, if they are interested, have important capabilities and expertise, or are part of the "formal team." But in the end, everything depends on that core group of committed people. Therefore, even before you begin, find a few partners who really share your values and passions.

Start small, grow steadily. Identify key practical issues to work on. Even executive leaders, intent on changing the entire organization's directions, can benefit from a strategy of starting small.

You must be willing to develop your own learning capabilities, and to be part of teams developing their learning capabilities. You must be open to the possibility of changing yourself.

Intended results and useful tools are more important than a detailed plan. With significant change initiatives, there are often no answers, and experimentation, observation and reflection are essential. However, practical tools and an approach with which to begin are also essential. Equally essential is clarity around the issues at stake and the aims of the undertaking. People will never commit fully if the goals have little real meaning to them.

If you're short on time and you're up against the wall, fix the crisis first. However, be mindful that reacting to the crisis is not enough. It will not lay a foundation for sustained learning.

Effective leaders understand that rather than driving change, they need to participate, be willing to change themselves. As they participate they also know that there will be challenges, and that their greatest internal resources will be devoted to dealing with the forces that can limit the momentum they have helped to unleash.

Activities at the end of this chapter encourage you to examine your personal definition of leadership, paying particular attention to leading change. This will assist in your further examination of "self as practitioner." Despite certain myths about leadership, i.e., you are born a leader, I believe leadership can be developed (Jackson, 1998). In the final chapter you will find an activity on values, which I find very helpful to developing a personal philosophy of leadership and facilitating organizational change.

PERSONAL DEFINITION OF LEADERSHIP

How do you define leadership? Please write your personal definition of leadership below. You may draw from the readings in this chapter, from any literature source, and from your own personal experience. Pay particular attention to the concept of leading organizational change.

_____

_____

_____

_____

_____

_____

_____

_____

_____

_____

_____

10 CHARACTERISTICS OF SERVANT-LEADER

Assess yourself on the ten characteristics of servant leadership.

Listening	Conceptualization
Empathy	Foresight
Healing	Stewardship
Awareness	Commitment to Growth of Others
Persuasion	Building Community

1. Which characteristics have you observed as critical to effective leadership of change in others? Think of a recent example.
2. Which characteristics have been most important to your leading and facilitating change? Think of a recent example.
3. Which characteristics are most challenging to you personally? Think of a recent example.
4. How might you work on and improve those that are challenging and develop more of the characteristics deemed effective in leading change?

ENDNOTES

[1] Adapted from John P. Kotter (May-June 1990). What Leaders Really Do, *Harvard Business Review*, pp. 103-111.

[2] Drawn from Bridges, W. (1996). Leading the de-jobbed organization. In F. Hesselbein, M. Goldsmith, & R. Beckhard (Eds.), *The leader of the future: New visions, strategies, and practices for the next era*: 11-18. San Francisco: Jossey-Bass Publishers; Senge, P. M. (1996). Leading learning organizations: The bold, the powerful, and the invisible. In F. Hesselbein, M. Goldsmith, & R. Beckhard (Eds.), *The leader of the future: New visions, strategies, and practices for the next era*: 41-58. San Francisco: Jossey-Bass Publishers; and Senge, P.; Kleiner, A.; Roberts, C.; Ross, R.; Roth, G.; & Smith, B. (1999). *The Dance of Change: The Challenges to Sustaining Momentum in Learning Organizations*. New York: Currency Doubleday.

[3] O'Toole, J. (1996). *Leading Change: The Argument for Values-Based Leadership*. New York: Ballentine Books, p. 11. See also Greenleaf, R. K. (1991). *The Servant As Leader*. Indianapolis, IN: The Robert K. Greenleaf Center. Note: Originally published in 1970 by Robert K. Greenleaf.

[4] This list draws from Greenleaf, R. K. (1991). *The Servant As Leader*. Indianapolis, IN: The Robert K. Greenleaf Center. Note: Originally published in 1970 by Robert K. Greenleaf; Spears, L. C. (Ed.). (1998). *Insights on Leadership: Service, Stewardship, Spirit, and Servant-leadership*. New York: John Wiley & Sons, Inc.; and Spears, L. C., & Lawrence, M. (Eds.). (2002). *Focus on Leadership: Servant-leadership for the Twenty-first Century*. New York: John Wiley & Sons, Inc.

[5] See Anderson, D., & Anderson, L. A. (2001). *Beyond change Management: Advanced Strategies for Today's Transformational* Leaders. Jossey-Bass Pfeiffer: A Wiley Company; Bridges, W. (1980). *Transitions: Making Sense of Life's Changes*. Reading, MA: Addison-Wesley Publishing Company; Bridges, W. (1991). *Managing Transitions: Making the Most of Change*. Reading, MA: Addison-Wesley Publishing Company, and Bridges, W. (2001). *The Way of Transition: Embracing Life's Most Difficult Moments*. Cambridge, MA: Persues Publishing.

[6] e.g., O'Toole, J. (1996). *Leading Change: The Argument for Values-Based Leadership*. New York: Ballentine Books; Senge, P.; Kleiner, A.; Roberts, C.; Ross, R.; Roth, G.; & Smith, B. (1999). *The Dance of Change: The Challenges to Sustaining Momentum in Learning Organizations*. New York: Currency Doubleday.

[7] This list draws from Covey, S. R. (1992). *Principle-Centered Leadership*. New York: Simon & Schuster.; Greenleaf, R. K. (1991). *The Servant As Leader*. Indianapolis, IN: The Robert K. Greenleaf Center. Note: Originally published in 1970 by Robert K. Greenleaf.; Hesselbein, F. (2002). *Hesselbein on Leadership*. San Francisco, CA: Jossey-Bass.; O'Toole, J. (1996). *Leading Change: The Argument for Values-Based Leadership*. New York: Ballentine Books; and Senge, P. M. (1996). Leading learning organizations: The bold, the powerful, and the invisible. In F. Hesselbein, M. Goldsmith, & R. Beckhard (Eds.), *The leader of the future: New visions, strategies, and practices for the next era*: 41-58. San Francisco: Jossey-Bass Publishers; and Senge, P.; Kleiner, A.; Roberts, C.; Ross, R.; Roth, G.; & Smith, B. (1999). *The Dance of Change: The Challenges to Sustaining Momentum in Learning Organizations*. New York: Currency Doubleday.

CHAPTER 10:
SELF AS PRACTITIONER

Who is the self that practices Organization Development? Parker Palmer, in *The Courage to Teach* (1998) poses the central "who" question. While technique is important, it is only part of the equation of successful OD practice. In addition to asking <u>what</u> shall we practice, <u>how</u> shall we use interventions in our practice, and <u>why</u> should we use these interventions, we need to ask the *who* question – who is the self that practices? How does the quality of my selfhood form, or deform, the way I relate to my clients, my practice, my colleagues, my world (p. 4).

The field of organization development is exciting. Organizational change is fraught with many challenges; even a change that appears to be quite simple deals with human and social dynamics. This field addresses the issues surrounding *people* and organizational change, for without organizational members doing something different, there is no change. All the best technology, and best planning cannot guarantee that people will embrace the change. Traditional organizations do not always acknowledge this, and indeed today, many traditional managers believe that "leading by fear" is the way to create change. Organization development has emerged to allow the voice of all organizational members to be heard and all organizational talent to be captured.

As a facilitator of organizational change, it is imperative to develop a personal philosophy or "credo" from which to operate. OD consultants are invited to intervene in numerous situations, some which will be more comfortable than others. Understanding your own assumptions about organizations and its members will help guide you in the process of working with clients. There may be times when it is best to decline engagement with a client whose values do not match your own. There will definitely be times when you need to deliver "bad news;" understanding how you perceive organizational data will guide you. The issue of content expert consultation versus process facilitation is one worthy of deliberation.

It is important to always be clear about who the client is, what their intentions are, and how you will aid them in meeting their goals. Being honest with the client (and with yourself) about your range of expertise is important to maintaining an ethical practice. For example, consider how you would deal with discovering the "real problem" is the manager/client that hired you? Would you do the job you were hired to do? Confront the manager? Select another option?

In this book, I've included several questionnaires and activities that hopefully have been helpful to developing your sense of self as practitioner. One of the outcomes of this book is to encourage you to develop and articulate a "personal philosophy" of organization development, a platform upon which to rest your OD practice. This final activity is designed to assist that process.

There is a lot more to say about organizational change. But for now, I'll simply end with "Best Wishes!"

SELF AS PRACTITIONER

Directions: Review the activities and notes you made in the book. Use these as guides for responding to the following questions. Engage in conversation with others on these questions and your responses. Reflect upon them as you encounter opportunities to facilitate organizational change.

Questions:

What is your personal vision statement?

What are the top three values that guide you in your life and work?

What commitment are you willing to make to an ethical practice of organizational change?

How will you maintain the balance between meeting the needs of a client and maintaining high ethical standards?

What is your personal motivation for doing this work?

What do you consider to be strengths that you bring to this work?

What do you consider to be weaknesses that you bring to this work?

What is your commitment to personal growth, personal mastery?

How will you practice reflective thinking (double- and triple-loop)?

What will you do if asked to provide service that is beyond your expertise?

How will you maintain client confidentiality? What will you do if asked to divulge confidential data about employees of your client?

How will you maintain a systems perspective, especially when faced with what appears to be a minor change within one department?

How will you engage with the client in the "discovery" process, and avoid "fixing the wrong problem?"

What commitment are you willing to make to admit when you have made a mistake? How will you turn that mistake into a learning opportunity?

What commitment are you willing to make to model diversity?

VALUES SORT[1]

From the following list of values (both work and personal), select the ten that are most important to you, as guides for how to behave, or as components of a valued way of life. Feel free to add any values of your own to this list.

__ Achievement	__ Advancement and promotion
__ Adventure	__ Affection (Love & caring)
__ Arts	__ Challenging problems
__ Change & variety	__ Close relationships
__ Community	__ Competence
__ Competition	__ Cooperation
__ Country	__ Creativity
__ Decisiveness	__ Democracy
__ Ecological awareness	__ Economic security
__ Effectiveness	__ Efficiency
__ Ethical practice	__ Excellence
__ Fame	__ Fast living
__ Fast-paced work	__ Financial gain
__ Freedom	__ Friendships
__ Growth	__ Having a family
__ Health	__ Helping other people
__ Helping society	__ Honesty
__ Independence	__ Influencing others
__ Inner harmony	__ Integrity
__ Intellectual status	__ Involvement
__ Job tranquility	__ Knowledge
__ Leadership	__ Location
__ Loyalty	__ Market position
__ Meaningful work	__ Merit
__ Money	__ Nature
__ Personal Development	__ Physical challenge
__ Pleasure	__ Power & authority
__ Privacy	__ Public Service
__ Purity	__ Quality of things I do
__ Quality relationships	__ Recognition (from others)
__ Religion	__ Reputation
__ Responsibility/Accountability	__ Security
__ Self-respect	__ Serenity
__ Service to others	__ Sophistication
__ Stability	__ Status
__ Supervising others	__ Time freedom
__ Truth	__ Wealth
__ Work under pressure	__ Work with others
__ Work alone __ Other	

VALUES SORT -- REFLECTIONS

Now, of these ten select <u>three</u> that are most meaningful to you, listing them below:

_____

_____

_____

Take a look at the top three values that you chose.

1. What do they mean, exactly? What are you expecting from yourself, even in bad times?
2. How would your life be different if those values were prominent and practiced?
3. What would an organization be like which encouraged employees to live up to those values?
4. How have these values guided you along your life journey? What inhibitors to living these values have you encountered?
5. Are you willing to choose a life, and an organization, in which these values are prominent?

Reflections:

_____

_____

_____

_____

_____

ENDNOTES

[1] Adapted from Senge, P.; Kleiner, A.; Roberts, C.; Ross, R. B.; & Smith, B. J. (1994). *The Fifth Discipline Fieldbook: Strategies and Tools for Building a Learning Organization.* New York: Currency Doubleday, pp. 209-211.

APPENDIX A:
CHRONOLOGY OF EVENTS THAT INFLUENCED ORGANIZATION DEVELOPMENT[1]

Event	Impact on the Field of Organization Development
1911 Frederick Taylor published *The Principles of Scientific Management*[2]	Introduced the scientific process of breaking jobs into small, repetitive tasks in an attempt to find "the one best way" to do each job; creation of piece-rate pay systems designed to increase motivation and prevent slacking off; simple, repetitive tasks minimized skills required to do the job. Became the model for the way to organize work.
1922 Max Weber wrote "The Essentials of Bureaucratic Organization: An Ideal-Type Construction"[3]	Introduced the concept of "bureaucracy" as the best, most efficient way to organize people; strong hierarchy of authority, division of labor, impersonal rules, and rigid procedures. Became the model for the way to organize people in organizations.
1916. Henri Fayol wrote *Administration Industrielle et Generale*[4]	Outlined five rules of proper management of organizations and the people within. Fayol became known as the founder of the classical management school.
1926 Mary Parker Follett wrote "The Giving of Orders"[5]	Advocated participative leadership and joint problem solving by labor and management.
1927-1932 Hawthorne Studies at the Hawthorne Plant of Western Electric Company. Subsequent reports on these studies: 1933, 1945 Elton Mayo[6] 1939 Roethlisberger and Dickson[7] 1950 Homans[8]	Discovery of social factors that affected productivity and morale; simple, repetitive jobs left workers with a sense of alienation; group norms had more power effects on productivity than economic incentives. Introduced concept of the whole person coming to work. Profoundly and irreversibly affected people's beliefs about organization behavior.
1938 Chester Barnard wrote *The Functions of the Executive*[9]	Presented insights from his experience; viewed organizations as social systems that must be effective (achieve goals) and efficient (satisfy the needs of employees); introduced concept that authority derives from willingness of subordinates to comply with directions rather than from position power.

Event	Impact on the Field of Organization Development
1939 Kurt Lewin, Ron Lippitt, and White wrote "Patterns of Aggressive Behavior in Experimentally Created Social Climates"[10]	Research found democratic leadership as superior to authoritarian and laissez-faire leadership in affecting group climate and performance.
1940s to 1960s Behavioral Sciences movement	The behavioral sciences movement, resulting from the Hawthorne studies, advocated participative management, greater attention to workers' social needs, training in interpersonal skills for supervisors, and a general "humanizing" of the workplace.
1947 Lewin, K. wrote "Frontiers in Group Dynamics"[11] 1951 wrote *Field Theory in Social Science*[12]	Lewin coined the term "group dynamics." Lewin's field theory and his conceptualizing about group dynamics, change processes, and action research profoundly influenced the field of organization development.
1946-1947 Beginnings of the laboratory training movement[13]	Laboratory training taught people how to improve interpersonal relations, increase self-understanding, and understanding group dynamics; focus on humanist and democratic values. This was a direct precursor to OD.
1946 Survey Research Center of the University of Michigan created.	Rensis Likert's dissertation, *A Technique for the Measurement of Attitudes* became a classic study that developed the widely used five-point Likert scale. Likert and colleagues created survey research and feedback, which constitutes a major stem in the history of OD.
1948 Laboratory Training movement	Work in laboratory training proposed shared leadership functions between leader and group members[14]; examined how resistance to change could be minimized by communicating the need for change and allowing people affected by the change to participate in planning it[15].
1940s-1950s Kurt Lewin and colleagues used Action Research in a variety of behavioral domains.	Action Research was applied to such areas as improving intergroup relations, community relations projects, leadership training, the study of resistance of change. Lewin promoted the concept of "no action without research, and no research without action."

Event	Impact on the Field of Organization Development
1950, 1956 Ludwig von Bertalanffy[16]	Introduced concepts of general systems theory.
1951 Carl Rogers wrote *Client-Centered Therapy*[17]	Introduced concept that individuals have within themselves the capacity to assume responsibility for their behavior and mental health provided with a supportive, caring social climate. The focus on effective interpersonal communications was applicable to superior-subordinate relations.
1951 Eric Trist and Ken Bamforth published "Some Social and Psychological Consequences of the Long-Wall Method of Coal-Getting"[18]	Working in British coal mines, Trist and Bamforth of the Tavistock Clinic, introduced the concept of organizations as sociotechnical systems—organizations are comprised of a social system and a technological system, changes in one system will produce changes in the other system.
1954 Abraham Maslow published *Motivation and Personality*[19]	Presented a view of human motivation in a hierarchy of needs—when lower order needs are met, higher-order needs become dominant.
1956 Blake, Shepard, and Mouton began work at Esso Standard Oil Company[20] 1962 Robert Blake and Jane Mouton published *The Managerial Grid*[21]	Using a sensitivity-type approach coupled with case study practice in applying behavioral theories, particularly Theory X and Y, 800 managers participated in an OD effort. The results were mixed. It was successful for helping to heal union-management issues; but lack of follow-up failed to produce a huge organization impact. Subsequent OD efforts in 1959 and 1961 had better results because they were based on the Managerial Grid and on a six-phase follow-up sequence.
1957 Chris Argyris published *Personality and Organization*[22]	Introduced concept that there is an inherent conflict between the needs of organizations and the needs of mature, healthy adults.

Event	Impact on the Field of Organization Development
1959 Frederick Herzberg et al published *The Motivation to Work*[23] 1966 Herzberg published *Work and the Nature of Man*[24]	Investigated conditions of work that result in experiences of satisfaction or dissatisfaction. Two factors were present. Job related, intrinsic "motivators" included interesting work, recognition, responsibility, and advancement. Environment-related, extrinsic "hygiene factors" included company policy and administration, supervision, salary, status, security, interpersonal relations, and working conditions. Herzberg contended that an absence of hygiene factors might lead to job dissatisfaction; however, their presence is not directly linked to job satisfaction, as are the motivators.
1960 Douglas McGregor published *the Human Side of Enterprise*[25]	Described Theory X and Theory Y assumptions. Theory X assumes people are lazy, lack ambition, need to be coerced into working. Theory Y assumes people want to do well at work, have the potential to develop, to assume responsibility if given the chance and proper social environment. Introduced concept of management role of changing organizational structures, management practices, and human resource practices to allow individual potential to be released. Built on Maslow's motivation theory and introduced practicing managers to concepts of need hierarchy and self-actualization.
1961 Rensis Likert published *New Patterns of Management* [26]	Presented theory of superiority of democratic leadership style in which leader is group oriented, goal oriented, and shares decision making within the work group. This contrasted with an authoritarian leadership style.

Event	Impact on the Field of Organization Development
1967 Rensis Likert developed "*Profile of Organizational Characteristics*"[27]	Advanced the survey feedback approach to include six sections: leadership, motivation, communication, decisions, goals, and control. These were surveyed within the overall framework of four organizational categories or systems: System 1 *autocratic*, System 2 *benevolent autocracy*, System 3 *consultative*, and System 4 *participative and consensus management*.
1966 Daniel Katz and Robert Kahn published *The Social Psychology of Organizations*[28]	Presented first comprehensive coverage of organizations as open systems.
1969 "OD Six-Pack"[29]	A series of six books summarizing the field of OD one decade after its inception; presented theory, practice, and values of the field.
1980's and 1990's Intensified pace of change	Changes such as the emergence of technology, company mergers, acquisitions, bankruptcies, downsizings, changes in the law, and globalization have created a new arena for the practice of organization development.
Holistic Approach to Change	Relying on traditional organization development techniques, practitioners are increasingly relying on applications that are more complex and multifaceted. There is a blur in exactly what is and what is not organization development.

ENDNOTES

[1] Adapted from Wendell L. French and Cecil H. Bell, Jr. 1999. *Organization Development: Behavioral Science Interventions for Organization Improvement*, pp. 63-65; Robert R. Blake. 1995. "Memories of HRD", *Training & Development*; Jane Srygley Mouton and Robert R. Blake. 1972. Behavioral Science Theories Underlying Organization Development. *Journal of Contemporary Business*, 1(3), pp. 9-22.

[2] Taylor, F. W. 1911. *The Principles of Scientific Management*. New York: Harper and Brothers.

[3] Weber, M. 1922. "The Essentials of Bureaucratic Organization: An Ideal-Type Construction". Reprinted in H. H. Gerth and C. W. Mills (trans. And eds.) 1946 *Max Weber: Essays in Sociology*. New York: Oxford University Press.

[4] Fayol, H. 1916. *General and industrial management*. London: Pitman. C. Storrs, translator.

[5] Follett, M. P. 1926. "The Giving of Orders". In H. C. Metcalf (ed.). *Scientific Foundations of Business Administration*. Baltimore, MD: Williams and Wilkins Company. See also H. C. Metcalf (ed.). 1941. *Dynamic Administration: The Collected Papers of Mary Parker Follett*. New York: Harper.

[6] Mayo, E. 1933. *The Human Problems of an Industrial Civilization* Cambridge, MA: Harvard University, Graduate School of Business, Division of Research; and Mayo, E. 1945. *The Social Problems of an Industrial Civilization*. Cambridge, MA: Harvard University Press.
Mayo, E. 1945. *The Social Problems of an Industrial Civilization*. Cambridge, MA: Harvard University Press.

[7] Roethlisberger, F. W. & Dickson, W. J. 1939. *Management and the Worker*. Cambridge, MA: Harvard University Press.

[8] Homans, G. C. 1950. *The Human Group*. New York: Harcourt, Brace & World, Inc.

[9] Barnard, C. I. 1938. *The Functions of the Executive*. Cambridge, MA: Harvard University Press.

[10] Lewin, K., Lippitt, R., & White, R. 1939. "Patterns of Aggressive Behavior in Experimentally Created Social Climates," *Journal of Social Psychology*, 10, pp. 271-299.

[11] Lewin, K. 1947. "Frontiers in Group Dynamics". *Human Relations*, 1(2), pp. 143-153.

[12] Lewin, K. 1951. *Field Theory in Social Science*. New York: Harper.

[13] See Edgar Schein and Warren G. Bennis. 1965. *Personal and Organizational Change Through Group Methods*. New York: John Wiley & Sons; Blake, R. 1995. "Memories of HRD", *Training & Development*, 49(3), pp. 22-.

[14] Benne, K. D., & Sheats, P. 1948. "Functional Roles of Group Members." *Journal of Social Issues*, 4(2), pp. 41-49.

[15] Coch, L. & French, J. R. P. Jr. 1948. "Overcoming Resistance to Change". *Human Relations*, 1, pp. 512-532.

[16] von Bertalanffy, L. 1950. "The Theory of Open Systems in Physics and Biology", *Science*, 3, pp. 23-29.
von Bertalanffy, L. 1956. "General Systems Theory", *General Systems: Yearbook of the Society for General Systems Theory*, 1, pp. 1-10.

[17] Rogers, Carl R. 1951. *Client-Centered Therapy*. Boston, MA: Houghton-Mifflin.

[18] Trist, E. L., & Bamforth, K. W. 1951. "Some Social and Psychological Consequences of the Long-Wall Method of Coal-Getting", *Human Relations*, 4, pp. 3-38.

[19] Maslow, A. 1954. *Motivation and Personality*. New York: Harper and Row.

[20] Blake, R. R. 1960. "Typical Laboratory Procedures and Experiments" in *An Action Research Program for Organization Improvement (in Esso Standard Oil Company.* Ann Arbor, MI: Foundations for Research on Human Behavior; Shepard, H. A. "Three Management Programs and the Theories Behind Them" in *An Action Research Program for Organization Improvement (in Esso Standard Oil Company.* Ann Arbor, MI: Foundations for Research on Human Behavior; Blake, R. R., & Mouton, J. S. et al. 1964. "Breakthrough in Organization Development". *Harvard Business Review,* 42(6) November-December, pp. 133-155.

[21] Blake, R. R., Mouton, J. S. 1962. *The Managerial Grid: A Framework for Assessing Managerial Orientations.* Scientific Methods, Inc.

[22] Argyris, C. 1957. *Personality and Organization.* New York: Harper and Row.

Argyris, C. 1962. *Inter-personal Competence and Organizational Effectiveness.* Homewood, IL: Irwin-Dorsey.

[23] Herzberg, F, Mausner, B., & Snyderman, B. 1959. *The Motivation to Work.* New York: Wiley.

[24] Herzberg. F. 1966. *Work and the Nature of Man.* New York: World Publishing Co.

[25] McGregor, D. (1960). *The Human Side of Enterprise.* New York: McGraw-Hill.

[26] Likert, R. (1961). *New Patterns of Management.* New York: McGraw-Hill; and Likert, R. (1967). *The Human Organization.* New York: McGraw-Hill.

[27] Likert, R. (1967). *The Human Organization.* New York: McGraw-Hill.

[28] Katz, D., & Kahn, R. L. (1966). *The Social Psychology of Organizations.* New York: John Wiley & Sons.

[29] The OD Six-Pack consisted of the following books published by Addison-Wesley Publishing Company in 1969.

Beckhard, R. *Organization Development: Strategies and Models.*

Bennis, W. *Organization Development: Its Nature, Origins, and Prospects.*

Lawrence, P., & Lorsch, J. *Developing Organizations: Diagnosis and Action.*

Schein, E. *Process Consultation: Its Role in Organization Development.*

Walton, R. *Interpersonal Peacemaking: Confrontations and Third-Party Consultation.*

Blake, R., & Mouton, J. S. Building a Dynamic Corporation Through Grid Organization Development.

REFERENCES

Albrecht, K. (1987). *The Creative Corporation*. Homewood, ILL: Dow Jones-Irwin.

Allesandra, T., & O'Connor, M. J. (1994). *People Smarts. Bending the Golden Rule to Give Others What They Want.* San Diego, CA: Pfeiffer & Company.

Amabile, T. (1983). *Social Psychology of Creativity*. New York: Springer-Verlag.

Amabile, T. (1997). Motivating Creativity in Organizations. *California Management Review*, 40(1), 39-58.

Amabile, T. M. (1996). *Creativity in Context: Update to the Social Psychology of Creativity*. Boulder, CO: Westview Press.

Amabile, T. M., Conti, R., Coon, H., Lazenby, J., & Herron, M. (1996). Assessing the Work Environment for Creativity. *Academy of Management Journal*, 39(5), 1154-1184.

Anderson, L. A., & Anderson, D. (2001). *The Change Leader's Roadmap*. Jossey Bass Pfeiffer: A Wiley Company.

Anderson, D., & Anderson, L. A. (2001). *Beyond change Management: Advanced Strategies for Today's Transformational* Leaders. Jossey-Bass Pfeiffer: A Wiley Company.

Anderson, L. A., & Anderson, D. (2001). Awake at the Wheel: Moving Beyond Change Management to Conscious Change Leadership. *OD Practitioner*, 33(3).

Argyris, C. & Schon, D. A. (1974). *Theory in Practice: Increasing Professional Effectiveness*. San Francisco: Jossey-Bass.

Argyris, C., & Schon, D. (1978). *Organizational Learning*. Reading, MA: Addison-Wesley

Armstrong, T. (2000). *Multiple Intelligences in the Classroom*. Alexandria, VA: Association for Supervision and Curriculum Development.

Axelrod, D. (1992). Getting Everyone Involved: How One Organization Involved Its Employees, Supervisors, and Managers in Redesigning the Organization. *The Journal of Applied Behavioral Science.* 28, 4, 499-509.

Bailey, D. & Dupre, S. (1992). The Future Search Conference As a Vehicle for Educational Change: A Shared Vision for Will Rogers Middle School, Sacramento, California. *The Journal of Applied Behavioral Science.* 28, 4, 510-519.

Beckhard, R. & Harris, R. (1967). The Confrontation Meeting. *Harvard Business Review*, 45, 2, 149-155.

Beckhard, R. & Harris, R. (1977). *Organizational Transitions: Managing Complex Change*. Reading, MA: Addison-Wesley.

Beckhard, R. (1969). *Organization Development: Strategies and Models*. Reading, MASS: Addison-Wesley Publishing.

Beckhard, R. (1975). Strategies for large system change. In K. Benne, L. Bradford, J. Gibb, R. Lippitt (Eds.), *Laboratory method of changing and learning*. Palo Alto, CA: Science and Behavior Books.

Bedeian, A. G. (1987). Organization Theory: Current Controversies, Issues and Directions. In C. Cooper and I. T. Robertson. *International Review of*

Industrial and Organizational Psychology. New York: John Wiley & Sons, pp. 1-33.

Belenky, M. F.; Clinchy, B. M.; Goldberger, N. R.; & Tarule, J. M. (1986). *Women's Ways of Knowing.* New York: Basic Books.

Bennis, W. (1969). *Organization Development: Its Nature, Origins and Prospects.* Reading, MASS: Addison-Wesley Publishing.

Bennis, W. (1993). *An Invented Life: Reflections on Leadership and Change.* Reading, MASS: Addison-Wesley.

Blake, R. R. (1995). Memories of HRD. *Training & Development,* 49(3), 22-.

Blanchard, K. (1998). Servant-Leadership Revisited. In L. C. Spears (Ed.), *Insights on leadership: Service, Stewardship, Spirit, and Servant-Leadership*: 21-28. New York: John Wiley & Sons, Inc.

Bleedorn, B. (1993). Toward an Integration of Creative and Critical Thinking. *American Behavioral Scientist,* 37(1), 10-19.

Block, P. (2000). *Flawless Consulting: A Guide to Getting Your Expertise Used* (2nd ed). Jossey-Bass/Pfeiffer.

Block, P. (2001). *The Flawless Consulting Fieldbook & Companion: A Guide to Understanding Your Expertise.* Jossey-Bass/Pfeiffer.

Bolman, L. G., & Deal, T. E. (1999). 4 Steps to Keeping Change Efforts Heading in the Right Direction. *The Journal for Quality and Participation,* May/June, 22(3), pp. 6-11

Bridges, W. (1980). *Transitions: Making Sense of Life's Changes.* Reading, MA: Addison-Wesley Publishing Company;

Bridges, W. (1990). *Transitions: Making Sense of Life's Changes.* Reading, Reading, MASS: Addison-Wesley.

Bridges, W. (1991). *Managing Transitions: Making the Most of Change.* Reading, MA: Addison-Wesley Publishing Company.

Bridges, W. (1996). Leading the de-jobbed organization. In F. Hesselbein, M. Goldsmith, & R. Beckhard (Eds.), *The leader of the future: New visions, strategies, and practices for the next era*: 11-18. San Francisco: Jossey-Bass Publishers.

Bridges, W. (2001). *The Way of Transition: Embracing Life's Most Difficult Moments.* Cambridge, MASS: Perseus Publishing.

Bridges, W. & Associates. (2002). *Leading Transition: Dealing Successfully with the Human Side of Change.* City of Anaheim Management Meeting, February 7, 2002.

Bryant, D. (1979). The Psychology of Resistance to Change. *Management Services,* March, 10-11.

Bryant, D. (1989). The Psychology of Resistance to Change. In R. McLennan. *Managing Organizational Change.* Englewood Cliffs, NJ: Prentice Hall, pp. 193-195.

Burns, J. M. (1978). *Leadership.* New York: Harper & Row.

Clark, C. (1980). *Idea Management.* New York: AMACOM.

Cooperrider, D. L., & Srivastva, S. 1987. Appreciative Inquiry in Organizational Life. In W. Pasmore and R. Woodman. (eds.) *Research in Organization Change and Development*, vol. 1, pp. 129-169. Greenwich, Conn.: JAI Press.

Cooperrider, D. L., & Whitney, D. (1999). Appreciative Inquiry: A Positive Revolution in Change. In P. Holman, & T. Devane (Eds.), *The Change Handbook: Group Methods for Shaping the Future*. San Francisco: Berrett-Koehler Publishers, Inc., pp. 245-261.

Covey, S. R. (1992). *Principle-Centered Leadership*. New York: Simon & Schuster.

Dannemiller, K. D. & Jacobs, R. W. (1992). Changing the Way Organizations Change: A Revolution of Common Sense. *The Journal of Applied Behavioral Science*. 28, 4, 480-498.

Drucker, P. (1972). *Concept of the Corporation*, Mentor Executive Library.

Emery, M., & Devane, T. (1999). Search Conference. In P. Holman, & T. Devane (Eds.), *The Change Handbook: Group Methods for Shaping the Future*. San Francisco: Berrett-Koehler Publishers, Inc., pp. 25-41.

Fahden, A. (1993). *Innovation on* Demand. Minneapolis, MN: The Illiterati.

Fahden, A., & Namakkal, S. (1993). The Art and Practice of Innovation: Changing the Way We Do Business in the '90s. Learning 2001: *Carlson Learning Company Journal*. Minneapolis, MN: 4, 1, 6-8.

Frame, R. M.; Hess, R. K. & Nielsen, W. R. (1982). *The OD Source Book: A Practitioner's Guide*. San Francisco, CA: Jossey-Bass Pfeiffer, p. 8.

French, W. L. & Hollman, R. W. (1983). "Management by Objectives: The Team Approach" in French, W., Bell, C., and Zawacki, R. *Organization Development: Theory, Practice and Research*. Texas: Business Publications.

French, W. L., & Bell, C. H. Jr. (1999). *Organization Development: Behavioral Science Interventions for Organization Improvement*, 6th ed. Upper Saddle River, NJ: PrenticeHall.

Gardner, H. (1983). *Frames of Mind: The Theory of Multiple Intelligences*. New York: Basic Books.

Gardner, H. (1999). *Intelligence Reframed*. New York: Basic Books.

Gibb, J. (1970). *The Basic Reader: Reading in Laboratory Training*. Detroit, MI: Province V, the Episcopal Church.

Gilligan, C. (1982). *In A Different Voice*. Cambridge, MA: Harvard University Press.

Gladwell, M. (2005). *Blink: The power of thinking without thinking*. New York: Little, Brown and Company

Greenleaf, R. K. (1976). *The Institution As Servant*. Indianapolis, IN: The Robert K. Greenleaf Center.

Greenleaf, R. K. (1991). *The Servant As Leader*. Indianapolis, IN: The Robert K. Greenleaf Center. Note: Originally published in 1970 by Robert K. Greenleaf.

Grossman, S. R., Rodgers, B. E., & Moore, B. R. (1988). *Innovation*, Inc. Plano, TX: Wordware Publishing, Inc.

Gutknecht D. & Miller, J. R. (1990). *The Organizational and Human Resources Sourcebook*, 2nd ed., Lanham, MD: University Press of America.

Haas, R. (1993). The Corporation Without Boundaries. In Michael Ray and Alan Rinzler, eds. *The New Paradigm in Business: Emerging Strategies for Leadership and Organizational Change.* New York: Jeremy P. Tarcher/Perigee Books.

Hadamard, J. (1945). *The Psychology of Invention in the Mathematical Field.* Princeton, NJ: Princeton University Press.

Hall, J., & Hammond, S. *"What is Appreciative Inquiry?"* www.thinbook.com.

Handy, C. (1993, Spring). Managing the Dream: The Learning Organization. *Benchmark*. X(1), 13-15, p. 13.

Harvey, D. & Brown, D. R. (2001). *An Experiential Approach to Organization Development* 6th ed. New Jersey: Prentice Hall.

Helgesen, S. 1995. *The Web of Inclusion.* New York: Doubleday.

Hersey, P. & Blanchard, K. (1993). *Management of Organizational Behavior.* 6th ed. Englewood Cliffs, NJ: Prentice Hall.

Hesselbein, F. (2002). *Hesselbein on Leadership.* San Francisco, CA: Jossey-Bass.

Hoffman, L. R. (1965). *Group Problem Solving. Advances in Experimental Social Psychology.* Vol 2., 99-132, p. 115.

Holman, E., & Devane, T. (1999). *The Change Handbook: Group Methods for Shaping the Future.* San Francisco: Berrett-Koehler Publishers, Inc.

Huse, E. G. & Cummings, T. G. (1985). *Organization Development and Change.* 3rd ed. St. Paul, MN: West Publishing Co.

Imai, M., & Heymans, B. (1999). Gemba Kaizen: Organizational Change in Real Time. In P. Holman, & T. Devane (Eds.), *The Change Handbook: Group Methods for Shaping the Future.* San Francisco: Berrett-Koehler Publishers, Inc., pp. 109-121.

Inscape Publishing, Inc. (2001). *Team Dimensions Profile®.* http://www.inscapepublishing.com.

Inscape Publishing, Inc. (2001). *Innovate with C.A.R.E. Profile Facilitator's Kit.* http://www.inscapepublishing.com.

Jackson, J. C. (1995). *Dimensions of Innovation: An Examination of the Factors of Personal Style and Idea Management in the Team Innovation Process.* Unpublished doctoral dissertation, Santa Barbara, CA: The Fielding Graduate Institute.

Jackson, J. C. (1998). Leadership Education: Debunking the Myths, *Journal of Management Systems*, Vol.10, No. 2, 43-54

Kanter, R. M. (1983). *The Change Masters: Innovation for Productivity in the American Corporation.* New York: Simon and Schuster.

Kanter, R. M. (Apr 1985). Managing the Human Side of Change. *Management Review*, 74(4), 52-56.

Katz, D., & Kahn, R. L. (1978). *The Social Psychology of Organizations* 2nd ed. New York: Wiley.

Katzenbach, J. R., & Smith, D. D. (1993, March-April). The Discipline of Teams. *Harvard Business Review*. 71(2), 111-120.

Kirkpatrick, D. L. (1988). *How to Manage Change Effectively*. San Francisco: Jossey-Bass.

Kirton, M. J. (1976). Adaptors and Innovators: A Description and Measure. *Journal of Applied Psychology*. 61, 622-629.

Kirton, M. J. (1987). Adaptors and Innovators: Cognitive Style and Personality. In S. G. Isaksen (Ed.) *Frontiers of Creativity Research: Beyond the Basics*. Buffalo, NY: Bearly Limited, pp. 282-304.

Knowles, M. (1990). *The Adult Learner: A Neglected Species*. Houston, TX: Gulf Publishing Company.

Knowles, M. (1983, Sept.) Making Things Happen By Releasing the Energy of Others. *Journal of Management Development*. Australia: University of Queensland Business School.

Kolb, D. A. (1976). *Learning Styles Inventory*. Boston, MASS: McBer and Company.

Kolb, D., Rubin, I., & McIntyre, J. M. (1984). *Organizational Psychology: An Experiential Approach to Organizational Behavior*. Englewood Cliffs, NJ: Prentice-Hall.

Kolb, D.A. (1985). *Learning Style Inventory*. Boston: McBer and Co.

Kotter, J. P. (1990). What leaders really do. *Harvard Business Review*, 68(3).

Kotter, J. P. (1996). *Leading Change*. Boston: Harvard Business School Press.

Kotter, J. P. (2002). *The Heart of Change: Real Life Stories of How People Change Their Organizations*. Boston, MA: Harvard Business School Press, p. 1.

Leavitt, H. (1965). Applied organizational change in industry. In J. March (Ed.), *Handbook of organizations*. Chicago: Rand McNally.

Lewin, K. (1951). *Field Theory in Social Sciences*. New York: Harper & Row.

Lewin, K. (1947). Frontiers in Group Dynamics: Concept, Method, and Reality in Social Science, Social Equilibria and Social Change. *Human Relations*, 1(1), June, pp. 5-41.

Lewin, K. (1952). Group Decision and Social Change. In G. E. Swanson, T. N. Newcombe, & E. L. Hartley (eds.), *Readings in Social Psychology*, Rev. ed. New York: Holt.

Lewin, K. (1958). Group decision and social change. In E. E. Macoby, T. M. Newcomb, & E. L. Hartley (Eds.), *Readings in Social Psychology*. New York: Holt, Rinehart & Winston, pp. 197-211.

Lewin, K. (1969). "Quasi-stationary Social Equilibria and the Problem of Permanent Change". In Bennis, W. G., Benne, K. D., and Chin, R. (Eds.). *The Planning of Change*. New York: Hold, Rinehart, Winston, pp. 235-238.

Lippitt, L. L. (1999). Preferred Futuring™: The Power to Change Whole Systems of Any Size. In P. Holman, & T. Devane (Eds.), *The Change Handbook: Group Methods for Shaping the Future.* San Francisco: Berrett-Koehler Publishers, Inc., pp. 159-174.

Likert, R. (1967). *The Human Organization: Its Management and Value.* New York: McGraw-Hill.

Lippitt, R. (1983). Future before you plan. In R. A. Ritvo & A. G. Sargent (Eds.), *The NTL managers' handbook.* Arlington, VA: NTL Institute.

Lippitt, R., Watson, J, and Wetley, B. (1958). *The Dynamics of Planned Change.* New York: Harcourt, Brace & World.

Marguilies, N., & Raia, A. P. (1978). *Conceptual Foundations of Organizational Development.* New York: McGraw-Hill.

Marston, W. M. (1928). *Emotions of Normal People.* New York: Harcourt, Brace Co.

Maslow, A. (1954). *Motivation and Personality.* New York: Harper and Row.

Maslow, A. (1968). *Toward a Psychology of Being.* New York: Van Nostrand.

Maurer, R. (2003). *Conditions for Change Assessment.* http://www.beyondresistance.com. Downloaded 6/16/03.

May, R. (1976). *The Courage to Create.* New York: Bantam Books.

McGee-Cooper, A., & Trammel, D. (2002). From hero-as-leader to servant-as-leader. In L. C. Spears & M. Lawrence (Eds.), *Focus on leadership: Servant-leadership for the twenty-first century*: 141-151. New York: John Wiley & Sons, Inc.

McGregor, D. (1960). *The Human Side of Enterprise.* New York: McGraw-Hill.

McLennan, R. (1989). *Managing Organizational Change.* Englewood Cliffs, NJ: Prentice Hall.

McWhinney, W. (1992). *Paths of Change.* Newbury Park, CA: Sage Publications.

McWhinney, W. (1993), June 4. In memory of Eric Trist. Personal communication.

Miller, J. R. (1993). Social Dynamics of Change. *Learning 2001.* Carlson Learning Company Journal. Summer.

Miller, J. R. (1994). Getting the Most From Supplier Relationships. *Training & Development,* 48(12):14-15.

Mink, O. G.; Shultz, J. M.; & Mink, B. P. (1991). *Developing and managing open organizations.* Austin, TX: Somerset Consulting Group.

Mink, O., Shultz, J. M., & Mink, B. (1991). *Developing and Managing Open Organizations.* Austin, TX: Somerset Consulting Group, Inc.

Mohr, B. (2001). Appreciative Inquiry: Igniting Transformative Action. *The Systems Thinker,* 12(1) at www.pegasuscommunications.com.

Morgan, G. (1993). *Imaginization: The Art of Creative Management.* Newbury Park, CA: Sage Publications.

Mouton, J. S., & Blake, R. R. (1972). Behavioral Science Theories Underlying Organization Development. *Journal of Contemporary Business*, 1(3), Summer.

O'Toole, J. (1996). *Leading Change: The Argument for Values-Based Leadership*. New York: Ballantine Books.

Osborn, A. (1963). *Applied Imagination* (3rd ed). New York: Charles Scribner's Sons.

Osciak, S. Y., & Milheim, W. D. (2001). Multiple Intelligence and the Design of Web-based Instruction. *International Journal of Instructional Media*, Fall 2001 v28 i4 p355(7).

Osland, J.; Kolb, D. A.; & Rubin, I. M. (2001). *Organizational Behavior: An Experiential Approach*, 7th ed. Prentice Hall.

Parker, P. J. (1998). *The Courage to Teach: Exploring The Inner Landscape of a Teacher's Life*. San Francisco: Jossey Bass.

Parnes, S. J. (1987). The Creative Studies Project. In S. G. Isaksen (Ed.) *Frontiers of Creativity Research: Beyond the Basics*. Buffalo, NY: Bearly Limited, pp. 156-188.

Personal Profile System® (1994) and *Personal Profile Preview®* (1996) are registered trademarks and published by Carlson Learning Company, Minneapolis, Minnesota.

Raven, B. H. (1974). "A Comparative Analysis of Power and Preference," in J. T. Tedeschi (ed.), *Perspectives on Social Power*. Chicago: Aldine.

Ray, M., and Rinzler, A. (eds.). (1993). *The New Paradigm in Business*, New York: Jeremy P. Tarcher/Perigee Books

Rice, K. A. (1965). *Learning for Leadership: Interpersonal and Intergroup Relationships*. London: Tavistock.

Rogers, C. (1961). *On Becoming a Person*. Boston: Houghton Mifflin.

Rost, J. C. (1993). *Leadership for the Twenty-First Century*. Westport, CONN: Praeger.

Ruschman, N. L. (2002). Servant-leadership and the best companies to work for in America. In L. C. Spears & M. Lawrence (Eds.), *Focus on leadership: Servant-leadership for the twenty-first century*: 123-139. New York: John Wiley & Sons, Inc.

Schein, E. H. (1980). *Organizational Psychology*, 3rd ed. Englewood Cliffs, NJ: Prentice-Hall.

Schein, E. H. (1987). *Process Consultation: Vol. 2. Its Role in Organization Development*. Reading, MA: Addison-Wesley.

Schein, E. H.. (1992). *Organizational Culture and Leadership*, 2nd ed. San Francisco, CA: Jossey-Bass Publishers.

Schein, E. H. (1997). The concept of "client" from a process consultation perspective: A guide for change agents. *Journal of Organizational Change Management*, 10(3), 202-.

Schein. E. H. (1978). The Role of the Consultant: Content Expert or Process Facilitator?" *Personnel and Guidance Journal*, 58.

Senge, P. M. (1990). *The Fifth Discipline: The Art and Practice of the Learning Organization*. New York: Doubleday Currency.

Senge, P. M. (1996). Leading learning organizations: The bold, the powerful, and the invisible. In F. Hesselbein, M. Goldsmith, & R. Beckhard (Eds.), *The leader of the future: New visions, strategies, and practices for the next era*: 41-58. San Francisco: Jossey-Bass Publishers.

Senge, P. M.; Kleiner, A.; Roberts, C.; Ross, R. B.; & Smith, B. J. (1994). *The Fifth Discipline Fieldbook: Strategies and Tools for Building a Learning Organization*. New York: Currency Doubleday.

Senge, P.; Kleiner, A.; Roberts, C.; Ross, R.; Roth, G.; & Smith, B. (1999). *The Dance of Change: The Challenges of Sustaining Momentum in* Learning *Organizations*. New York: Currency Doubleday.

Sheehey, G. (1995). *New Passages: Mapping Your Life Across Time*. New York: Ballantine Books.

Sherman, S. (1995). Wanted: Company Change Agents. *Fortune*, December 11.

Sloan, A. P. Jr., (1963). *My Years with General Motors*, Doubleday.

Smith, N. I., & Ainsworth, M. (1989). *Managing for Innovation*. London: Mercury Books Division of W. H. Allen & Co. Plc.

Sonnenberg, F. K. (1991, August). *Cultivating Creativity*. Executive Excellence. 8(8), 13-14.

Spears, L. C. (Ed.). (1998). *Insights on leadership: Service, stewardship, spirit, and servant-leadership*. New York: John Wiley & Sons, Inc.

Spears, L. C., & Lawrence, M. (Eds.). (2002). *Focus on leadership: Servant-leadership for the twenty-first century*. New York: John Wiley & Sons, Inc.

Trist, E. L., & Emery, F. E. (1960). Report on the Barford Course for Bristol/Siddeley. July 10-16, 1960 (*Tavistock Document No. 598*). London: Tavistock Institute.

Trist, E., Higgins, G. W., Murray, H., Pollock, A. B. (1963) *Organizational Choice*. London: Tavistock.

Tuckman, B. W. (1965). Developmental Sequence in Small Groups. *Psychological Bulletin*. 63, 384-399.

Tuckman, B. W. (1977). Stages of Small-Group Development Revisited. *Group and Organizational Studies*, 2, 419-427.

Vaill, P. B. (1989). "Seven Process Frontiers for Organization Development" in Sikes, W., Drexler, A. B., & Gant, J. (eds.) *The emerging practice of organization development*. La Jolla, CA: Copublished by NTL Institute and University Associates.

Van Gundy, A. (1984). *Managing Group Creativity*. New York: American Management Association.

Van Gundy, A. (1987). Organizational Creativity and Innovation. In S. G. Isaksen (Ed.) *Frontiers of Creativity Research: Beyond the Basics*. Buffalo, NY: Bearly Limited, pp. 358-370.

Wallas, G. (1926). *The art of thought*. New York: Harcourt, Brace.

Weisbord, M. R. (1983). "Organizational Diagnosis: Six Places to Look for Trouble With or Without a Theory" in French, W., Bell, C., and Zawacki, R. *Organization Development: Theory, Practice and Research*. Texas: Business Publications.

Weisbord, M. R. (1992). *Discovering Common Ground*. San Francisco: Berrett-Koehler.

Weisbord, M., & Janoff, S. (1999). In P. Holman, & T. Devane (Eds.), *The Change Handbook: Group Methods for Shaping the Future*. San Francisco: Berrett-Koehler Publishers, Inc., pp. 43-57.

Wheatley, M. J., & Kellner-Rogers, M. (1996). *A Simpler Way*. San Francisco: Berrett-Koehler Publishers.

Woodman, R. W., Sawyer, J. E., & Griffin, R. W. (1993). Toward a Theory of Organizational Creativity. *Academy of Management Review*. 18(2), 293-321.

www.odnetwork.org.

www.wmbridges.com.

Wycoff, J. (1991). *Mindmapping: Your Personal Guide to Exploring Creativity and Problem-Solving*. New York: Berkley Books.

Zemke, R., & Zemke, S. (1984). 30 Things We Know for Sure About Adult Learning. *Innovation Abstracts* (6), 8, March 9.

ABOUT THE AUTHOR

Janet Cooper Jackson received her Ph.D. from Fielding Graduate University. She is an Associate Professor of Organizational Leadership at Chapman University. Prior to joining academia, Dr. Jackson spent over twenty years in the corporate world. Dr. Jackson's interests include women and leadership, servant leadership and organizational change. Her publications include: "Leadership Education: Debunking the Myths", *Journal of Management Systems*, December 1998. "Women Middle Manager's Perception of the Glass Ceiling", *Women in Management Review*, 2001; and *The Organizational and Human Resources Sourcebook*, University Press of America, Second Edition, 1990 (co-author Douglas Gutknecht). Dr. Jackson lives in Orange County, California with her husband and is surrounded by family, including three grandchildren.